The Mandela Revolution

The Mandela Revolution

A British Soldier's Inside View of His Rise To Power

By Huw Lawford

Pen & Sword
MILITARY

First published in Great Britain in 2021 by
Pen & Sword Military
An imprint of
Pen & Sword Books Ltd
Yorkshire–Philadelphia

ISBN 9781 3 9900 9 058

A CIP catalogue record for this book is available from the British Library.

Printed and bound by CPI Group (UK) Ltd, Croydon, CR0 4YY

MIX
Paper from responsible sources
FSC® C013604

Pen & Sword Books Limited incorporates the imprints of Atlas, Archaeology, Aviation, Discovery, Family History, Fiction, History, Maritime, Military, Military Classics, Politics, Select, Transport, True Crime, Air World, Frontline Publishing, Leo Cooper, Remember When, Seaforth Publishing, The Praetorian Press, Wharncliffe Local History, Wharncliffe Transport, Wharncliffe True Crime and White Owl.

For a complete list of Pen & Sword titles please contact

PEN & SWORD BOOKS LIMITED
47 Church Street, Barnsley, South Yorkshire, S70 2AS, England
E-mail: enquiries@pen-and-sword.co.uk
Website: www.pen-and-sword.co.uk

Or
PEN AND SWORD BOOKS
1950 Lawrence Rd, Havertown, PA 19083, USA
E-mail: Uspen-and-sword@casematepublishers.com
Website: www.penandswordbooks.com

‘The time comes in the life of any nation when there remain only two choices – submit or fight. That time has now come to South Africa. We shall not submit and we have no choice but to hit back by all means in our power in defence of our people, our future, and our freedom.’ Nelson Mandela’s statement from the dock at the opening of the defence case in the Rivonia Trial, Pretoria Supreme Court, 20 April 1964

‘I am not prepared to lead White South Africans and other minority groups on a road to abdication and suicide. Destroy White South Africa and our influence, and this country will drift into faction strife, chaos and poverty.’ President P.W. Botha address at the opening of the National Party Natal Congress, Durban, 15 August 1985

Contents

Prologue

On 27 April 1994, South Africa went to the polls. This was the first general election in which all South Africans were allowed to vote, and the landslide victory for the African National Congress allowed Nelson Mandela to be inaugurated as President on 10 May 1994. The movement for change, although figure-headed by the African National Congress, had many constituent parts. It was a multi-faceted quasi-coalition of political beliefs and races, from the simmering black activists in the townships surrounding Johannesburg and Cape Town to the liberal white crusaders in the leafy suburbs of the cities and in the universities.

This is not the whole story of how the 'Rainbow Nation' was formed, but it tells a story of one part of the revolution; a vital part, that had to occur to give legitimacy to the new South Africa both at home and abroad. It highlights the political necessity that drove a process and the seemingly inevitable failure that it became. Not a failure of the process itself, but a failure that had to occur to permit acceptability; it resulted in the end of South Africa as a hegemony.

This account focusses on how the military forces supporting the Apartheid regime and those committed to its overthrow came together to form a new national force, reflecting the new multi-racial, multi-faith democracy. The process appeared unacceptable in some measure to all sides, but the political instruction in 1994 was that there was to be the integration of the South African Defence Force and the armed wings of the African National Congress and the Azanian People's Liberation Army to form the South African National Defence Force. The consequence was a new military, weaker than before and no longer able to stamp its authority in sub-Saharan Africa, but one that truly reflected the colours of the Rainbow Nation.

Within the revolution, there was a small detachment from the British armed forces that was charged with assisting this transition. Many have reflected that what its members were asked to oversee was the equivalent of the political instruction to merge the Irish Republican Army with the British Army in the wake of the Good Friday Agreement. They were required to oversee and assist a process that included everything from the assessment and selection that took individuals from the three assembly areas, to the basic and specialist training to allow individuals to begin the integration process. The team, often acting individually, had to troubleshoot across the whole of the country. Theirs is a story of highs and lows, of sudden death, breakdowns and ultimately hope.

This is a personal account of three years spent in the middle of this staggering transitional experiment. It was Security Sector Reform and Disarmament, Demobilization and Reintegration before such processes were coined by the United Nations, and arguably it was considerably more successful than any such venture attempted by the UN. This is also a book that demonstrates how success and failure can occur simultaneously.

Chapter 1

We Live In Interesting Times

The two machine guns were carried on an open-topped truck, which was well concealed behind a blackthorn hedge. The reconnaissance had been thorough, and the truck was located in dead ground, unable to be seen by the two sangars[1] protecting the old police station that overlooked the Blackwater River in Middletown, County Armagh, Northern Ireland. The Intelligence staff had suggested that there was a high probability of a terrorist incident that Friday evening, but there again this was the same warning that was received every Friday afternoon as the staff at Headquarters finished for the weekend.

It was about ten o'clock and I had just settled down to sleep after a busy day. I was anticipating an even busier one tomorrow as we prepared to mount a major clearance operation on a Command Wire Improvised Explosive Device on the border of the Republic and Northern Ireland. Expected or not, the sudden noise of the machine guns firing was immense and ripped through the unusually balmy evening. Tracer fire seemed to fill the small quadrangle between the mortar-proof accommodation blocks, the kitchen and the old police station itself. The incoming bursts were met by fire from our own machine guns from the sangars sited on the roof of the old police station and from the 'supersangar'[2] erected in the south-west corner of the base covering the border itself. It was a cacophony amplified by the enclosed space of the quadrangle. Added to this, there was a dull thud of an explosion; fortunately, this was not another type of attack but the sound of the road-closing barrier being deployed. This 1-tonne barrier was dropped by means of a small explosive charge and would close the border to any vehicle that was trying to cross to or from the Republic. It was part of the Standing Operating Procedure in the event of an attack on the base.

As I ran across the quadrangle from the mortar-hardened accommodation block to the Operations Room, more through necessity rather than any notion of valour, everything seemed to slow down and years of training just took over. This was what was supposed to happen and, very much in retrospect, it was rather satisfying to experience it.

I burst, somewhat unceremoniously, into the Operations Room and saw a vision of serene calmness. The Operations Officer, my Battery Captain, Chris Wood, was master of the situation; issuing instructions, gleaning accurate information that he then passed on to the Battalion Headquarters, 10 miles away along the Monaghan Road in Armagh. The room was tiny and improvised from what had been the police sergeant's office in quieter and more peaceful times. Chris was on duty with two signallers supporting him, manning the Battery and Battalion communications. One of our intelligence JNCOs happened to be there too, having popped in for a chat on this Friday evening. Chris had already sent the initial contact report and was now sending information as soon as he was able to confirm facts.

The contact report is a well-proven tool. Its opening serial is 'Contact, Wait Out'. This is intended to keep everyone else off the radio net, alert commanders to an incident and allow a picture to be built slowly as facts are ascertained. By drip-feeding information to the Battalion Headquarters, the chances of proving the old adage that the first report is inevitably wrong can be reduced. The situation was clarifying: two machine guns had engaged our base; we had returned fire and no casualties had been sustained. The target had been the base itself, which had been sprayed with a copious amount of ammunition, as well as the small sangar on the border crossing point. An updated report was sent containing the time of the incident, confirmation of no casualties and estimated number of rounds incoming and outgoing. Assistance was requested from the Royal Ulster Constabulary, scene of crimes staff, tracker dogs and helicopters with powerful illuminating equipment. This was all communicated to the Battalion Headquarters. No response is necessary initially.

Indeed, no response is necessary in the initial stages of an incident, but when things have settled down then one would expect some form of dialogue with the Battalion Headquarters. All was quiet. Chris and I exchanged glances. Perhaps communications with Armagh were down? It happened frequently, especially in the days before the hand-held digital communications technology of today.

OK, send the radio messages again. All remained quiet. Ring the Battalion Operations Room on the secure telephone line. Still nothing. So ring the Battalion Operations Room on the insecure telephone line. Again, nothing. Then the penny began to drop. It was highly unlikely that all forms of communication were down. It was more likely that the Battalion Headquarters' staff were glued to the television or quietly snoozing.

We had just been attacked, fortunately with no casualties. The noise had been immense, so had woken everybody in the town. It was approaching closing time in the local pubs, where the majority of patrons were from the Republic, not through any sense of misplaced loyalty but because the prices were much lower, and we, the British Army, had just dropped the barrier preventing them from crossing back home. Still there was no answer.

It was not as though the Battalion could do much. There was a general policy that if there were no casualties, then no supporting element – be it forensic or search – would move down the Monaghan Road at night, for fear that the incident had been a 'come on' for a deliberate ambush. Even so, that decision could not be made because we could still not get through. The Battery Quartermaster Sergeant (BQMS) and his staff were desperately trying to assemble the pulleys and winches to get the barrier up and the road open, obstructed by the fact that the instructions seemed to be written in Japanese and we were gunners, not engineers! In the meantime, there was an ever-swelling crowd from the pubs outside the base, being held in place by a small number of the Battery under the capable command of a staff sergeant multiple commander who was attempting to reassure and inform, but mainly bluff, the crowd into staying calm and orderly. We did not need any 'aggro' that night, which would have been very easy bearing in mind that the IRA volunteers had just 'razzed up the Brits' and our own local populace, let alone their friends from across the border, were anything but loyalists.

The challenge of informing Battalion was solved by the intelligence JNCO, who remembered that his predecessor had told him that sometimes the Battalion Operations Room staff would not hear the radio or telephone if the television was on – such a reassuring image! However, the fax machine in the Operations Room sounded like a steam train, so that would be worth a try. Success! A fax with very large letters spelling 'CONTACT WAIT OUT' was sent and had a remarkable effect. The radio burst into life and, albeit to a sleepy sounding operator, the details were passed on. Within a few minutes, the Battalion Operations Officer, a disarmingly pleasant Parachute Regiment officer, rang up rather sheepishly with a splutter of weak excuses. Regardless, communications and the chain of command had been restored. The next thirty minutes was a stream of telephone calls from various commanders and, now very attentive, staff officers.

The crowd was by now getting vocal and a few projectiles were being thrown towards the thin green line. Time was of the essence. Cars from the Republic were having to do U-turns in the main road as the crossing was blocked and the duty policeman, who had drawn the short straw to stay overnight with us, was not inclined to go out and put up any 'Road Closed' signs. We were literally stuck in the middle. I donned my body armour and helmet, grabbed my rifle and went out to see what I could do. In reality, it was more to be seen and to encourage rather than anything else. The BQMS was sweating and swearing in equal amounts, especially as he realized that he and his party were labouring in the direct line of sight of the now-vacated firing point from across the border. The barrier was inching up, not enough to let traffic through but sufficient I thought to let pedestrians through in about ten minutes. I went back to see teams on the ground, and as I were assessing the situation, we received a reasonable amount of verbal abuse from the now larger, more beer-fuelled crowd. I gave quick orders, making it clear that I wanted to open up a reasonable gap and control the press of people moving towards the BQMS and the crossing. I would deploy another multiple[3] to line the route and protect the BQMS – I was not too sure how accommodating he would be to the wisecracks of the returning locals, cheered by a clear show of strength from the 'volunteers'.[4]

My heart sank as I went back into the Operations Room to give orders to the multiple commanders. Ahead of me was a bank of CCTV screens that covered the outside of the base and various areas of 'dead ground' in the immediate vicinity. On the CCTV covering the main street was a steady stream of locals exiting the pub after the final last orders, but in the midst of them was an articulated lorry towing a long trailer, upon which was a very large and expensive motor yacht. Now this was in County Armagh, the south-central part of Northern Ireland. One just did not see yachts; tractors aplenty, but not yachts. Anyway, for whatever reason, this yacht and the accompanying large lorry was now trying to squeeze through a large crowd of Irishmen who were becoming less than happy. The lorry driver eventually realized that he could not proceed forward, back, left or right. He was stuck. The crowd was also stuck, and the potential for things to get ugly was growing by the minute.

However, the bizarre appearance of this errant yacht began to take the post-pub horde's collective mind off the blocked road. We opened a gap and, with a line of soldiers picketing the route, the crowd moved seamlessly through them, underneath the barrier held in position by a very tired BQMS and across the border. They were quite absorbed by the yacht, seemingly oblivious to what had happened an hour previously, and completely ignored the soldiers. As on many previous occasions, Northern Ireland had a habit of producing the most unusual situations that could calm down a heated situation and are also a source of stories for the future.

This incident happened in the first few weeks of a six-month operational tour, and it was clear to me that this had been our initial test. The swift reaction of the sangar sentries and the manner in which the incident as a whole was handled, including the following chaos, clearly demonstrated that we were ready for pretty well anything that Northern Ireland could throw at us. This resulted in us being able to deter any direct action on my two bases, even though it was at the height of the IRA threat as its members roamed the border area with the lethal Barratt 0.5in sniper rifle[5] and the Mark 15 mortar,[6] both of which claimed lives before, during and after our tour in the Middletown area.

* * *

At this time I was commanding 42 (Alem Hamza) Battery in the 22nd Regiment Royal Artillery (The Welsh Gunners). We had been deployed to Northern Ireland as the Armagh Roulement Battalion for a six-month tour starting in early April 1993. The ARB was normally a Gunner or Armoured Corps regiment that formed three sub-units that were attached to two of the Home Service battalions of the Royal Irish Regiment (the old Ulster Defence Regiments), the third sub-unit reinforcing the roulement infantry battalion at Bessbrook Mill, the Bessbrook Roulement Battalion. My Battery was to reinforce the 8th Royal Irish, who had their Battalion Headquarters in Drummad Barracks in Armagh. We were to operate from two Royal Ulster Constabulary stations in Middletown and Keady. I had the Battery Headquarters and three troops[7] in Middletown, plus a small headquarters element and two troops in Keady.

* * *

The six-month tour ended, we returned back to our regimental barracks in Lincolnshire and after several weeks' leave settled back to regimental life. I had assumed command of my Battery at the beginning of the year in the very week that we commenced our pre-deployment training to Northern Ireland. Therefore, my experience in command had been totally operationally focused – which was great because that is the reason one joins the Army. I had been given command of a reinforced battery with almost 160 soldiers; the normal strength was just under ninety. All necessary equipment was in place and the soldiers were motivated. But what a sobering experience it was coming back to a peacetime routine. My command was reduced to its peacetime establishment and our return coincided with another round of redundancies (Options For Change Phase 3). These redundancies were part of the programme to reduce the numbers in the armed forces to the optimum levels for the post-Cold War era. Unfortunately, a great tract of my SNCOs were removed. In addition to those I lost to redundancies, I lost more as the Commanding Officer had to move SNCOs between batteries to maintain a balance of talent across the regiment. There were also further cuts in Defence expenditure, which involved limitation on mileage, training, ammunition and so on. All in all, it was a most disheartening time.

My Battery Captain, Chris Wood, who had continued to be an exceptional Operations Officer throughout the tour, was rewarded with the appointment of Adjutant – leaving yet another gap. Then, in January 1994, my brightest young captain decided to leave the Army and asked me to help him with his references. It was not looking too good. The headhunter to whom I was to provide references rang me the following day. We chatted pleasantly, I provided him with the required references and then, for no particular reason, I casually asked about my own prospects? How was the job market at the moment? Would I be marketable? We continued to talk, and before I knew it, we had agreed to meet.

I was at that age when I had just qualified for my Army pension but had not yet been required to send our children to boarding school,[8] and therefore I had yet to fall into what is known as the 'boarding school trap'. Maybe it was time to go? I had had a great time thus far, but with cuts to the size of the Army coming on an almost annual basis, would I be the right side of the selection criteria for promotion to lieutenant colonel, and then would I be lucky enough to be selected for command of a regiment? It was a highly competitive environment and the unknowns were growing.

I met the headhunter and, upon my return, decided that it would only be fair to speak to my Commanding Officer. Chris Wood advised me when there was a suitable opportunity, so I went into the CO's office. He was a big, dominating man. He spoke with a soft Welsh accent and always had a ready wit, almost as ready as his temper, which was legendary and easily ignited. I did not prevaricate; I told him that I was seriously considering leaving the Army and thought it fair to inform him and seek his opinion. After a silent pause, what came next was typically unbalancing. He was calm, reassuring and avuncular. He could see my reasoning and understood the arguments, both for and against. But he then said I was a bloody idiot. He could not promise anything, but assured me that my reports would stand me in very good stead for promotion and command. Much would be decided by what appointment I did next, but it would have to be high-profile and demanding, with a strong reporting chain, and it would be well within my ability. I left reassured that I was apparently on the right track, but not much closer to making a decision. I was sure, however, that this was not an attempt at appeasement but an honest opinion.

* * *

These were the days when everything was done by signal, letter and telephone, or occasionally by fax. Shortly after my interview with the CO, I saw a signal had been flagged up by Chris with the note 'BC 42 – this might appeal'. It was a signal asking for volunteers to go to South Africa to assist with the creation of the new South African National Defence Force. The UK was providing a British Military Advisory and Training Team (BMATT), which was to have the majority of its members as majors and captains. There were specific requirements, depending on one's specialty. For the gunners it requested a major, post sub-unit command, a graduate of the Army Command and Staff College,[9] and the officer also had to have had air defence and field artillery experience. That reflected my experience and seemed like a wonderful opportunity, so, ignoring my father's advice of never volunteering for anything in the Army, I put my name forward. Thinking nothing more of it, I returned to my paperwork.

* * *

Three years previously I was at the Army Command and Staff College at Camberley. Sage words were that you worked as hard at Camberley as you intended to do for the rest of your Army career. Looking back, that meant that those who reached the top of the Army had natural ability and were able to join in all the plethora of activities – be it playing sport, acting in the pantomime, writing for the underground newspaper or throwing themselves into the social whirl of a 'thirty-something' collective – and still float effortlessly to the top of the pile. Others tried too hard, cut themselves off and ended up leaving the Army early, frustrated, not a little bitter but no surprise to the other members of the course. The majority of us played hard and worked sufficiently diligently to be neither graded a star nor a dullard. I would include myself in the majority, and looked back with fond memories to that year, 1990.

The course had a wonderful eclectic mix of people. There was a complete cross-section from the British Army, several Royal Marines, and the course was further supplemented with token Royal Navy and Royal Air Force officers. But the real added value was from the international contingent, which made up one-third of the course. There were the serious North Americans, who took a while to realize that in the British Army you can relax and be yourself, and were quite horrified to see that the heresy of questioning the norm was encouraged. The Europeans had all attended their own Command and Staff Colleges and so were well ahead of us on the doctrinal aspects of soldiering, especially the Germans. Then we also had students from the Middle East (both Arab and Israeli), the Far East, Africa and South America. Everyone was able to contribute at some stage of the course; for example, the Israeli student had unique ideas of counter-insurgency (I am not sure how well the use of bulldozers would have gone down with the local population in Belfast!) and the officer from an African country had a very novel take on the interpretation of battlefield interrogation. Perhaps the most defining moment was when two officers, one each from India and Pakistan, gave a presentation of fighting at high altitude, and it was clear that they had been on opposing sides fighting over the same glacier.

In the real world, things were moving quickly; in fact they appeared to be almost out of control. Within months of finishing Camberley, the first Gulf War had kicked off and many of my fellow students were busy putting into practice their new-found knowledge. That year, 1990, was an unbelievable time to be at the Staff College. We were lucky enough to have the top figures in the political, academic and military worlds to address us, and to comment and try to explain what was happening in the wider world. In June, the Berlin Wall was dismantled; in September, the 'New World Order' was announced by President George Bush Snr; in November, Margaret Thatcher was deposed. The Soviet Union was creaking at the seams and the Warsaw Pact members were in turmoil. The strategic environment of East versus West, capitalism versus communism, NATO versus the Warsaw Pact glaring at each other across the North-West German Plain, had all gone in a matter of months. What had been the norm since I left Sandhurst[10] had disappeared, to be replaced by who knows what? It was an exciting, puzzling but overall an exhilarating time. And something occurred in February 1990, several thousand miles away, that was, in retrospect, an opening scene for all these epoch-changing activities. This was without doubt global headline news, but it seemed more a story of great fascination rather than one that would have a direct impact on me. On 11 February 1990, Nelson Rolihlahla Mandela was released from Victor Verster prison, near Paarl, in the Cape Province of the Republic of South Africa.

In his closing address to the course at Camberley, the Chief of the General Staff, commenting on the rapidly changing world picture, said that 'we live in interesting times'. He explained that this was widely assumed to be an old Chinese curse, although he went on to explain that although no direct reference can be found for this saying, it can be roughly translated as 'rather live as a dog in peaceful times than live as a human in turbulent times'. He was right because, from this particular Staff College course, we were all to see what is quaintly termed 'active service' in some if not all of the first and second Gulf Wars, Bosnia, Kosovo, Sierra Leone, Iraq and Afghanistan, as well as, of course, Northern Ireland. From that day, we entered a period where we ceased to be 'Nobby No Medals' or 'swishers',[11] and in the next 15 years we were all to gather a chest-full of medals.

* * *

At the end of April 1994, the first proper nationwide elections were held in South Africa. It was a sobering and humbling sight to see a nation's people, especially those who had been denied their rights in the past, go so calmly and determinedly to the polls. The sight of hundreds of the black population queuing stoically for hours to cast their first true vote was impressive. The result was inevitable and the African National Congress (ANC) won a landslide victory with almost 63 per cent of the votes cast. As required by the Interim Constitution, the ANC formed a 'Government of National Unity' with the National Party, the old white governing party, and the Inkatha Freedom Party, which was the political figurehead for the Zulu kingdom. The first act of the new National Assembly was to elect Nelson Mandela as President. There was a new government, a new leader, a new national anthem and a new flag; dawn rose over a new South Africa – the Rainbow Nation. Most importantly, the sky had not fallen in, as a minority had expected, and the transition was relatively peaceful. There was no widespread civil unrest; it was a mark of both the old South Africa and the new South Africa that the people of all persuasions did not want a civil war. There was no appetite for another Zimbabwe.

* * *

Very shortly after the election, the signal asking for volunteers to deploy to South Africa had been circulated; the very one for which I had put forward my name. At home, regimental life accelerated apace, and I had soon forgotten about the signal and my volunteering. One evening we had a Regimental Dinner Night, and the CO asked if Trisha, my wife, and I would offer a bedroom and host the outgoing Honorary Regimental Colonel, a very gregarious major general, as we had known him for many years. As always, it was a great evening of good food, too much wine and games galore. Eventually it was time to leave and extract the general from a huddle. It took a while, but we were soon walking back to our house, a short ten minutes' stroll for what would normally take five minutes. The general asked for a quick whisky, to settle his stomach, before retiring, and whilst we were sitting in the drawing room ruminating, he suddenly changed tack and said that he understood that I had volunteered to go to South Africa after considering my future in the Army. There was a pause, and then he stated that he hoped I would have an invigorating time there and that I would enjoy the challenges that it would throw at me, as without doubt there would be many. But learn well, he said, and come back, as it was me that he and the new Honorary Regimental Colonel would want to command the regiment when the opportunity arose. And with that he stood up, excused himself and retired to bed. I was flattered, and went to bed with a smile on my face. I saw him next morning for a fulsome breakfast in the chaos of trying to get the girls away to school. He was again charm personified, chatting to Trisha and me about everything under the sun but avoiding anything to do with the regiment itself.

The next afternoon, 13 May, the CO summoned me to his office. I expected it to be an opportunity to discuss anything that had been mentioned the previous evening at the inevitable whisky-aided download from the outgoing Honorary Regimental Colonel. I was wrong; as I entered the office, he told me that I had been selected to go to South Africa and that I should be prepared to move in four days. He understood that my position would be one of those that would be accompanied in due course, although at this stage there was no date for when families would follow. That would be decided once it had been deemed safe for them to do so. I then received the necessary rebuke for vacating my Battery at such short notice and without a successor being nominated, and there being little likelihood of one being available for several months, etc. I was then told to depart without further ceremony, book a farewell lunch/dinner with the Adjutant, see the Quartermaster about moving, see the doctor about inoculations and malaria prophylactics. Then he added, 'You had better tell your wife!' There was a 'well done' and 'good luck' chucked in at some point, but it was lost in the tidal wave of questions that started to rush around my head.

Trisha was at the time completing her PGCE[12] training at Bishop Grosseteste College, near Lincoln, and was due to complete her course in the summer. It was now early May and I could be off in a couple of days. Flexibility may be a principle of war, but it can wreak havoc in any form of domestic arrangement. There were so many conflicting stories coming out of South Africa about trouble in the townships, the reaction of the extreme sections of the white population and the potential for a slide into civil war; it was hardly the picture of domestic bliss. We had discussed the idea of my volunteering to go to South Africa, but we did not really think anything more about it and certainly had not actually planned for such an event.

I managed to have Trisha dragged out of a lecture by assuring the member of staff that I had to speak to her urgently, at the same time reassuring her that there had not been an accident or drama in the family. Trisha came to the telephone clearly concerned, assuming I had wrecked the car or something equally dramatic, regardless of the disarming summons. Once I had reassured Trisha that nothing was amiss, I told her we were off to South Africa. There was a silence, and to be fair a stunned silence. I duly swore her to secrecy and to use the opportunity to think about all the questions before we saw each other again that evening. Trisha's response was immediate, saying that, if we decided to accept this posting, we would not put the girls into boarding school; I had to promise we would take them with us.

Four days' notice was slipped to seven days, and then on 23 May I received a signal stating that I would deploy on 4 June, so there was a little more time but not much.

Chapter 2

New World, New Role

In the run-up to the South African general election of April 1994, a National Peacekeeping Force (NPKF) had been established to meet the anticipated serious security challenges. A Commonwealth Peacekeeping Assistance Group (CPAG), which had included some British advisors, had been formed to assist in the training of the NPKF. The experience of forming and delivering the NPKF had been varied, so in many respects any lessons from the CPAG would be able to give valuable insights into the mission and environment into which we were about to embark.

The NPKF was formed from military members of the South African Defence Force (SADF), the uMkhonto weSizwe – MK, the armed wing of the African National Congress – and the Transkei, Bophuthatswana, Venda and Ciskei (TBVC) defence forces. The concept was sound, in that any deployment of the NPKF would be seen to have representation from all the contributing parties in South Africa. However, integration down to platoon level for any organization has its difficulties regardless of the situation, as any commander of a multinational force will recount. In the case of the NPKF, the challenges were underlined by the inherent racial tensions as the Apartheid regime was in its dying throes. Accusations of obstinacy and retribution were frequent, and there were reported instances of SADF personnel refusing to obey orders from non-SADF NPKF officers and a general lack of discipline across the force. Originally, the SADF recommendation was for six months' training, but with bureaucratic wrangling and protracted negotiations this was reduced to just seven weeks. Consequently, it was considered only partially ready for its deployment in mid-April, just a fortnight prior to the election.

There must have been lessons identified by the British participants in the CPAG, but even if the command element of the British Military Advisory and Training Team had been briefed, nothing trickled down to us. Of course, the situation in South Africa in late April and early May was still fluid and politically very sensitive. There were many important factors that needed to be considered across Whitehall, between the Foreign and Commonwealth Office and the Ministry of Defence, and of course there was dialogue between the Transitional Executive Council and the British High Commission in Pretoria. Everyone was talking to each other, which was good, but nobody thought about talking to us whilst we waited to deploy.

On 8 April 1994, the Transitional Executive Council approached the United Kingdom to contribute to the smooth transition of the military in South Africa from the Apartheid-era SADF to the new South African National Defence Force (SANDF) that would encompass all recognized armed elements. The request was summarized in the term BMATT, a British Military Advisory and Training Team; could the United Kingdom provide a BMATT to help? There had, after all, been BMATTs in Botswana, Lesotho, Mauritius, Swaziland, Namibia and Zimbabwe. It was a term that was recognized throughout sub-Saharan Africa and seen as a positive step forward rather than a conduit for foreign intrusion. The concept of the British Military Advisory and Training Team (South Africa) – BMATT (SA) – was born.

* * *

The task of bringing together so many armed forces under the umbrella of the new South African National Defence Force was clearly both a significant and very sensitive task. There was a clear advantage to having some form of international engagement to assist in the legitimization of the process. There had been a request by the South African government for the UN to provide observers for the transition process from Apartheid, and this evolved into the United Nations Observer Mission in South Africa (UNOMSA). For the elections, apart from the CPAG helping to train the NPKF, there were other observer missions, from the Commonwealth – the Commonwealth Observer Mission in South Africa (COMSA) – the European Union and the Organization of African Unity. But it was decided that there was a need for a team of neutrals to take an active role in the integration process rather than just being passive observers; an unbiased team that could report directly to the national political leadership on the progress of the military integration – a rare formalization of telling truth to power.

The task of merging disparate groups, who had opposed each other for decades, directly and indirectly, into a homogenous defence force was a major challenge. It was to be a national activity, planned and executed by the SANDF, but involving external neutrals to provide an honest assessment and consequently an external stamp of approval. There was a requirement to oversee the integration process, advise and assist in all aspects of education and training to ensure transparency and fairness. Robust and honest external validation would provide credence to the process to both internal and external audiences. One of the key elements to the end state had to be that the SANDF was trusted by its own population – the same population whose majority would claim to have been suppressed by its predecessor, the SADF.

* * *

Deploying such a small team to another country is routine business for the British Army, and there was a well-oiled machine that enabled all this to happen seamlessly. The British Army was used to operating all over the world in a variety of deployments. It was not just bound to defensive operations within the NATO context. It had of course another reputation, and that was for fighting in small wars. Since the end of the Second World War, fuelled mainly by the withdrawal from Empire, it has fought all over the globe in a series of counter-insurgency operations from Borneo to Malaya, from Cyprus to Kenya, then to Aden, and so the list goes on. The 'Troubles' in Ulster were another example of how the British Army could switch its attention from the North-West German Plain, with the emphasis on high-intensity armoured warfare, to low-intensity, predominantly infantry operations in support of a civil power where force had to be used legally, clinically and proportionately, often in a hugely complex urban setting. Armoured warfare per se, prior to the Gulf War in 1990–91, had not been conducted since the Korean War, and then only in small-scale operations. During the 1970s and 1980s, the Army had been committed to Cold War deterrence in Germany and regular deployments to Northern Ireland. Of course, the Falkland Islands conflict was the exception, but this served to demonstrate – to those who needed to understand – that the United Kingdom was capable of much more than just picketing the inner-German border.

But everything changed with the collapse of the Soviet Union and the Warsaw Pact. Suddenly the Red Threat vanished, and there were three armoured divisions facing eastwards with no tangible threat. The first Gulf War in 1990–91 allowed the armoured capability of the British Army to be demonstrated in the hundred-hour lightning campaign, but it was over almost before it had started. The cannibalization of spare parts from tanks and armoured vehicles of the divisions remaining in Germany to keep the two armoured brigades mobile in the Gulf raised many an eyebrow. That, however, is not for debate here. What was demonstrated was that the Army could do a job anywhere in the world, and consequently the need to maintain our expeditionary capability grew in importance. Here was the answer to what the Army could now do following the end of the Cold War and a reduction in the intensity of operations in Northern Ireland. As if on cue, the disintegration of Yugoslavia began with the horrors of racial butchery in Bosnia, and would continue through to the subsequent ethnic cleansing in Kosovo. It was clear that there was a distinct role for the Army, and the Armed Services as a whole, in hugely complex areas of conflict prevention and conflict resolution.

The world had gone from the perverse stability of the Cold War and the post-Second World War struggle between capitalism and communism, to what President George Bush Snr would label the New World Order. The stability of the Cold War was indeed perverse, although there was a string of brutal wars fought around the world fuelled by ideology, but these were fought by proxy. They were clashes supported or orchestrated by the superpowers, but clashes that did not see the superpowers fight directly against each other. The list was seemingly endless, encompassing the Middle East, Vietnam and wars throughout Africa, including the overt US support to South Africa in the early days of its involvement in Angola. But once the lines of conflict had gone and only one superpower remained, things changed dramatically. The stability created through the balance and counter-balance of two rival superpowers had gone, and for a while there was a void that began to be filled by rising nationalism and religious intolerance. The world after the Cold War was more unpredictable and unstable, and warfare became asymmetric.

Peacekeeping could be a catch-all for the employment of the British Army. It requires professional soldiers, highly trained and educated officers and the ability to work internationally within a multinational political-military environment. Some nations such as Canada recognized this as a wonderful opportunity to maintain their military capability whilst being seen to be doing good. Subsequently, the Canadians became one of the backbones of United Nations peacekeeping. There are distinct definitions and environments to peacekeeping. It suits some nations, but the more passive nature of the operation does not come naturally to the British Army. For hundreds of years, the British Army has been more comfortable with intervention and prefers operating kinetically, not shying away from using lethal force. Although the United Kingdom had always supported United Nations peacekeeping, it is not a major contributor. However, there was one occasion when, at the height of the Bosnian crisis, the United Kingdom was the greatest contributor to peacekeeping, with over 10,000 troops deployed. This, however, was at a time when the United Kingdom and France were holding the whole UNPROFOR (United Nations Protection Force) mission together. The mission, flawed from the start, failed politically, and it was not long before the United Nations Blue Berets were thrown away and replaced by camouflaged helmets as NATO took on the security role from the UN. The mission moved from that of the hobbled, and eventually disastrous, protection of humanitarian relief to conflict resolution with the ability to conduct kinetic operations. This form of conflict resolution, achieving peace by using a chain-mailed fist in a kidskin glove, better suited the British Army.

The other option was conflict prevention through soft power. This is proactive and allows the United Kingdom to enable other nations to establish and maintain domestic security. This in turn allows them to contribute to external security by becoming a contributor to multinational peacekeeping operations with international organizations such as the UN, the Organization for Security and Co-operation in Europe (OSCE), NATO or the African Union (AU). It can be done by training individuals within the United Kingdom at academic institutions by means of scholarships, or through military institutions such as the Royal Military Academy Sandhurst, the staff colleges or the Royal College of Defence Studies. It can also be tailored so that the military, police or civil servants can receive specific training to suit the assessed requirement; for example, pilot training or Explosive Ordnance Disposal training. Another option is the export of training with a benign military presence, which can better be described as Defence Diplomacy. The British military has an excellent reputation worldwide and is the partner of choice of many countries, and not just members of the Commonwealth. It would be true to say that the British military can be both professional and empathetic. Its members can operate anywhere, and they do not need a huge logistic machine to support them. They can adapt and, within reason, slip into the local way of life. Directly and indirectly, the British have been doing this for hundreds of years. One of the most popular vehicles for the delivery of such capability is a BMATT. BMATTs have operated worldwide, and generally nations recognize them as a product; not quite

Coca Cola, but nevertheless recognized by governments throughout Africa and the Far East. The influence that a deployed BMATT delivers to an Ambassador or, more likely, a High Commissioner, is immense. BMATTs traditionally are trusted, both for their discretion and for not peddling a national line. They are there to do a job, and that job can differ considerably from nation to nation.

* * *

But the task to face BMATT (SA) was unique. It was an advisory and training team, but without an advisory or training task. It was to play a neutral role in a political process played out in a military environment, and witness and report on the merger of four principal players into a homogenous and representative defence force; this was an expansion of the participants of the NPKF. The four principal players were the South African Defence Force (SADF), the uMkhonto we Sizwe (MK, the armed wing of the African National Congress), the members from the Transkei, Bophuthatswana, Venda and Ciskei (TBVC) defence forces and the Azanian People's Liberation Army (APLA, the armed wing of the Pan African Congress). Later, and in far smaller numbers, these were to be joined by the Kwazulu-Natal Self Protection Units.

* * *

The South African Defence Force was formed in 1957, when it replaced the Union Defence Force. The SADF had two primary duties: to counter insurgency in all forms and to maintain a conventional military force to defend South Africa's borders. The SADF was organized on a traditional structure, with one principal exception, which was that the medical capability – which generally is a distant element of each service – was combined under one command. The South African Medical Service (SAMS) was given equal status to the South African Army, Navy and Air Force.

In 1961, shortly after the formation of the SADF, South Africa became a republic. The new Republic of South Africa removed the Queen as Head of State and left the Commonwealth. The last Governor General became State President, and there began a legislative adoption of the Apartheid regime. The rising opposition to Apartheid both at home and abroad is well known, and as a result the SADF was used regularly to suppress violent opposition in direct support of the South African Police. It was often the case that the SADF would move in to restore order in the townships once the police had lost control.

In addition to their internal security role, the SADF were deployed for many years in supporting Pretoria's political allies in the Mozambican, Zimbabwean and Angolan civil wars, as well as in regular conflicts along the border and in South West Africa during the Namibian independence struggle. This period, which saw the rise of African nationalism, saw the SADF expand in both numbers and capability. The SADF, which had been formed with around 25,000 personnel, soon saw its numbers increase to over 83,000. The UN-imposed arms embargo provoked the development of a very capable and sophisticated arms industry, which enabled South Africa to become militarily self-sufficient. South Africa could demonstrate that its armed forces were immeasurably better in all regards than those of any of its neighbours, and indeed of any other African country.

The SADF was a conscript force, and this burden fell predominantly on the white population. It is interesting to note that in line with the perversity of Apartheid, Asians and 'Coloureds' with mixed ancestry were also eligible to serve, but this was a very small minority. However, the 32nd Battalion (the Buffalo Battalion) was raised with the soldiers being predominantly Angolan nationals with a connection to the National Liberation Front of Angola (FNLA); the officers and senior non-commissioned officers were mainly white. The 32nd Battalion fought with distinction in Angola, and again in the Namibian independence war. It was withdrawn to South Africa in 1989 and then, following an incident in Phola Park in 1992 where members of the public were shot and killed, was disbanded in March 1993. Its members, who could not return home, were retired to a camp near the town of Pomfret in a very isolated part of South Africa.

The SADF grew into a sophisticated and very effective force within the African environment. It could field the whole range of capabilities in its full-time forces and through its extensive Citizen Forces (CF), which were based on the traditions of the old Boer Kommandos and the British territorial regiments. The CF units enjoyed some ironically traditional names belonging more to the time of the Dominion than that of the Republic: the Cape Town Highlanders Regiment, the Transvaal Scottish Regiment and the Transvaal Horse Artillery. These very traditional regiments, not surprisingly recruited from the English-speaking population, had clear British ancestry. During the height of the internal unrest, the National Party government was increasingly concerned that the Cape Town Highlanders were more likely to be sympathetic to the liberal opposition and would be unwilling to suppress unrest in the townships. To address this, the regiment received drafts of Afrikaners and National Party supporters who could be relied upon; this assured that the character of the regiment was changed.

During the fighting in Angola and Namibia, the SADF won the clear majority of the tactical battles, but was eventually strategically unsuccessful and had to be withdrawn back to South Africa. Concurrently, the nature of the threat was also changing towards a counter-insurgency campaign being conducted by the MK and APLA, challenging the Apartheid regime by force of arms. It was estimated that by 1984 there were 6,000 MK and APLA volunteers in exile being trained and armed in many countries, including Ethiopia, Uganda, Tanzania, the Soviet Union, Cuba and Warsaw Pact countries. The volunteers had support and camps in neighbouring Mozambique, Lesotho, Zimbabwe and Zambia. These camps became targets for the SADF, who launched cross-border strikes which proved very effective in disrupting any large-scale insurgency.

By the end of the Apartheid regime, the SADF was the most sophisticated force in Africa, well equipped and able to operate successfully in both conventional and counter-insurgency warfare. It had been successful militarily and had crushed any insurgent opposition with ease. It had operated within South Africa in support of the deeply unpopular South African Police Service, but had learnt to moderate its actions for the most part and sought to defuse township violence rather than inflame tensions. Now Apartheid was at an end, its political bedrock had ceased to exist. As a non-inclusive force, the SADF had to change, and change as fundamentally as the political tide.

* * *

The uMkhonto we Sizwe (Spear of the Nation), abbreviated to MK, was the armed wing of the ANC and was formed on 16 December 1961 in the wake of the Sharpeville massacre. This marked the end to the totally non-violent protest movement that the ANC had originally envisaged. In June 1961, the ANC had warned the South African government that if there was no movement towards constitutional reform, then it would institute a resistance policy. Nelson Mandela referred to this change during his trial in Rivonia: 'The time comes in the life of any nation when there remain only two choices – submit or fight. That time has now come to South Africa. We shall not submit and we have no choice but to hit back by all means in our power in defence of our people, our future, and our freedom.'

On the evening on which it was founded, the MK initiated a series of bomb attacks in all major cities in South Africa. This was the beginning of its low-level bombing campaign against institutional targets such as pass offices, electrical pylons and police stations. The South African regime was swift to respond, and soon the MK leadership and command structure had to move into exile. This exile not only gave the MK the ability to secure training areas outside South Africa, but also allowed them to gain international support. MK recruits soon began to leave South Africa to join newly formed units within the neighbouring African countries, the front-line states. As their training progressed, elements joined in actions against the Rhodesian Army, and soon the MK was allied formally to the Zimbabwe People's Revolutionary Army (ZIPRA). The numbers moving into exile surged in 1976 after the increasing civil unrest in South Africa, and these elements were labelled the 'student soldiers' or the 'June 1976 Detachment'. By 1977, the MK felt confident enough to begin to infiltrate scores of trained personnel back into South Africa.

In response, the South African government increased its counter-insurgency activity against the MK. This move varied from increasing National Service to two years for white South Africans to conducting cross-border interdiction raids against MK training camps. These raids were so successful that in Angola the MK was forced to relocate many of its camps to the north of the country. It was during this period that the MK evolved and looked to create a more sophisticated structure to enhance its internal security, improve its ability to survive increased counter-insurgency activities of the South African government, increase the levels of direct and indirect international support, and conduct more ambitious offensive operations within the country. This evolution was called Operation Mayibuye.

The development of a Special Operations Division and an Intelligence Division (MKIZA) saw an increase in the effectiveness of insurgency operations inside South Africa, with bombings of the Sasol oil refinery complex in 1980 and the Eskom power plants in 1981. There were also attacks on police stations (Booysens, Soweto and Soekmekaar), a bold attack on the Voortekkerhoogte military complex in Pretoria in 1981, physical clashes with the police in rural areas (Derdepoort and Rustenberg) and car bomb explosions outside both the South African Air Force and Military Intelligence headquarters in Pretoria in 1983. The tempo of operations continued throughout the 1980s, with a steady increase in both rural and urban areas. In 1987, there were two major successes: a car bomb outside the Johannesburg Magistrates' Court and a mortar attack on the alleged 'secret' South African Air Force's 3 Satellite Radar Station at Klippan in the Western Transvaal. The MK was also involved in operations in support of fellow freedom fighters, working closely with Frelimo, ZIPRA and UNITA forces. These all contributed to a wide experience of both conventional and insurgent operations gained by the senior MK personnel.

One of the ironies of the armed struggle against Apartheid was that incidents against the civil population did not receive international support and, if anything, drew adverse comment. So whilst there was an almost universal criticism of the Apartheid regime and an increasing demand for it to cease, there was not the balancing support for any action against the population or infrastructure that was not purely political and passive in nature. Therefore, with a few notable exceptions, the MK actions were generally small-scale in nature and had an insignificant effect on the economy or the population. There was, however, a constant series of attacks on isolated communities, especially farmsteads.

Throughout this time, it was clear that the MK was the military wing of the ANC and that it was supporting a political struggle. It therefore had the trappings of a revolutionary force in that the commissars were present at all levels and, in theory, acted as deputies to military commanders. In its manifesto, the MK stated its intent that it would carry on the struggle for freedom and democracy by methods which were necessary to complement the actions of the established national liberation organizations. It made it clear that all its members were to place themselves under its political guidance to support the cause of national liberation.

As the political impetus towards regime change gathered pace under President de Klerk, formal talks began in 1990 that laid the path towards the general election in 1994. However, neither party discussed the status of the military forces until November 1993 because each side valued its armed forces as an insurance policy; perhaps more as a symbolic gesture and proverbial security blanket. The retention of an armed force was a reminder of what could happen if negotiations failed. But once the negotiations started, the MK, having been front and centre of the 'liberation' movement, was to play a pivotal role in the negotiations for and the process towards the fully integrated SANDF.

* * *

Transkei, Bophuthatswana, Venda and Ciskei were four independent 'black homelands' that the Apartheid government established. The intent was to form self-governing territories, each of which was tribally homogenous. Once they were fully functioning, the homelands were nominally declared independent from South Africa. With forced relocation, the long-term intent of the Apartheid government was to remove the whole of the black population from South Africa into these homelands. As part of this overall programme, each homeland had its own defence force,[1] which was established with the assistance of the South African government and the SADF. Consequently, the training system and overall operating standard were similar or identical to the SADF. These defence forces were responsible for the internal security of their respective homelands. It was an unfortunate consequence that these forces became more involved in politics, and each had at least one coup during their brief existence. However, with the culture of the TBVC forces very much anchored in that of the SADF, their members were easily incorporated into the SANDF when the homelands ceased to exist, and 11,000 were available to be integrated into the SANDF in 1994; by 1998 the figure was 7,243. The TBVC forces provided a significant number of black officers and non-commissioned officers who had important functions in the formation of the SANDF. An interesting observation is that although these homelands were termed 'black homelands', that was merely a label. This was demonstrated by the appointment of Major General Ron Reid Daly as the commander of the Transkei Defence Force, the same man who had commanded the Selous Scouts, the notorious Special Forces regiment of the Rhodesian Army.

* * *

The Pan Africanist Congress (PAC), now known as the Pan Africanist Congress of Azania, is still active in South African politics, although it is losing support steadily, polling fewer than 38,000 votes in the 2014 election compared to the 243,478 votes it received in 1994. The party was formed as part of the schism in the ANC following the adoption of the Freedom Charter in 1955. Whereas the ANC campaigned for a non-racial South Africa, the PAC was more extreme, as suggested by the inaugural speech by Robert Sobukwe in 1959, when he made it clear that he wanted government of the Africans by the Africans, with an African majority democratic rule being established. Shortly after this, in April 1960, following the Sharpeville massacre, the PAC – along with the

ANC – was outlawed by the South African government. In September 1961, the PAC formed a military wing, the Azanian People's Liberation Army (APLA). This was three months before the formation of the MK, and the APLA set out from the beginning to be extremist. The APLA (or Poqo as it was originally called) made no effort to minimize civilian casualties, and was the most militant of the various resistance movements.

APLA went through many transformations and was constantly at war with itself, especially after the death of Robert Sobukwe in 1978. The internal conflicts within the PAC and APLA resulted in military activity ceasing for a long period, the turmoil lasting until 1985 when the APLA began military activity again. APLA operations included the attacks on the South African Police in Sharpeville (1986) and the Soweto Police Training College (1987). Notoriously, in 1986 the APLA coined the infamous slogan of 'one settler, one bullet'. This was universally condemned, and the PAC still attempts to distance itself from any association with this rallying cry. It did mark a further shift by the APLA away from other resistance movements, in that it continued attacks predominantly against white civilians even in the period after the release of Nelson Mandela. The majority of attacks were against farms, although the group claimed responsibility for attacks on restaurants and even against St James Church in Cape Town in July 1993, in which twelve people were killed and 148 injured.

When the APLA was invited to integrate with all the other constituent parties to form the SANDF, the Maoist-Revolutionary faction declined and most of its members returned to exile. However, the APLA formally ended its armed struggle in 1994 and 6,000 APLA personnel were identified to enter the integration process. By mid-1995, 2,569 had reported to De Brug, and by 1998 the figure had risen to 3,713.

* * *

The self-defence and self-protection units evolved out of the demands from various communities who felt that they were subject to excessive tribal violence which was met with either indifference or partisanship of the local police. The mission of these units was to provide protection to the various communities, and through their presence an element of law and order. The MK had proposed to train self-defence units but had none of the manpower, structure or resources (especially weapons) to achieve this venture. Consequently, local volunteers, who were mainly undisciplined, took on the task and often the units became more of a hindrance and a problem than a solution. In 1990, the Inkatha Freedom Party (IFP) established itself as a major political force under the leadership of Chief Mangosuthu Buthelezi, with its power base in Kwazulu-Natal. The IFP had been part of the ANC from its foundation in 1975, but it broke away in 1979 and the relationship between the two political parties deteriorated steadily, even though Chief Buthelezi had been a prominent member of the ANC. It did not take long before rival supporters became involved in violent clashes. As a consequence, the IFP formed self-protection units, and right up to the 1994 general election there were regular clashes between the ANC self-defence units and IFP self-protection units. In the late 1980s, the SADF trained many Zulu members of the IFP to act in self-protection units. The intent was for these units to operate against the armed members of the United Democratic Front (UDF) and the Confederation of South African Trade Unions (COSATU), both of which were surrogate fronts for the exiled ANC. There were many clashes, and SADF-trained IFP members were implicated in the Trust Feed massacre in 1988 and the Boipatong massacre in 1992. The self-protection units were amalgamated into the KwaZulu-Natal Self Protection Force (KZSPF), and by 1998 a total of 1,788 members of the KZSPF had joined the integration process.

Chapter 3

The Devil In The Detail

It soon became apparent that it was necessary to approach the move to South Africa as a two-phase operation. Firstly, I needed to pack what I would require as if I was departing on a six-month deployment, but with the addition of a selection of civilian and sports kit. It would be winter in South Africa, but I had little idea of what that meant, apart from the knowledge I had gained from my cousin in Pretoria, who said she had never seen snow on the High Veldt. A quick check suggested that the daytime temperatures would be in the twenties Centigrade and the evenings would be cool – in fact better than the weather we were having in Lincolnshire in June. So it would be an easy pack – several books, a camera (new) and a radio would be the luxury items. The Quartermaster had arranged several sets of tropical combat suits for me – it is Africa and the temperate kit would be too warm, I was assured – and he also chucked in a couple of bush hats and several extra water bottles for good measure. The second phase would be to identify what we would need as a family in South Africa, but as I had no idea where we were to live, that phase would have to wait a bit.

My next stop was the medical and dental centres. It would be fair to say that I was filled with more than a normal amount of trepidation as I walked in. On my first tour of Northern Ireland, an enthusiastic dentist had decided that two of my wisdom teeth looked as though they might run a risk of impacting at some time in the future. Rather than wait and see, he decided that it would be better if he yanked them both out then and there – just in case. I was not best pleased, and I still to this day think that it was unnecessary. They say many complaints are psychosomatic, and as I crossed the threshold I was convinced I felt a twinge in my remaining wisdom teeth. This time, however, all was well. The dentist took a long time to complete her inspection before announcing that there was no need for any form of dentistry and that my teeth should be in fine fettle for the next year. She was concerned that I was going to Africa and was determined that for however long I was to be there, my teeth were not going to be the cause of any anxiety. It did seem somewhat over-protective, and I resisted the temptation to remind her that South Africa had a very good reputation for all things medical; after all, I remember that Christiaan Barnard conducted the first heart transplant operation in Cape Town. I kept quiet. Having sharp, pointed instruments in one's mouth was a remarkably effective way of suppressing sarcastic remarks.

Next it was a visit to the doctor. Again, there was a thorough inspection, this time with coughing, squeezing, prodding and listening, which resulted in me being passed fit for deployment. What he was concerned about was the number of injections that I needed and the narrow window of time before I could deploy. Therefore, I was to become a pincushion in the coming fortnight, and I was pumped with inoculations for yellow fever, typhoid, typhus, tetanus, polio and hepatitis A, B and C. I was given malarial prophylactics and all measures of pills and potions. At the end of it, I was ready for Africa and all that it would throw at me. The cocktails of inoculations, however, knocked me flat on my back, and I had to retire to bed for twenty-four hours with a raging fever and feeling like death; a perfectly normal reaction to having so many foreign bodies injected into my precious sealed and normally balanced system.

On 23 May, a signal came into the regiment confirming the movement dates. The advance party – which was to consist of the Commander, Brigadier Dick Trigger (late Parachute Regiment), the Deputy Commander, Colonel Paul Davis (late Royal Hampshire Regiment) and the immediate Headquarters staff – would fly on 1 June. The remainder of us would fly on 4 June. The signal went on in very brief detail to describe our task before finishing with a reassuring paragraph that said 'a briefing pack is being assembled to give greater background to the New South Africa, an outline of the BMATT task, a map and job specifications'. We would find out what we were supposed to be doing, in outline at least, upon arrival. But most importantly, the signal stated that the 'South Africans have asked that team members deploy with Mess Kit or Dinner Suit (or women's equivalent)'. There was not a lot about what we would need on a day-to-day basis, but at least we would be able to dine correctly attired.

The signal continued that BMATT (SA) was to be thirty-one strong, drawing from all three services. There was to be a Commander with a small HQ element, comprising senior service representatives from the Royal Navy, Army and Royal Air Force, plus one other RAF officer who would be the senior representative for the medical services. The remainder of us were to represent the various arms and services – in my case, I was to look after all aspects of the artillery, both field artillery and air defence artillery. There were infantrymen, an armoured corps officer, a sapper, a signaller, an intelligence officer and so on. One thing that was stated but not made clear in the signal was that a small element would become a permanent presence; in other words, they would be posted to the mission for at least two years and therefore would be accompanied by their family, whereas the others would be on a six-month rotation. Although I had been told that I was one of the permanent members, rather worryingly there was nothing on paper to this effect.

The first stage of the process would be to establish the team in Pretoria, where briefings and orientation would take place. Most of the team would then deploy to the Assembly Area/Personnel Maintenance Office and Reception Depot (PMORD) near Pretoria but some, to be detailed by the Commander, would deploy to Hoedspruit Assembly Area, 'some 150km NE of Pretoria', wherever that was. Then came the interesting sentence: 'At end of initial PMORD phase, [the] team will deploy to HQs/Training Schools throughout RSA to continue task.' So we knew where we would start the initial phase, but not much else. As to what we were supposed to do at this PMORD, one hoped that would be covered at the 'briefings and orientation' sessions.

* * *

It was of course not just a question of my moving, but in due course also Trisha and the girls, although when the move would take place – and indeed to where – was not made clear. It was a pretty unsettling period, and the whole tortuous issue of leaving a wife and family with a regiment whilst I was posted overseas began to become clear. There were the practical issues. Trisha was on the last stage of her PGCE, which was due to finish in July at about the same time as the girls were to finish their school year. The signal of 23 May had stated that 'those deploying married accompanied should not expect to move their families before 1 Jul 94. BMATT admin party will select housing which will be fully furnished. Further instr[uction]s for married accompanied personnel to fol[low].' While this was as vague as could be, it at least gave a 'not before date', which with Trisha's course and the girls' end of term was ideal. If the housing was to be fully furnished, then it would mean putting the majority of our possessions into storage. There was also the issue of when it would be safe for families to travel and what possessions could or should be taken. It became clear that 'to follow' was to be the mantra.

I was able to get hold of someone in the logistics centre in Andover who was knowledgeable in the practicalities of intercontinental moves, and he stated that BMATT (SA) had been classified as a Loan Service posting. This meant that there was to be a Memorandum of Understanding signed between the governments of UK and South Africa which would spell out the details of responsibilities and provisions, and detail where costs would fall. From this would come the Terms and Conditions of Service, which was binding on the UK personnel and covered all the UK administrative details. This would cover pay, allowances, movement and freight entitlements, housing requirements, education for children, medical, dental and legal provisions, and so on and so forth. This sounded very good, but when I asked to see a copy, I was told that it had not yet been drafted, let alone discussed. However, as BMATT (SA) was to be established at the request of the hosting government, and being cognizant that South Africa was a wealthy country, it had been decided that we should base our initial entitlements on BMATT Kuwait. Just why I am not sure, but that was to be the case. This meant that I had a source as a planning guide for movement of freight. I spoke to the Quartermaster, who as always was a great sounding board, especially when armed with some form of authoritative paperwork. He perused the documentation for Kuwait and said that I should apply for sea freight – which would take about six weeks from leaving the regiment to arriving in our abode in South Africa – and airfreight, which would be quicker, taking about a week. For the initial journey, I would be entitled to three suitcases – or more realistically, two suitcases and a Bergen.[1] Everything else would go into storage.

At least we had something to work on. Boxes started to arrive, and we began to work our way through the house, prioritising items: storage; sea freight; airfreight (about 1 metre square); my flight baggage and the family flight baggage (three suitcases each, with no Bergens). The garage became the hub of activity as time ticked away. Of course, in all our previous moves we had a new address for our move – for which we could arrange change of address cards, set up utilities, phone lines and so on. On this occasion we had no idea where we would be living. The storage items would just be stored, and the sea and airfreight would be collected to be sent to South Africa once we knew its final destination. Details became trivial, the key being to get as much as possible sorted before I set off for Heathrow.

* * *

On 4 June I was at Heathrow Terminal 3 with a South African Airways Business Class ticket in my hand, a trolley loaded with two suitcases and my faithful Bergen, and about to meet the main party of the new team in the lounge. Both BA and SAA had several flights going to South Africa, either Johannesburg or Cape Town, each evening, so the departure lounge would be full. How is one expected to meet up with people you have never met before? This is one of the advantages of being in the British Army, and the answer is obvious – haircut and jacket. Short hair, not too short, and what would seem to be homogenous tweed or herringbone country jackets, or the timeless blazer. Bingo! There were five obvious suspects when I walked in, and an old face I had not seen for a while. To be fair, Cheryl had a very young and pretty face. I had first met her when she had been Assistant Adjutant of our sister regiment in Dortmund and I was a new, wet-behind-the-ears young subaltern joining my regiment. She was great fun then, and it was really good to see her again. We then began to corral the others, and mentally ticked their names off the list one by one as we married faces to names. Several glasses of wine later, we were boarding the aircraft, each of us wondering what lay ahead.

It is something unique to the military as to how you can bond just upon meeting. All of us were in the same position, lacking a clear brief, but were all now heading to South Africa for a somewhat tantalizing mission.

The team had been scattered around the cabin. I sat next to a charming South African businessman on the plane, who introduced me to Pinotage wine and biltong (dried cured meat). He was excited about the changes facing the whole of South Africa, but at the same time he was realistic. However, he felt the strengths of hard work would always bring rewards and he was not going to 'run away', as he saw it. His family had been in South Africa for over a century, it was his home and, perhaps most importantly, he saw himself as an African.

The sun rose as we entered Zimbabwean airspace, and the massive fiery ball that is sunrise in Africa dominated the eastern horizon. I had not seen a sunrise like it. 'Another new dawn in Africa,' my companion joked. 'You will soon learn that no day is ever the same in Africa.' He was not wrong.

* * *

We arrived somewhat tired but expectant, as for most of us this was our first time in Africa. It was a Sunday; there was a blue sky and a gentle wind, with temperatures creeping up the teens to settle at about 20°C. The airport was large and very much like any other around the world. It was bustling with new arrivals, as all long-haul flights seemed to arrive within thirty minutes of each other. On the concourse stood a British Army Warrant Officer dressed in his stone-coloured barrack dress uniform, looking and acting as though he was an old hand even though he had only arrived three days previously. We were shepherded out to the waiting transport in the huge car park outside Johannesburg International Airport, formerly known as Jan Smuts International Airport and later to be renamed O.R. Tambo International Airport. I do not know quite what I expected, but the smart, modern buildings, acres of cars all shining brightly in the sunshine and infrastructure with all the trappings of a modern Western society was a little unsettling. I was expecting something else, but I could not actually articulate what it was.

* * *

Travelling west from the airport in the Johannesburg suburb of Kempton Park towards Johannesburg itself, then turning north on the N3 towards Midrand, we passed the signs to Alexandra. Alexandra, one of the townships that surrounded Johannesburg, had seen its fair share of troubles, especially during the unrest following the Soweto riots in 1976 when nineteen people had been killed. Seeing the shacks of the townships nestling so close to the road signs for Sandton City, one of the wealthier parts of Johannesburg, gave us perhaps the first indication of the scale of the challenge that we were about to face. But no sooner had we noticed the first signs of poverty than the next things we saw were the glittering buildings of the high-tech companies that lined the road through Midrand on the way to Pretoria. There were contradictions already, and we had only just arrived. We wound our way into Pretoria, with its mixture of colonial buildings, high-rise blocks and the 'shabby chic' residences with elegant façades topped off with silver-painted corrugated iron roofs. It was a busy city with smart shops, impressive public areas and an amazing sense of space, the like of which I had seen previously only in the US and Canada. We then arrived at our destination, the Pretoria suburb of Voortrekkerhoogte. We were to be initially billeted at the South African Army Staff College, or rather in its barracks.

It was a question of dumping suitcases and having lunch before launching into the briefings. There was an element of death by vu-foil; PowerPoint was still in its infancy. We were given an introduction to the now-formed SANDF and learned about the structures of the four services. This was like going back to Staff College, the only difference being that there was unlikely to be a test at the end. Following that, we had a series of presentations about the recent history of South Africa, up to the negotiations between the ANC and the National Party, and events after that. We had the Multiparty Negotiating Forum (MPNF) explained to us, which had seen the inclusion in the discussions of the white right-wing parties, the Pan African Congress (PAC), the KwaZulu homeland government and delegations from the 'traditional leaders'. It was the MPNF that ratified the Interim Constitution, and then saw the Transitional Executive Council oversee the move to the elections in April 1994. There was a huge amount of information to take in, but we were very lucky to have as our guide, amongst others, Mark Malan from the Institute of Security Studies in Pretoria. Mark had been an officer in the SADF before turning to academia. He was able to put things into context to a military audience with ease; he spoke with an authority and confidence that came from experience. I was lucky to work with Mark again some twelve years later in West Africa.

Finally, we had an address from the Commander on what he expected of us and the outline of the first couple of weeks. It was clear that everyone was feeling their way forward and that, even though the process seemed to have been very well planned, progress had been slow. The impression given was that everyone had been awaiting our arrival. It was lamentable that we were the one group within the process who knew the least, having only a gossamer-thin understanding of what was needed, and yet all the others were looking to us to make the process work!

* * *

At this stage it is worth reviewing how the situation in South Africa had evolved. The 1993 Interim Constitution provided for and directed for the formation of the SANDF, which was to be an integration of the SADF, the defence forces of the former TBVC states, the military forces of the ANC (MK) and PAC (APLA), and subsequently the self-protection units of the Inkatha Freedom Party (KZSPF). The body that oversaw the transitional period was the Convention for a Democratic South Africa (CODESA). which delegated the responsibility for the delivery of the transition to the Transitional Executive Committee (TEC), which consisted of various sub-committees, one of which covered defence. The TEC approved the establishment of the Joint Military Co-ordinating Committee (JMCC), which was to scope the creation of the new Ministry of Defence and look at the issue of integration and defence policy. It was, most importantly, the forum in which former officers of the constituent parts of the new SANDF would meet and work together, although in reality the forum was dominated by SADF and MK leaders. This is important to note, as criticism by MK officers in later years that the SADF just absorbed the other parties does not acknowledge that this was a joint decision agreed to by all parties. In the coming years, the reality was that the SADF dominated the process numerically and technically, although the political leverage was firmly in the hands of the MK through the ANC majority in parliament.

The task ahead of the SANDF was considerable. It was required to integrate the non-statutory forces with the statutory forces in order to create a fully integrated conventional defence force. In other words, it had to create a regular armed force by merging armed forces that had been combatting each other over the previous decades. This was an immense task in itself when the constituent pieces were taken into consideration. Within the existing structure of the SADF, the members of the non-statutory forces were to be integrated to form the SANDF. This was after each member had been allocated an appropriate rank and appointment, and having received sufficient 'Bridging Training' to carry out their appointment effectively. In theory, once an individual had been attested, he or she would cease all ties with their previous force and relatively seamlessly become solely a member of the SANDF.

This would have seemed a logical and fair way to proceed if it was a paper exercise, but the reality was quite different. The members of the MK and APLA, the military wings of the ANC and PAC respectively, were allies in the struggle against Apartheid but not necessarily the best of friends through their political ideology; they would have to be integrated slowly, carefully and with full acknowledgement of the differences between them. To manage this, it was decided to assemble the MK and APLA forces in geographically separate locations. There was an additional challenge of integrating, albeit later in the process, members of the self-protection units of the Inkatha Freedom Party, known as the KwaZulu Self-Protection Force (KZSPF), which whilst originally allied to the ANC had undergone a painful schism and clashed regularly and with considerable fatalities in KwaZulu Natal. At least these elements of the non-statutory forces were unified through their involvement in the struggle against the Apartheid regime, although at the time the KZSPF had been operating against ANC members and had received assistance from the SADF. Then there were the former members of the TBVC homeland forces to be integrated. At least this would be relatively easy, as their training and structure had been modelled on the SADF. All of them had to be integrated with the former members of the SADF, who had been waging a security campaign both internal and external to South Africa against the MK and APLA, whilst aiding the TBVC forces and the KZSPF. The SADF was predominantly comprised of Afrikaners and had been staunch supporters of the previous regime. That is not to say that all the Afrikaner members of the SADF were right-wing supporters, but the image was quite clear. Mixing together all these potentially volatile elements would be dangerous. In reality, the process would have to be handled with extreme care as there was a great risk of an explosion at every twist and turn of the process. Add to all this the political imperatives and the uncertainty which gripped the country, and it was a very audacious ambition.

A question that was often asked was how would we have reacted if the British government had given instructions that the British Army was to be integrated with members of the IRA? It was a question that was best left unanswered.

* * *

The process by which this integration was to occur was to be deliberate, and it was to be the priority task for the Minister of Defence and the SANDF after the election. Initially, the Integration Committee of the SANDF, under the chairmanship of Lieutenant General Nyanda, now Chief of the Defence Force Staff, thought that the assembly and integration process would be completed by the end of 1994. However, it soon became clear that this would be impossible and the process was then given an additional three years to be completed. It had to be made to work, as the spotlight was on the SANDF, both internally and externally. A successful integration would be heralded worldwide as a triumph for President Mandela's new South Africa, an example of how conflict could be resolved in a unified, progressive and harmonious way.

Naturally, the integration process was to be complex but fundamentally fair. In simple terms, it had three phases: assessment, placement and training. Of course, each part of the SANDF had different detailed entrance criteria, but in no way different to any other armed force around the world. The requirements for an air force pilot were naturally different to those for an infantryman, for an engineer in the navy or for a surgeon in the medical services. The criteria for each speciality in the old SADF had followed international norms, so the requirements should be straightforward. At all costs, the spectre of discrimination had to be avoided.

It was identified early on in the process that there were some members of the MK who had left the country and gone into exile many years previously. They were not amongst the top echelons of the organization, but had served loyally and without a doubt in some hardship. They carried illnesses and injuries sustained during their service, and most probably would not be able to continue to serve in the new statutory force. There would have to be a medical discharge system developed and an entitlement to a pension established. At the other end of the scale would be those who clearly had never gone into exile and most probably had just joined the MK or APLA as a stepping-stone to the future. It was estimated from the Certified Personnel Register – the list of certified members of the MK – that 30 per cent of those registered had joined after 1990, and therefore had never gone into exile and had not seen any form of active military service. There was a whole series of scenarios which would have to be considered, discussed and a fair and transparent policy formulated. As always, the devil would be in the detail.

The integration process also had to run in parallel with a streamlining exercise for the SANDF. In 1994, the anticipated numbers available for integration were identified as 90,000 SADF, 22,000 MK, 6,000 APLA and 11,000 TBVC. At this stage there were no figures for the KZSPF. The SANDF would have to expand through integration whilst at the same time looking to reduce its numbers to a level dictated by a review of the standing force required to meet South Africa's new security environment. This would mean downsizing by some form of demobilization. There was a planning figure to reduce the size of the integrated SANDF by about 30,000. This was going to be a very politically sensitive process no matter how it was handled, and consequently the policy endorsement for downsizing came later on in the process. This lack of early political endorsement would cause uncertainty, a great deal of mistrust and consequently disruption.

* * *

The integration process had to be simple. It had to be based on a series of steps that logically took an individual into the Personnel Maintenance Office and Reception Depot (PMORD), through assessment and placement, to an initial training establishment and finally a specialist training establishment. At the end of this process, the newly integrated personnel could join their unit or assume their appointment. The process followed a logical sequence and was tailored to the individual. After assessment, an individual would be placed in a rank and his or her training requirements would be dictated by the qualifications and experience they had demonstrated during their assessment. This process would have four bespoke streams – Army, Navy, Air Force and Medical Services – allowing each arm to concentrate on their specialities and unique qualification requirements.

* * *

There was, of course, an additional stream for the senior leadership, of one-star general rank and above. Clearly, these individuals would seek senior appointment on the staff or in command. Their previous political and practical leadership experience would dictate less of the standard training and more of a focused period of mentoring, to allow the transition of these senior figures into the new SANDF structure as soon as possible. This process had already started and was largely complete by the time BMATT (SA) arrived, as it had been necessary to have senior non-statutory personnel in place during the transition and the deployment of the NPKF during the elections. A good example of this was the appointment of Lieutenant General Nyanda as Chief of the Defence Force Staff in 1994; he was subsequently made Chief of the South African National Defence Force in 1998.

The integration process for the Navy, Air Force and Medical Services was quite straightforward, mainly because the numbers of non-statutory forces applying to transfer were limited and the positions available were very specialized in nature. It was planned that the process would be relatively simple and the placement of individuals into their tailored training packages would be of a short duration. In the more advanced cases, for example that of a surgeon or a pilot, assessment and proof of qualification was required so that a plan could be identified for any remedial training necessary to bring the individual up to the standard which was internationally expected. It would be important to bring forward such high-profile individuals into the training programmes as soon as possible, as their progress and integration would be essential for the SANDF to demonstrate results. This would be part of the necessary communication plan for internal and external consumption.

The big challenge was to be the integration process for the Army. The Army represented the lion's share of the non-statutory forces and embraced the whole spectrum of specialities, from infantry to armour, artillery, engineers, signals, intelligence, logistics and so on. It also had the challenge of having the greatest number of personnel who would serve in the lower echelons – the classic foot soldiers. At any moment in time, any army in the world can be distilled down into the basic denominator of infantry. Every soldier needs to be an infantryman first and a specialist afterwards. The requirement would be for all non-statutory personnel to be able to complete the basic training required of an infantryman, regardless of whether the individual be subsequently placed as an officer, a senior or junior non-commissioned officer or a private soldier. As with the other services, this stage of basic training would be known as Phase 1 Bridging Training. On top of this, the individual had to receive training in his speciality, which would be called Phase 2 Bridging Training. It was not long before the scale of the integration process began to be realized because all this training could only begin once an individual had been assembled, processed and placed.

In the planning for the integration process, which was run by the Joint Military Co-ordinating Committee (JMCC) prior to the election, it had been decided that, unlike in previous examples of integration, the non-statutory forces would not all be assembled for processing at the same time. There would instead be a series of call-ups. This meant that the majority of the MK and APLA personnel would spend up to a year living back in South Africa before being called forward for assessment.

* * *

The Commander, along with his Chief of Staff, Squadron Leader Ian Jenkins, RAF Regiment, and the Chief Clerk, Mr Smith, were ensconced in the SANDF Headquarters, which was the South African equivalent of the Ministry of Defence in Whitehall. It was determined that the Commander would engage with Ministers and the Chiefs of Staff at the strategic level, whilst each of the services would have a senior BMATT (SA) representative. Colonel Paul Davis would be the Army representative, based in the Army Headquarters, as well as being BMATT (SA) Deputy Commander. The remainder of us would focus on the PMORDs and begin, concurrently, the process of validation with our various directorates.

The remainder of the team was to deploy to the three PMORDs – there was an additional one to those listed on the signal of 23 May. The principal location was Wallmannsthal, where the MK was mustered, with two additional locations in Hoedspruit at the South African Air Force base near to the Kruger National Park – some five-and-a-half hours' drive east from Pretoria – and De Brug, near Bloemfontein, a six-hour drive to the west. The latter was the assembly area for the APLA. The Commander nominated small teams to deploy to the two subsidiary sites, but his main effort was Wallmannsthal; the mechanics of all the tasks would be the same, but without doubt the political and media interest would be on Wallmannsthal as it was just 60km north of Pretoria and took about an hour to drive there.

* * *

The Commander intended that BMATT (SA) would become fully operational on 13 June, giving us one working week to get briefed, orientated, administered and ready to execute our mission. It was to be a steep learning curve. He then outlined the tasks, which were threefold: to validate, monitor and adjudicate. They were briefed as follows:

> The BMATT (SA) was to validate the criteria and standards for the SANDF. The criteria and standards would determine the initial assessment of personnel integrating into and their employment in the SANDF, selection onto training courses, the content of the courses and the criteria for student success or failure. The JMCC had set the criteria and standards, and the BMATT (SA) would have to validate the criteria and standards against international norms.
>
> The BMATT (SA) was to monitor assessment, selection and training across all four arms of the SANDF to ensure that they complied with the standards already set and validated. The personnel were to ensure that they were applied in an even handed way during 'Bridging Training' (the main part of the process by which non-statutory forces make the transition from non-conventional to a conventional force).
>
> Finally, the BMATT (SA) was to adjudicate if disputes arose between parties involved in the integration process. Within this, it was acknowledged that it was the ambition of all parties to the integration process that disputes should be avoided. However, in the event of a dispute, the BMATT (SA) 'line' should be taken into account by all parties to the dispute and respected by all.

> If there was still a dispute, the issue may be referred to a more senior forum, at which there should also be BMATT (SA) representation.

In addition, a possible secondary task was identified for BMATT (SA) personnel to assist with the training and instruction, but only if this did not conflict with the three primary tasks.

Chapter 4

First Days

The day wore on. More and more information was being pumped into us and, although we were now grasping the enormity of our task and the expectation being placed on our small team, we were approaching information overload. In retrospect, it would have been much easier if the background information, especially the political intent, had been sent to us in advance. But hindsight is always a great thing. For the remainder of the first day we had some discussions with the Deputy Commander, Colonel Davis, who was focusing on the Army integration issues, how he saw our initial engagement and his thoughts on the structure of the team in the coming months. One soon realized that he and the Commander were trying to create something out of very little information. It was reassuring to see that the senior ranks were equally surviving from hand to mouth, but at the same time somewhat disconcerting that nobody really had any idea of what we were facing once we commenced operating. There would be no template, and the impression that BMATT (SA) made in the initial days would be up to our combined initiative.

What we were about to experience in the PMORDs, the assessment and placement procedures and the subsequent integration process had never been done before. There was no right or wrong way of operating. One needed integrity, hard work, honesty and a clear and very unambiguous understanding of what was right and wrong. Added to these characteristics was the certainty that any decision made was going to upset someone. This was not going to be an appointment where a huge number of friends would be made. It was, like in so many cases in the Army, a case of having to engineer it as the occasion demanded. Nevertheless, if a steady job with a manageable routine had been sought, then one would not have joined the Army.

The first of many surprises came that first day in Pretoria in our follow-up meeting with Colonel Davis. In a very much 'get to know each other' session, he was giving his opinion on the subsequent responsibilities and challenges each of us would face in the period of Bridging Training. He informed the Royal Military Police officer, Jeremy Green, that he would have a relatively straightforward task as the numbers estimated to apply to join the military police were small. His 'cap badge' appointment was therefore likely to be limited and he would definitely be on a six-month tour. The same would apply to Al Sommerlad, the Intelligence Corps captain, and to Nick Richardson, the Sapper. Colonel Davis then turned to me and said that I would be responsible for the integration of both the field artillery and the air defence artillery. The former was based in Potchefstroom and the latter in Kimberley, so it would mean a fair time on the road. He then said that my post was also a six-month appointment. Needless to say, this came as somewhat of a shock, and I retorted that if this was the case then something would need to happen quite quickly as the whole of my possessions were in the process of being split up between storage, sea and air freight. I also just imagined the conversation I would have to have with Trisha and the girls. Fortunately, my shock was equalled by one of the infantry officers, James Sawyer, who was informed that he was about to spend two years at the Infantry School in Oudtshoorn, when he was due to start his staff training at the Portuguese Staff College in eight months' time. Colonel Davis resolved the matter a few hours later; he clearly was a cool character and, along with the rest of us, was to be well tested in the coming months.

Colonel Davis went on to say that he was uncertain where I would be best placed. I was the most qualified of the deployed majors, so there might be a greater role for me at the PMORDs and in Pretoria. This was due to a certain extent to the very good reputation of the South African Artillery, which was recognized as being highly professional, and so it was assumed that their integration process would be straightforward. I might therefore end up quartered in Pretoria and visiting Potchefstroom and Kimberley on a regular basis, rather than being quartered in Potchefstroom or Kimberley. So eventually it looked as though I was here for two years.

* * *

Our accommodation was also a surprise, which I suppose is a typical example of British understatement. It was a barrack block with twenty-odd beds to a room, sheets and blankets folded and ready on a bed frame, concrete floors and the thin curtains that bedeck such accommodation the world over. I am not saying that I need five-star comfort, and I have happily enjoyed such facilities when on exercise or pre-deployment training. I have slept in very interesting places in the past, including a very warm night in a piggery on one occasion, although after four weeks in the field I am sure neither I, nor my crew, nor the pigs objected to the smell. But somehow this was completely unexpected. We had, after all, been flown across in business class, and we knew that the South Africans had a mess system similar to our own, so why the barrack block? It led to an interesting first night which, surprisingly, was quite cold. We were all to a man wrong-footed by the South African winter weather. Yes, we realized that, although it was June, this was the middle of the South African winter. It was cold at night, and cold at 2,000 metres above sea level has an additional bite to it. I suppose I should feel embarrassed by this incredible lack of forethought, but I was not alone; we all had suffered from collective assumptions. I remember reading Andy McNabb's *Bravo Two Zero* book and being amazed at how the SAS managed to deploy to Iraq, be dressed in completely the wrong kit and thus suffer exposure and frostbite. Well here we were, shivering in a barrack block, expecting to have been received into a comfortable mess; the only advantage was that nobody was trying to kill us.

We awoke early next morning to a glorious day with a bright blue sky and not a cloud in sight, but very cold. We got up, showered, shaved and put on our uniforms for the first time – to a man dressed in jungle combats, issued for Africa. They were good, lightweight and could dry easily from one's body heat; ideal for Brunei or Belize, but frankly, in June in South Africa I would have loved my old temperate combat kit with that thick, warm jacket. However, that was not to be. We collectively took the decision that we were British after all, so we would enjoy this bracing weather. And damn it, we were not going to let the locals know that we were cold! The locals, I would add, were the students of the Army Staff College. They were emerging from their rondavels and heading to the mess for breakfast, wearing greatcoats and looking warm. We were freezing but making the effort to appear delighted to be in such a wonderful climate. Monty Halls, our Royal Marine, made a point of asking if the swimming pool was open and expressed considerable dismay when learning that it was closed for the winter. He could not understand why, with such sunny weather, a refreshing dip should be denied. I am sure we fooled nobody, but at least it provided a subject for conversation.

We were informed later in the day that we were being moved into the mess in Voortrekkerhoogte,[1] about a mile away. Much muttering of ironical disappointment was heard, but not too loudly. In the meantime, we boarded minibuses to take us across Pretoria to the British High Commission on Hill Street in the suburb of Arcadia.

Pretoria is a typical city; bustling, cosmopolitan and an architectural array of old and modern, although it would be correct to substitute old for colonial and Cape Dutch, the latter being a beautiful style of building in an Afrikaner style dating from the seventeenth century. There were high-rise buildings and impressive sandstone structures, such as the magnificent Union Buildings designed by Sir Herbert Baker in the English monumental style. It is a modern city similar to many in the USA, with a grid system in the centre. But within it there are some stark reminders of the country's unique history. On our way to the High Commission, we passed the Voortrekker Monument, a huge granite monolith. It reminded me of the Leipzig monument erected in 1913 to commemorate the centenary of the Battle of the Nations. The Voortrekker Monument was designed to commemorate the Voortrekkers who left the Cape Colony between 1835 and 1854 to found the Orange Free State and the Transvaal. It is a deeply significant memorial for the Afrikaners, and although it has much symbolism of white supremacy and the idea that Western civilization is triumphant, the ANC government declared it a National Heritage Site in 2011. In 1994, however, it gave the impression of retrenchment and resistance to the seismic changes that were occurring all around it.

We continued our journey to Arcadia, the 'playground of the Gods', which is, I suppose, a very apt name for the diplomatic quarter; Pretoria hosts the second-highest number of embassies in the world after Washington DC. It is an area of wide avenues and an eclectic mix of buildings, and no greater contrast could there be between that of the British High Commission and the US Embassy. The British High Commission hid behind the grandeur of the façade of the colonial period. Behind this façade was a highly technical world, but it oozed the charm and sophistication that the Foreign and Commonwealth Office used to hold in such high esteem. It emitted elegance, superiority and a sense of belonging. The US Embassy, by comparison, was a metal and glass architectural monstrosity that seemed quite out of place.

At the High Commission, passports and identity cards were produced and checked and we were permitted to enter the inner sanctum. A jovial Royal Navy petty officer welcomed us and gave us a very cursory country briefing. There was no Defence Adviser or High Commissioner to greet us, and we were left wondering why on earth we were there. Then a Foreign and Commonwealth Office (FCO) official arrived and gave a thoroughly underwhelming brief on the political situation. In comparison to that which we had received from Mark Malan the previous day, it was quite naïve – and that is being polite. That was the sum of our briefings by Her Majesty's representatives.

Looking back, and accepting that any comparison is invidious, I can honestly say that we were not prepared for what we were about to encounter. I suppose that the South Africans who briefed us were able to deliver a very good political scene-setter, but they did not think to prepare us for Africa. After all, they were African, they understood how things worked and had grown up understanding the culture and nuances of the different peoples who made up South Africa. To them it was in their blood. By the same token, the British briefs were wholly inadequate because the High Commission staff appeared unable to brief about South African culture and the nuances of tribal relationships because it was either not in their remit or, more likely, was irrelevant to them in their cosseted diplomatic world. Without doubt, our FCO colleagues were comfortable in their life in Pretoria, with its leafy suburbs, shopping malls and first-world comforts. There was no need to understand the difference between a Xhosa, a Tswana or a Zulu, or the political doctrine that served a member of the MK, APLA or KZSPF. We left the High Commission thoroughly deflated. We had the sense that, with the lack of any senior representation in the briefs, we were an inconvenience thrust upon them. It was quite bizarre that there should be such a disconnect. On the one side, we were a hugely important element of the integration process, a process that had to work, and yet, to the official British presence in South Africa, we seemed to be an irritating intrusion into their cosy world. It did not bode well for future relationships between BMATT (SA) and the British High Commission.

* * *

That evening we moved to the mess in Voortrekkerhoogte. Here we were allocated single rooms with a bed, lockers and a sink, and there was an adjoining shared shower. It was an interesting but workable combination. Most importantly, it was warm and therefore instantly homely. The mess had anterooms and a large dining room, and was more of a transit or garrison mess than a regimental mess, but with a welcoming bar. Home had been found for the time being. It was good to mix with South African officers, but the lack of a black face was a constant reminder of what we were about to embark on. In fact, there were some who were far from welcoming and they, after a few drinks, lost no time in telling us that people thought BMATT were nothing more than a bunch of 'Kaffir lovers'.

So, after a couple of days in country we were not much the wiser. But wisdom then came from an unusual quarter. Many of the South African officers we met in the bar in Voortrekkerhoogte were very balanced and soundly grounded following many years of operations. They really welcomed speaking to fellow soldiers from nations other than Israel and Taiwan, which until recently were the only countries to regularly work with South Africa. There is a common understanding between soldiers, regardless of the nation they serve. The same hardships are experienced, the same emotions felt, and the same camaraderie is expressed. The one thing soldiers do is to speak directly. We began to gather an insight into the challenges ahead and the nuances required to deal with the non-statutory forces. Over a beer together, we began to learn what we, as BMATT officers, needed to be aware of and how to approach our task. We also began to understand that there was no desire to fight a civil war in South Africa. The consensus amongst those with a modicum of common sense was that change was necessary, no matter how bitter a pill it would be to swallow, and that the future would be dictated by those prepared to manage change. We were like sponges absorbing everything.

* * *

The rest of the week passed in a blur as we prepared ourselves for the task ahead. There was a mountain of administration to be tackled, both British and South African. One such task was to attend the South African Medical Services (SAMS) clinic in Army Headquarters, as it had been identified that we might not have been given the right inoculations! The doctor, while sympathetic, said that we ought to have an additional inoculation against yet another strain of hepatitis which was particularly prevalent in the High Veldt. He also announced, as some form of compensation, that there was no need to take the malarial prophylactics we had been prescribed as malaria had been wiped out in South Africa, except in some areas in and around the Kruger Park.

One evening that week, the BMATT (SA) Army contingent was invited to an icebreaker at the Army Headquarters Mess. This would be the opportunity to meet the South African officers with whom we would be working closely at the PMORDs, most of whom were from the various arms and services directorates. At this stage, it was exclusively the ex-SADF officers, and in my case I met three officers from the Directorate of Artillery. The regimental extended family is worldwide, and the three gunners stood out with their regimental insignia, which were very similar to mine. Although formal relationships had fallen away with the exit of South Africa from the Commonwealth, it was clear that the traditions and regimental lineage were still there, even though much effort had been made by the Apartheid government to purge the British traditions from the military. The three officers in question were Colonel Jacques Jacobs, the Director of the South African Artillery, and Lieutenant Colonels Leon Phillipson and Andre Eckard. I count myself very lucky that I was to work with three such highly experienced, intelligent, forward-thinking and honest officers. After the initial small talk and tiptoeing around sensitive issues, we just formed a great relationship and spent the evening laughing and swapping gunner stories. Their operational experience was fascinating, having fired their guns in anger for many years in Angola and South West Africa. My operational experience was predominantly infantry-based. I noted this straightaway as an area that I would need to watch in the future if there was disagreement on the syllabi for the Bridging Training. It is demeaning for any soldier to suggest that his opposite number has no 'real experience' in any area. I was determined that this would not be an issue, and to be fair to them all, it never was.

In our conversations, it was clear that the South African Artillery had already put a huge amount of effort into their planning for the assessment and placement process and in how to approach the Bridging Training. They acknowledged that there would be difficulties, but they collectively exuded a positive attitude and clearly wanted to manage change as opposed to throwing up obstacles in front of inevitable progress. We agreed to meet at the Directorate in the coming weeks so that they could brief me on their overall plan and start the validation process. They wanted to impress one point on me, which was that they wanted to maintain standards. They were the right of line[2] and took great pride in their professionalism. They were prepared to spend more time in Bridging Training to ensure that the new officers and soldiers were able to execute their duties to the accepted standard and, most importantly, safely.

Looking around the room, it was clear that not all of my contemporaries were having such an easy time. There were some who were, unhelpfully, being as difficult as their hosts, while others were being blamed for all the troubles in the new South Africa. It was quite obvious that the role we were going to be asked to play would require, or in some cases demand, a huge amount of diplomacy and sensitivity on our part, whilst also requiring us to grow a hard skin. Some of the ex-SADF personnel, who were not going to accept the way business had to be done, would have to be dealt with in due course. One of the key requirements in these early days was to try to establish an open and workable relationship. There was no need to rise to the bait, be it deliberately cast in front of one or not. One of our team, Al Sommerlad, had managed to pick up a particularly obstreperous companion. Quite unreconstructed and well fuelled by the alcohol that was flowing freely, this individual was haranguing Al about the Afrikaans language and how important it was. Al could not avoid the diatribe, and eventually agreed to a wager that in a month's time he would be able to have a conversation with the fellow in Afrikaans for a set number of minutes, but Al's caveat was that this would be followed up by the same period of time in Zulu, a language with which his South African host was unfamiliar. The immediate group fell silent and interest was engendered across the whole room. And so the evening continued …

* * *

We arrived at Wallmannsthal early in the morning in a couple of self-drive minibuses. Wallmannsthal was about an hour's drive from the mess in Pretoria. When we arrived for the first time, it was really like entering a new world. The PMORD was like nothing I had ever seen before.

Having turned off the motorway from Pretoria, one approached the Wallmannsthal PMORD along a typical dirt road. These roads are not like the very rare dirt roads that are found in Britain, which tend to be the reserve of farms and military training areas. In South Africa, these roads actually make up the majority of roads away from the towns and main arterial routes. They are easy to drive on and a 4x4 vehicle is not needed, but care needs to be taken when they take on the appearance of corrugated iron as it is very easy to lose control, especially if you are travelling too fast.

There is very little rain in winter on the High Veldt, and the road was very dusty as we entered the typical bush land of the Northern Transvaal. Sun-dried, yellow-brown dirt stretched as far as the eye could see, broken up by low scrub and spindly low trees. The area was dissected by fencing, low normal wire fencing and then high wire fencing, which we soon understood was for livestock, most probably game. Eucalyptus and blue gum trees grew in patches; they had been imported from Australia to provide their uniquely straight timber for use in the mines. Gradually, the fencing took on a more military appearance and we were soon entering the huge Wallmannsthal complex.

Wallmannsthal was a large logistical base that had played a major role in the force generation process during the recent war years. Its arid setting reminded me of some of the US bases I had seen in Texas. We were to operate in a large fenced area with extensive concrete aprons and a huge hangar surrounded by a plethora of small outbuildings. There were various other satellite buildings in the complex and then a series of lines of Army tents, almost but not quite marquee-size. It looked quite innocuous, but the fencing was highly official, topped with efficient-looking barbed wire – and there were armed guards on duty. It was an area busy with people, some in civilian dress, others uniformed and every cap badge imaginable on display. We parked and were escorted into the hangar. This was divided into many sections, each appearing to have a specific purpose, although many of the signs, and indeed the language being spoken, was Afrikaans. There were administrators, doctors and medical staff, police representatives both civil and military and the entire caravan of the State.

We were welcomed, briefed and then shown around the complex, where each section was introduced to us and it was explained how each fitted into the process. This was the core of the whole administrative operation. It appeared well organized and there was a constant hum of activity, with ardent-looking individuals clutching clipboards moving purposefully about. They were clearly working by routine, and once work finished they would, to a man, shut down their computers, put away their papers and board the buses and cars to head back to Pretoria. The only twenty-four-hour activity was to be found in the Operations Room and Guardroom. We were then led outside, where for the first time we saw the assembly area.

The assembly area of the PMORD consisted of row upon row of khaki tents, divided into distinct clusters. In the centre of each cluster, there appeared to be a cookhouse and an administrative or headquarters tent. There were thousands of people in there, most of whom were dressed in blue boiler suits. Some also had the old-style brown SADF parka.[3] The shock was that fences topped with barbed wire surrounded the whole area and mounted infantry patrolled the perimeter. When I say 'mounted infantry', I mean infantrymen properly mounted on horseback. This gave the impression of the PMORD being more of a prisoner-of-war camp than an assembly area for those voluntarily joining the integration process – and this was a camp just for the non-statutory forces (in this case the MK). There was no SADF or TBVC presence 'behind the wire'. The statutory forces were clearly kept on one side[4] and non-statutory forces on the other, so the parallel of whites outside, blacks inside was easily and disturbingly drawn. With the delays in starting the whole process and the different criteria being used for the TBVC,[5] the MK personnel within the wire were quickly becoming restive. There was no buzz of optimism emanating from the assembly area; rather one sensed a bubbling resentment that nothing was about to change quickly. There was undoubtedly an atmosphere of distrust inside the wire, which matched the great tension amongst those in the hangar and outside the wire. Wallmannsthal was to be the real interface of the integration process, and it would have to provide the solution to it or face the consequences.

Things had so far obviously not progressed smoothly. We were briefed about the violence in the camp and told that many of the essential documents that were needed to commence the process were still missing. A car that had been bringing many of the personnel files from the ANC Headquarters to the MK leadership within the camp had been seized and the files either burnt or discarded. These files were essential for the identification of individuals and provided supporting evidence for these same individuals to enter the integration process. The overall state of affairs was not quite as optimistic as the leadership in Pretoria thought.

The lack of so many files meant that the first step of the integration process, which was to be pre-screening, was going to run into difficulties before it had even started. If the Certified Personnel Register, which had been compiled by the non-statutory forces, could not be cross-referenced by the necessary documents, then individuals would have to provide the required personal documentation themselves. The whole verification process was deliberate enough without essential documents being lost, mislaid or stolen. To compound matters, the older members of the MK, who had been in exile, were known by several different names: their real name, an alias that was known as the 'MK name' and in some cases an additional 'combat name'.

The purpose of having three names was quite logical within a non-statutory force structure. Security is paramount, because it is constantly under threat from military, police and intelligence services action. The more dispersed and complex the structure, the more difficult it is to identify, and therefore the chances of infiltration and interdiction are reduced considerably. By changing a given name to that of an alias, it becomes easier to move around, provided that the identification papers are properly replicated. This makes the job of the intelligence services harder and often results in only one individual being arrested rather than all the members of a particular cell. The 'combat names' were varied, plentiful and quite exotic, and were in effect nicknames. Later during the process, I was working with a very bright and colourful individual who was very proud of his 'combat name' of Stalin. I suggested that it was not a very lucky name, but he laughed this off, saying that he was proud to share the name with such a great man. I was later to be proved right.

Whereas the vast majority of those waiting to join the process were proud of their time with the MK in exile and were waiting their turn to enter the integration process, there were others who had used their time within the organization to conduct less-straightforward 'freedom fighting' activities. Amongst them were a few who had committed murder, rape, armed robbery and other crimes, which were separate to any of the 'insurgent' activity. They had used the cover of insurgency to conduct criminal activity for personal gain. The South African Police Service was keen to identify these individuals and interview them about their criminal activities. Needless to say, there was a large risk attached to this, but as was shown later during the period of the Truth and Reconciliation Committee, activities carried out in the political cause were different to those carried out with criminal intent. Although BMATT (SA) was not involved in this area of activity, there was very close supervision by the government and political officials from both sides of the old divide. This did not interfere unduly with the process once it began to function, but it was always in the background.

What was missing was an effective communications plan to inform and to explain what was going on, when and how. It was clear that at the strategic level there was a full understanding of the overall intent and the mechanism of the integration process, but although much had been promulgated and discussed through the media, there was still uncertainty on the ground. This was being exacerbated on a daily basis by the delays and disruptions. This was initially seen in the difficulty of getting individuals back to South Africa and then into the PMORDS, let alone once at the PMORDS and getting them into the process. There were huge logistic challenges in providing the life support for the estimated 16,000 MK personnel about to enter the integration process. Although centres such as Wallmannsthal had been designed to process thousands of national servicemen, much of the equipment had been disposed of in the defence cuts which followed the end of external operations. It was suggested that the SADF could only supply about an eighth of the necessary beds needed and some 60 per cent of the large tents. This resulted in MK members having to be brought into the process in tranches, which created further frustration.

Then, within this confusion and mounting distrust, a foreign military team arrived.

The BMATT team stood out because of our uniforms – especially James Sawyer's, who, as a member of the Royal Regiment of Fusiliers, was sporting his beret topped with the red-tipped hackle.[6] It was a source of universal wonder, especially as James was very tall and the hackle could not be missed. We were adding to the uncertainty in the camp, but at least most people had heard of us. We were universally referred to as BMATT, and really from our initial day at Wallmannsthal that name stuck – no more BMATT (SA). We were, after all, the only BMATT in the country and the only one that mattered to all the different parties. They had all heard of us, but not everyone knew what our role was to be, not that we were completely sure of it ourselves.

We realized that there was a potential role for the BMATT team straight away. It was considered that if BMATT members could introduce themselves to the various groups inside the wire and brief the intended process at the PMORD within the context of the overall integration process, then this could go some way to diffuse the increasing tension and feelings of distrust. At least BMATT members would have the credibility that came from being a neutral. It was thought that MK personnel would receive the messaging better from BMATT rather than hearing it from another SANDF representative or one of the commissars.[7] Although we would hopefully be reiterating what had already been briefed, it was considered that this information coming from BMATT would inject badly needed confidence and reassurance and, perhaps more realistically, would allow time to let the process start to function. Everyone wanted and needed a start as soon as practically possible.

Chapter 5

Into The Lion's Den

In winter, the High Veldt is bone dry. The soil is baked hard and everything seems brown, yellow or even a dull green, almost lifeless. The days are brilliantly clear and there is rarely a cloud in the sky. The daytime temperatures are very pleasant, in the high teens and early twenties Centigrade, but as the sun sets, they plunge. When the sun slides behind the hill, it is replaced by the deep blue night sky that is soon illuminated by the brilliance of the southern constellations. Away from the cities and the associated light pollution, the night sky is so much more spectacular than seen in the Northern Hemisphere.

There is little wind in winter, so smoke and industrial pollution rises and stays there. Wood smoke or smoke from cheap coal fires is the product of the thousands of stoves and open fires upon which the population in the poorer areas are dependent. This smoke hangs above the populated areas in a brown haze; it is particularly noticeable in the early morning and at dusk, crouching above the tin roofs, accompanied by a bitter, acrid smell. It is very noticeable when you approach Soweto from the west along the N12, passing the last of the platinum mines en route to Johannesburg. A brown shimmer on the horizon comes into view, gradually getting bigger and more defined, and then the shantytowns can be seen on the edge of the township, topped by this brown cloud.

This phenomenon was repeated on a smaller scale at Wallmannsthal. The winter was cold, and many of those in the assembly area had returned from exile in warmer African countries or had spent months back in South Africa prior to being called to the camp. Now in tented accommodation, the cold of the High Veldt was unavoidable, the fires produced the brown smog and the smell of wood-smoke penetrated everything. Later in my career, I remember the amazement of seeing Ghanaian soldiers on guard duty in Accra dressed in thick parkas and wearing woollen balaclavas, complaining that it was so cold. It was at least

25°C, but to them it was still cold. They would have suffered dreadfully had they been in Wallmannsthal.

* * *

Our orders were to go into the camp to communicate and reassure. We were to go in on our own, accompanied only by a couple of liaison staff, and speak to those inside the wire. We did not have a particularly comfortable feeling about this, being aware that there were still weapons in the camp. We were going to go through the perimeter area, guarded by the mounted infantry, and into the compound where the new SANDF did not operate. We were clearly going to be seen as coming from outside of the wire, the old SADF side; no matter how one tried to repackage the issue, we were still white people delivering a message from the statutory forces to the non-statutory forces. We may have had a different uniform, but we were still outsiders and would easily be associated with whatever regime an observer from inside the wire might choose. We were to be 'piggy in the middle', a role that we would soon realize was the purpose of BMATT.

The camp had been divided into sectors, with a brigade style grouping of battalions, for administrative purposes. Although these were battalions in name alone, it gave some organization and structure to a grouping of irregular forces. There was a chain of command which provided a system of control that allowed those inside the wire to be fed, clothed, watered and accommodated in an orderly manner. It also provided the structure to receive basic military training whilst waiting to be called forward to the integration process. We had discussed the way we would approach the task of talking to the personnel behind the wire, deciding that we would deal with one battalion group at a time. We would ask the commander to assemble his troops in a hollow 'C' shape, ask him to introduce us and instruct them to listen. Questions would be answered if appropriate, or, more likely, answers would be relayed back through the commander in a follow-up session. The MK commanders were uncomfortable with this approach because it meant they did not own the script. It has to be remembered that the MK was a military wing of a political organization, so there was a more questioning attitude amongst the leadership. We could well open up issues that the commander would not want discussed, and could inadvertently challenge a pledge or statement that he had made. It seemed a fluid situation, which we did not and could not control. It could turn ugly and, if so, then it was unlikely that we would be able to walk away. There certainly was no question of providing us with any protection, not even a pistol as a self-protection weapon, for that would demonstrate that we had no faith in the system and did not trust those 'inside the wire'. We took great comfort in the fact that we had a very small Union Flag sewn onto our jungle combats – surely this would protect us?

The way we decided to handle this situation was to stick to the facts of how we understood the process was to proceed and, most importantly, what our role was in this process. No observation must be made on events prior to this presentation, and there was to be no room for comment or opinion. We were a neutral party working for the good of the new South Africa – and from the moment we entered the compound we were on our own.

It was an interesting challenge, but one that could be achieved by keeping cool – and by avoiding confrontation. I ruminated on the best way to address the first battalion. The officers would have been in exile, so they would have a vested interest in the success of the process, but this would be balanced by frustration as a result of so many delays. In addition, the political nature of the non-statutory forces could well lead to them trying to use BMATT as a lever to get more concessions. The rest of the soldiers presented even more of a contradiction. The majority of them had not been in exile. We knew that many had joined the MK after 'hostilities' had ceased. Their commitment to the process would be skin-deep, more linked to getting paid employment than anything else. Of course there would be an element of those who, if they had been born earlier, would have gone into exile with all the genuine political conviction of their seniors, but the majority had been brought up in the townships at the time of the school strikes and civil unrest. Some would have been serial rioters, while others would have been either verging on or involved fully in criminal activity. Therefore, I assessed that my priority would be to engage and ensure they understood the process ahead, to deliver the message in simple, practical terms, pitched mainly to reassure. And of course, we had no script.

The distrust was palpable, and it would be too easy to be considered trite or offhand and therefore a mouthpiece for the statutory forces. I decided it was absolutely necessary to treat them as fellow soldiers and to work with them in an atmosphere of respect. Some form of balance had to be struck, and I was still pondering this as we walked towards the gate to the compound.

* * *

We strolled through the gates and into a different world. In many respects, the MK leadership had done a good job in mustering the troops and creating a semblance of order and structure. The personnel who were inside the wire were still dressed in a variety of clothing; predominantly blue overalls, with some having items of the old-style brown SADF uniforms. Issuing uniforms to these soldiers should have been a priority task so as to give them a feeling of unity and belonging. It is an idea often scoffed at by the liberal classes sitting comfortably at home and passing regular criticism on the armed forces, mocking the uniform and suggesting that all members of the services are somehow unreconstructed and would fall apart without the comfort blankets of military clothing. Sadly, these 'armchair' commentators have never had to bring together members from all sectors of society into a structured body with a clear, unambiguous chain of command, regardless of class, race or religion, and hone them into a homogenous body that would stand and fight both for their country and for each other. Uniformity is key to this, not just in the clothing but also in the conditions and the respect that is fostered. With that, I am talking of the British Army, the French Army or any regular army in the world. Give a soldier a uniform and he is made to feel part of the organization. Here we faced a still rag-tag bunch of non-statutory forces being brought together in order to embark on an integration process. Although at this moment in time, their demeanour and appearance were far short of what would be needed, that was understandable. However, this was the raw material with which we would have to work. Apparently, it had been decided that the new uniform would be issued once an individual had been accepted into the process and was in the actual Bridging Training. Right or wrong, this was the policy decision, and whilst the process was still failing to swing into effect, it added to the feeling of segregation and a lack of belonging which was becoming more marked.

I had pushed aside these distractions and returned to the reality I was facing. We split up and went off to different parts of the camp to meet with the various battalion groups. The intent was to deliver our message to as many as possible on one day. I approached my first group and was introduced to the commander of the battalion, who was also the Commissar. He was a tall, striking man and I would have placed him in his late 50s. He combined the authority of age with a firm physique. He was short on words but managed to combine a formal welcome with an undercurrent of suspicion. This was easily identified when I looked past him to see several hundred black faces staring at me without a glimmer of welcome.

He took me forward to what was a parade ground of sorts, a square of dirt surrounded by tents. It was a warm afternoon. The first battalion I was to address was assembled in a hollow 'C', standing up and following my every movement. There was no overt atmosphere of hostility from the assembled men, but neither was there any goodwill.

Treat them as soldiers, I reminded myself. Even better, treat them as if they were my own soldiers.

The commander and I approached the battalion and he introduced me as BMATT. BMATT was a term that was to stick as a collective noun, regardless of whether you were on your own or as a body; at this stage, I suppose it showed that the leadership was briefed, but I was not sure my audience had any idea what BMATT was. He then told the battalion that I wanted to talk to them, and stood back. This was an unexpectedly very short introduction. I asked him if he could have his men relax, and ideally sit down as I intended to speak for a while. He was somewhat surprised by this request. I suspect that he was more used to formally addressing his troops, based on his experience in the Soviet Bloc, where he would have spent his formative years in exile. Nonetheless, he agreed and, with much shuffling and the creation of a considerable amount of dust, my audience sat down and continued to stare at me.

It is interesting to think back to this moment. I might have made a huge mistake by having walked into the centre of that group of men. I was here, the only white face, standing and about to address several hundred black men who were sitting. Was I not about to recreate my own mini-Apartheid? But it was too late now; keep on moving forward, I told myself, and I started to address them.

It is said that the secret of public speaking is to stand up, speak up and then shut up. Treat them as soldiers, I had thought; even better, treat them as if they were my own soldiers. But as soon as I opened my mouth, I regretted it.

'Hello boys,' I started, 'my name is Major Lawford from BMATT.' There was an audible murmur, and the commander grabbed my shoulder and led me back. 'Are you being funny?' he asked. 'Why do you use such racist terms?' It dawned on me that the term 'boys' could be construed as racist. I had a flashback to the opening sequence of the bestseller *Wheels* by Arthur Hailey, when a strike was called through the use of that same word. 'Think quickly,' I thought. I stood back and, summoning all the composure that Sandhurst had bequeathed to its officer cadets, said calmly, 'I apologize if I have caused you, or any of your soldiers, any offence. However, I wish to address your soldiers as I would address my soldiers, and in the British Army the expression "boys" is considered to be one of association and respect.' I paused and assumed a poker face. The commander stared for a while, clearly weighing up the issue, and so I continued, 'And I would be very grateful if you could explain that to them so that we may proceed.' In my Army career, I have often heard the phrase 'and his backside was going sixpence, saucepan, sixpence, saucepan'. I was able at that moment to appreciate its meaning!

The commander addressed his troops along the lines that I had requested, and then I continued. During the next fifteen minutes or so, I talked through who I was, what BMATT was and what our role was in the integration process. I spoke simply and slowly, and tried to avoid too many British Army idiosyncrasies and acronyms. I kept their attention, and even on occasions managed to raise a laugh. I finished and declined questions, suggesting instead that they raise them through the chain of command, and they could then be brought to BMATT. I turned and walked back to the commander, pleased that I was still breathing and feeling as if I had lost three stone in weight.

The commander was standing apart from his officers. I walked up to him, thanking him for the time he had given and hoping that the address had helped to clarify some of their issues. I suggested that we could meet again and said that I would be very happy to answer any of his questions. He just replied with a warning to be careful what I said. I held out my hand, but he ignored it and refused to make eye contact. It was clear I needed to leave, so I asked for an escort to the entrance, which he gave me, and we left each other on what I considered to be not the best of terms. In fact, I was inwardly furious; I felt his behaviour was quite out of order. Accepting that I could have been more sensitive in my introduction, I still thought I had delivered a good message, reinforcing what his political leadership had delivered. The commander had really given me an unsettled feeling and I was quite out of sorts by the time I passed through the gates.

What did not help was that I had clearly taken longer than my colleagues, who had by then all disappeared back to Pretoria. Fortunately, our liaison officer, a delightfully irreverent ex-Rhodesian, Lieutenant Colonel Bert Sachser, was waiting and clearly read my mood. He suggested that we have a cold beer before heading back and led me to a makeshift mess tent secreted in the dead ground behind the hangar complex, well out of sight of the central buildings of Wallmannsthal. I was very grateful for the company and a cold can of lager. He probed, and I unloaded my tale of that afternoon. I recounted my meeting with the commander, the difficult start to the brief, the brush-off at the end and, what really got under my skin, the fact that the damned man would not even look me in the eye and shake my hand. Sachser let me rant before asking me for the name of the commander. At that point he grabbed a couple more beers and roared with laughter. He then proceeded to tell me that I was a complete idiot; did I not realise that the commander was a Zulu? 'No' was my response. 'Well, you fool,' he continued, 'that was a sign of respect. If he had looked you in the eyes, then you would have been in trouble! Did they not tell you anything at the High Commission?' I did not bother to answer.

* * *

The first week finally came to an end, and we felt both blooded and a little more confident about the tasks facing us. We had met our immediate opposite numbers from the statutory forces, but although I had been lucky, others in the team had not enjoyed the experience. It was clear that in some areas there would have to be a tremendous investment in establishing a working relationship. We had been inside the wire and had met an element of the non-statutory forces. Inside the wire, discipline – or rather the maintenance of discipline – was going to be key, especially when the process began. There would be the inevitable disappointments and in some cases, without doubt, outright rejection.

* * *

With time ticking away, there was still no discernible movement forward in the process at Wallmannsthal. Pressure was building and the need to start something was tangible. We had identified two priority areas that needed to be addressed as a matter of urgency. Firstly, there needed to be agreement by all parties on the selection criteria and process to be used for each arm and service; secondly, and most importantly, there was a need to establish a point of contact within the non-statutory forces who was sufficiently qualified to assist each team with the selection process.

It was essential to have the triumvirate of statutory force, non-statutory force and BMATT to work together to be able to present a united front in the assessment and selection process in Wallmannsthal and the other PMORDs. The statutory force and BMATT relationship had been established, albeit in some cases with a definitely fractious nature.

There were loose contacts between the non-statutory forces and both the statutory forces and BMATT, but this contact was unofficial. At the higher echelons of the SANDF, where many of the senior leader groups of the MK had already been integrated, the relationships had already been forged. This early relation was necessary, creating a unified policy at the political and strategic level. But it was divorced from the reality inside the wire, and therefore from the vast majority of the non-statutory forces.

This process of identifying potential candidates had already been started, with the MK leadership providing a list of candidates for each arm and service whom they considered to be professionally qualified and able to walk the difficult path between the statutory forces, BMATT and their own people. They would need to be an arbiter, a salesman and an interpreter, and it would literally require them to have a foot on either side of the wire.

The candidate for the point of contact within the military had been identified after an interview with the Director and a senior MK officer. I met him at the Directorate in Pretoria as soon as possible, and then again at Wallmannsthal. His name was Xavier Requana from the Eastern Cape.

Xavier was dressed in the old brown uniform of the SADF, with a brown bush hat firmly wedged on his head. He was about 5ft 9in tall, of medium build, and looked fit. However, the striking thing about him was his eyes; they went everywhere, taking in everything, darting here and there, but with a look that indicated a sharp mind and a good sense of humour. He was undoubtedly nervous; the only black man amongst a group of large white men. With the exception of Xavier, everyone else was well over 6ft tall and had been rugby players in their youth. Andre was dressed in brown fatigues, the other South Africans wore the smart stone-coloured South African Army barrack dress uniform and I was in the bright green disrupted-pattern British Army jungle combat suit.

Xavier's nervousness was understandable, for a plethora of reasons, but he would have to overcome this quickly if he was to play his necessary role. He must have been conscious of the divisions surrounding him: colour, uniform, background and politics, combined with the fact that he was amongst those who a few years previously he would have considered as a legitimate target. The suspicions must have been the same on the other side. Xavier was a member of the MK, and was, until a few years ago, nothing more than a terrorist to the ex-SADF officers. This was the first time I had experienced this dilemma, which would be in the background of every aspect of the integration process – and indeed for many years to come – and it reminded me of the question I was asked at the very beginning, whether I would be happy if the IRA was to merge with the British Army? Here, facing each other, were past enemies, who had been prepared to fight each other to the death should civil war break out in South Africa. The positive aspect was that they had not fought a civil war, and although each had lost friends in the 'struggle', they needed to put the past behind them and look together to the future.

The relationship between all sides had to be forged immediately. There was no need for everyone to be the best of friends but what was needed was an agreement to work together as a team on the problems facing them.

The issue of highest priority was to place Xavier. He needed to be a legitimate part of the machine as soon as possible so that, as the formal non-statutory force representative, he could lend his approval and therefore authority to the plans. His role was essential because the ex-SADF officers and I had come from a similar background; university-educated, professional soldiers and experienced artillerymen. We looked at problems in a similar way, so our views on what qualities were needed across the rank structures within the artillery were pretty well the same. This was based on familiar structures and doctrine, and the South African Artillery was to keep the same organization, ethos and training regimen as before. Why fix something when it is not broken? Of course, this presented a dilemma in itself. Many would say that as the organization was not to change, then surely the integration process was a case of the SADF absorbing selected non-statutory force personnel? But that would not be a true integration process; it would not mark a new beginning and certainly would not be acceptable politically or to the nation as a whole. There had to be a tangible display of integration of equal partners.

What we were looking at was the next generation of men[1] to serve the guns. It is a simple fact that the most valuable commodity in any army is not the equipment or the technology, but the person who uses it. That person has to be fit and able, and he or she must be clothed, fed, quartered, trained and be prepared to fight for their country and possibly pay the ultimate price. But that goes hand in hand with the contract that the soldier will be looked after, respected and valued, and from this comes morale; as Napoleon, another well-known gunner, said, in battle the morale is to the physical as three is to one. To achieve this, standards would have to be maintained. There was to be affirmative action, but the intent was not to turn this into positive discrimination. To go forward together, however, we needed to understand Xavier and his background.

Xavier then described to us his life's journey. He was a bright young man who was motivated, as were many of his generation, by the anti-Apartheid struggle, but he was not a stay-at-home protester content to *toyi-toyi*[2] at any opportunity. He went into exile, and so impressed the leader group with his potential that he was selected for a leadership appointment and sent overseas for training. This included three years at the Soviet Artillery Academy, follow-on training in Cuba and a Combined Arms Training Course in East Germany. He spoke Russian, German, Spanish, Portuguese, English, Afrikaans (under duress) and a handful of native South African languages. He was an impressive individual. I later asked him about his time in Russia and how he coped with the Russian winter. He laughed and said that it was the most miserable time in his life; he spent the winter exercises wrapped in as many clothes as possible, hiding in the back of the command post away from the wind. It must have been miserable beyond all measure.

His experience was going to be a massive bonus. The non-statutory forces did not have any formed artillery units, but they had enjoyed access to Soviet heavy weapons such as the Grad-P 122mm light portable rocket system and the 120mm PM-43 mortar. Some would have had experience on the D-20 howitzer, but not as part of the MK armoury. All their training was based on Soviet doctrine, which had significant differences with that used by the South African Artillery, the latter following to all extents and purposes the British doctrine. We had to ensure that during the assessment of non-statutory forces, questions had to be predominantly slanted towards Soviet equipment and practice. Xavier said that whilst the majority of the artillery leader group had been trained in the USSR or other communist countries, there were several who had attended courses in East African countries as well as India and Pakistan. They would have been exposed to both Soviet and Western equipment and doctrine. Regardless of the nationality of training or equipment, there are still a handful of fundamental artillery skills that are common to all. These consist of the ability to site a gun or mortar, along with knowledge of the sighting system on any type of artillery, the type of ammunition used, the calculations required to deliver a projectile at the right place and right time, the simple calculations required for an observer and the use of artillery in the combined-arms battle. These common skills are used throughout the various ranks, but as an individual progresses in rank, he adds another level of knowledge. A gunner will know about his part of the equipment in detail and the whole weapon system in general, while the

NCO in charge of the equipment knows about each part of his equipment in detail and the gun position in general. The young officer will know about each part of the gun position in detail and the artillery system in general, and the knowledge skill-set continues to expand until you get to the commanding officer – and everyone knows that the CO knows everything about everything!

The Directorate staff had already done their homework and suggested a series of selection tests that would culminate in an interview. The tests would be set out sequentially and take an individual through from the knowledge expected of a junior member of a gun crew to that of a JNCO, SNCO, warrant officer, junior officer at the gun position, junior officer as a forward observer and up to that of a battery commander, which would cover fire planning and combined-arms tactics.

The success of the system could only be judged once we had been able to correctly place a variety of candidates. If the system was able to propel candidates into training at the right level, then it would be seen as a fair and transparent method. For that to work, Xavier would have to identify potential candidates inside the wire from his own knowledge, as well as from the records provided by the MK. Because of the cellular structure of the MK and the fact that personnel had been dispersed in camps all over the continent, it was impossible for Xavier to have known all the candidates in person. His first task was thus to try to ascertain where they were in the system and, if they had been called to Wallmannsthal, where they were located in the camp. So Xavier had two immediate tasks – to endorse the selection and assessment process, and then to find the individual gunners in the camp. With the latter he was fortunate in that, as artillery training had only been given to those in exile, the initial candidates would be the more mature and experienced men.

The Directorate staff proposed that they set up the personnel selection tests in a series of tents at Wallmannsthal the following week. We would then be able to see the practical tests and review the written papers, as well as finally discussing how we would conduct the interviews. Xavier and I would have to be completely happy with the content because once we agreed to the process, there could not be a change. Fortunately we were all in agreement, so Xavier set off to find the candidates.

Chapter 6

Welcome To The Machine

Having spent a couple of days delivering the initial brief to various groups, my next major project was to validate the assessment and selection procedure that the staff of the Directorate of Artillery had drafted. Once I was satisfied, there was to be an official signing ceremony. Whereas it could be suggested that this ceremony was somewhat superfluous and a distraction, it was in fact important to be able to demonstrate not only progress towards the start of the process but also a visible display of agreement between the representatives of the ex-statutory and ex-non-statutory forces and BMATT. It was a tangible display of progress being made. There would be many excuses and opportunities to derail the process in the future, but for now there needed to be progress.

I must admit that in many respects this was a relatively easy exercise because the Directorate staff had already done all the hard work. They had put a huge amount of effort into producing a fair, balanced and transparent programme of selection criteria and Bridging Training. Keen to have an expert cast his eyes over the programmes, I asked to study them at my leisure. I drove to BMATT HQ in the South African National Defence Headquarters and faxed the programmes to the Royal School of Artillery at Larkhill, near Salisbury, asking the technical and training staff there to assess the training propositions and give me a series of speaking notes.

* * *

We had arrived at our second week in South Africa, and the intention now was to agree on the selection and assessment process and to have the outline plan for Bridging Training agreed and signed off at a ceremony scheduled for the Friday. Once this had been achieved, there should be no reason why the integration process could not start. But whilst we were ready to begin, we could not proceed until Xavier had located the candidates and confirmed their eligibility.

The provisional list circulated by the MK had identified candidates for each arm and service. There were two assumptions; firstly that any name on the list had to be on the Certified Personnel Register, and secondly that the names were based on a record of service that catalogued the candidate's training and experience. However, there was an expectation that candidates would 'slip' onto the list because they were a 'friend of a friend', so there was only a limited confidence in the veracity of the various lists. But there was no time to do an audit; the integration process had to start, and any ambiguities would have to be addressed during the process itself. This meant that the assessment and selection process had to be fair, transparent and, to a certain degree, flexible.

Xavier had done a good job and had met almost all of those who were on the initial list. He had checked that the candidates had undertaken some form of artillery training, but in some cases he was unsure of a name or had been unable to meet an individual. As far as we were concerned, our immediate task as the artillery selection board was to assess the candidates. Once successful, the candidate would have to go through the confirmation of his identity with a series of background and administrative checks. When all this had been completed, he would receive an identity card and the South African equivalent of a National Insurance number. The latter would permit the individual to appear on the SANDF system and, most importantly, to be paid. This administrative minefield was someone else's problem.

Xavier, Andre Eckard and I reviewed the list of artillery candidates again. Andre had been appointed as the Directorate's lead for the assessment process. We drew up a list of names which we believed would be an ideal initial artillery leader group. Once successfully accepted, our intention was to get these candidates into formal training as soon as possible. So Xavier's task was to go back inside the wire to locate these individuals and ensure that their names appeared on the list for the first tranche of candidates to be called forward the following week.

I had a reply from the Royal School of Artillery, which had endorsed the proposed training. They commented that there were more proposed courses than we would run for the Royal Artillery, but they acknowledged that with the task in hand, and with many of the more experienced non-statutory personnel having had a Soviet background, it was more sensible to be over-prescriptive than to base the training on assumptions.

There was also the need to ensure that the end product of the training was an ex-non-statutory force officer or soldier who was able to stand next to his ex-statutory force contemporary and be able to do his duty efficiently, and above all safely. There were some detailed, technical questions requesting clarification of terminology, and these were forwarded to the School of Artillery in Potchefstroom. None of the questions would interfere with the process, and therefore the Bridging Training programme could be agreed and formally signed off.

There was one requirement of Bridging Training which was a major challenge and applicable to all leader groups, regardless of arm or service. The training courses would have to be taken sequentially and the number of courses an individual had to complete was dictated by his allotted rank. Therefore, the higher the rank a candidate was granted, the longer he would be lost to the training system. Taking aside the initial generic basic training package, an artillery officer would have to complete all the courses of a normal career progression from second lieutenant to major or lieutenant colonel, dictated by the rank into which he had been appointed; but they had to be done sequentially.

The Bridging Training requirement for a major, having first completed his basic officer training, would involve completing the Command Post Officers Course, the Gun Position Officers Course, the Battery Second-in-Command Course and then the Battery Commander Course. Each course was between four and six weeks long, and therefore – with an element of rest, leave and a chance for some practical application of the newly learnt skills – a major selected from the first tranche of candidates would not be in position for almost eighteen months, and even that would depend upon all the courses being perfectly scheduled. It was therefore imperative that we selected leaders early and had them processed and entering the training system as soon as possible. The fundamental task for the successful candidate was to absorb ten years of career training in eighteen months, and to top this it had to be acknowledged that the candidate came from an irregular force. It was a tall order.

It was unreasonable to expect that members of the non-statutory forces, with their staccato, hotchpotch mixture of training and limited application, could simply walk into the shoes of their colleagues from the well-trained and experienced ex-statutory forces alongside whom they were to serve. The mantra of 'we must not let standards slip' was not a backdoor means of discrimination, or an obstruction to progress, but a simple safety mechanism. Unless there were well-trained personnel at both the gun position and the observer line, then a 96lb high explosive shell would be fired blindly over 20km, with inevitable fatal consequences. There was only a minority of non-statutory force members who said that sequential training was unnecessary and that a hybrid course would suffice; the majority to whom I spoke were in agreement. They had all had artillery training, to varying degrees of proficiency, and even those who had spent three years in Russia would agree that training was an absolute necessity, no matter how long it took. But time was of the essence. Ex-non-statutory force members had to be seen to be integrated and filling appointments in the SANDF. There had to be visible results.

There was an advantage to organizing the Bridging Training in this way. By having the ex-non-statutory force members attend the standard artillery courses, they would be receiving training alongside their ex-statutory force colleagues. This was because the routine life of the SANDF was continuing and the current force members had to be trained and moved continually throughout the military machine. Without doubt, integration through combined training was a bold step forward, but realistically there were insufficient resources to run parallel programmes. There would inevitably be problems as the various parties came into direct contact within the confined space of the classroom, but this could be tackled in due course, and indeed this was one of the specified tasks for BMATT. Therefore, there would not be any hybrid courses. The artillery Bridging Training was to be conducted as part of the extant SANDF artillery career course programme.

A tacit challenge facing the integration process was the management of the statutory forces. All parties had recognized that there were undesirable elements within all the merging parties, and there was a conscious effort to get rid of them before the process started. The integration process was difficult enough without individuals from any of the parties being obstructive. The early experience from the National Peacekeeping Force had demonstrated that there were some unreconstructed elements in the SADF. At the same time, there were hotheads in the non-statutory forces who would be only too keen to disrupt or to goad the white officers and soldiers. Leaving these individuals aside, there was also a communication exercise to be conducted on the core of the ex-SADF who had opted to stay in the SANDF. Whilst they had committed themselves to the process, there was a fear of 'affirmative action' – the political replacement of the old by the new with no real, honest attempt to place the best person for the job. Balancing the need to show both progress and change with competence, there were plans to ease the transition by having an ex-non-statutory force senior appointee supported in his appointment by good combined staff. It was in everyone's interest to avoid token appointments and instead to create a system that would provide mentorship and support within which the future leaders could progress. Ideally, the future leaders would be chosen on merit, not on colour or politics.

All this was a long way ahead, but our immediate issue was to prevent the ex-SADF personnel from being marginalized. All the focus was on the ex-non-statutory forces, but it was the former SADF personnel who would have to continue to provide the core of the armed forces for the foreseeable future. Their concern was palpable. Most realized that as the SANDF swelled its numbers with the integration process, there would have to be a downsizing exercise to reflect the size and structure of the SANDF that the nation needed and, of course, could afford. The ex-SADF personnel also realized that the bulk of the cuts would fall amongst them. There was a sugar-coating in that they had worked for years with the knowledge that while the salary might not be brilliant, the pension and healthcare benefits that they received were. As a future downsizing would be in the form of redundancy, many planned on leaving the SANDF and did not see that the future would present too many issues. But if there was a wholesale 'affirmative action' regime, regardless of training and competence, then there was a danger that the floodgates would open and many ex-SADF would resign and walk away without waiting for redundancy. There was a fine balancing act, and I was conscious that once the centre of gravity shifted from the PMORDs to the Bridging Training, then my own priority would have to be adjusted to focus not on just the non-statutory forces, but on the existing SADF personnel as well.

* * *

We gathered outside a couple of army marquees. The temperature was rising steadily, the sky becoming hazier, but there was no sign of rain, and delightfully very little humidity. What there was in abundance was dust; a light brown powder dust that pervaded the whole area. It was generated by thousands of pairs of boots marching around, compacting the earth and generating a cloud within which a body of men were submerged. Occasionally, a dust cloud would be seen moving eerily across the compound, but from within there would emerge the noise of soft chanting. Nobody would appear, and then the chanting would fade into the distance. The gentle breezes which caressed the High Veldt deposited the dust in a very equitable manner.

The Artillery Assessment and Selection Centre was an important title for two dusty marquees, but as dusty as they were, they were fit for purpose. The first marquee was for the practical test, the second for the written assessment and interview. Andre and WO1 (RSM) Boulter, the Regimental Sergeant Major of the Artillery School, showed Xavier and I around the finished product. Mr Boulter was an archetypal RSM and would have been a bonus to any army. Smart as a button – even in the dust – confident, knowledgeable and wrapped in constant good humour, he could talk to anyone. He was a Rhodesian by birth, and like so many of his countrymen had made his way south after the end of the Bush War. He had been in the Rhodesian Light Infantry, but had always had a hankering for the artillery so changed his cap badge when he joined the SADF. He was to be a great asset to the integration process. Many of his family had stayed in Zimbabwe and he had an incredibly practical, yet optimistic view of the future. Xavier and I both warmed to him immediately.

Mr Boulter had gathered together a collection of equipment that had come from both Soviet and British artillery systems. The South African Artillery had used the Second World War-vintage 5.5in and 25-pdr guns to great effect until they had been replaced, only recently, by the hugely impressive G5 and G6 howitzer systems. Pieces of artillery equipment from the gun position and some artillery observer tools were laid out on the floor of the marquee. There were firing tables, gun-sights, parts from a recoilless rifle, lanyards, protractors, gunners' quadrants and all sorts of other paraphernalia, including Soviet fire plan calculators. The items were laid out in an order, which started at those a junior gun crew member would recognize and progressed to those with which a battery commander would be familiar, especially had he been trained in Russia. Each item was clearly numbered, and a candidate would be handed an answer sheet onto which he would enter the name or description of the article. It was a very simple but highly effective test. A candidate would in effect recognize items which corresponded with his likely training, experience and rank.

However, the preamble to this would be that the candidate would have already been identified in a rank by the MK, which Xavier would examine and either concur with – because he knew or knew of the individual – or pass no judgement should the individual be unknown to him. Occasionally he would mark someone for attention because he knew there was some problem. This gave us a fair idea in advance into which rank range a candidate would be likely to fall. After the practical test, the candidate would undertake a second, written test. There were five sections to the paper, sequential and progressive: JNCO, SNCO or warrant officer, junior officer, middle ranking officer, major and above. As with the practical test, the further an individual progressed, the more training and experience he had. Finally, the marks from the practical and written tests would give us a reasonably good idea of what experience the candidate had and what should be his rank. The final interview would confirm this, and at the end of this three-stage process an offer of appointment would be made.

The Director would chair the interview panel for majors and above, while Andre would chair for junior candidates; Xavier and I would be board members to both. Our role was not only to ensure transparency and fairness but also to ask questions, especially if we felt there was a need for clarification or when no clear-cut decision was made. After the interview, we would confer and sign the offer, which confirmed sponsorship by the artillery, then ask the candidate to come back in and formally present our recommendations. In the event of us not agreeing, Xavier and I would interview the candidate once again, then we would reconvene to come to an agreement.

After a few minor adjustments to the practical display suggested by Xavier, and some amendments to the written paper, we were all more than satisfied. The Directorate and the Artillery School had devised an imaginative, balanced and ultimately fair assessment and selection process. It had inherent flexibility to allow an individual to demonstrate his knowledge based on a range of previous training and experience, and as a final arbiter the interview would confirm or otherwise the potential of the individual. It was not only a test but also a means to assess whether an individual was fit to receive what could be up to two years of intensive training. The difficulty would not be in placing a candidate who was able, but in deciding what to do with a candidate who was not.

* * *

At the end of the week, we were to take part in the ceremony to sign off the agreed plans for Bridging Training. For each arms and service there was to be a representative of the Directorate, MK and BMATT, under the chairmanship of a senior BMATT officer who would sign a Memorandum of Understanding (MOU) between the Republic of South Africa and the United Kingdom. Each element of this MOU detailed the selection requirements by rank and the prescribed Bridging Training they would receive. It was the official document, which was to be the reference for all the integration activity upon which we were about to embark. Once signed, it was an official bilateral agreement.

On Friday we were given the timings when we were to be present at one of the satellite buildings where the ceremony was to take place. It was a hot day and the sun was beating mercilessly off the concrete apron. There was a huge crowd around the building, and much activity. There were photographers everywhere, while several staff officers were looking very concerned and running around clutching papers, disappearing and reappearing on a seemingly endless conveyor belt. I met up with Andre and we continued to wait. Xavier was not required, as there was a MK official who would sign all the MOUs on behalf of the non-statutory forces. We both agreed that this was a shame because the three of us were about to set off on quite a journey together. However, being soldiers, we just accepted this. Xavier had managed to swing a weekend pass as compensation, so he was particularly happy.

The South African colonel who was clearly running the event popped out of the building, looking and behaving like the White Rabbit from *Alice in Wonderland*. 'Artillery!' he yelled. We came across and he shepherded us into the building.

Waiting inside was a bank of photographers with a cluster of bright lights, which had cranked the internal temperature of the building up to a very uncomfortable level. There was a long table covered in a red cloth, with five seats arranged behind it. The backdrop was a huge camouflage net, upon which were hung the Union and South African flags. In front of each seat was a book and pen, and seated in the middle was the chairman, looking very hot and not a little uncomfortable. I must admit I was surprised to see the senior RAF officer, a wing commander who had an incredible number of hours in the F-4 Phantom; but there was no commander. Urged forward by the White Rabbit, Andre and I shook hands with the other members of the board and took our seats. We were asked to sign the MOUs one at a time, and as each person put pen to paper there was an explosion of camera shots.

All done. With no speeches. Ushered out again into what felt quite a cool midday, Andre and I went our separate ways, looking forward to formally starting the integration process on Monday. But no commander at the launch event? Odd!

* * *

The following Monday we assembled expectantly in Wallmanstahl. This was to be the day when the integration process was to start. Although this had already begun for the members of the senior leader group and certain specialists, today was the long-awaited official start of the process. The bureaucratic machine at the PMORD had trundled forward, panting and wheezing at every step, but it now stood ready. The large hangar was bursting at the seams with mountains of paper files and anxious clerks ready to check, crosscheck, enter and push buttons to produce the raw data to support the process. The clerks would produce a personal file of each candidate for the assessment boards, which would be updated at every stage and, if all went according to plan, would eventually contain the letter offering an engagement in the SANDF. This file would then be checked again and passed to the next branch to allow the attestation of the individual and the swearing of the oath of allegiance. From there, more staff would continue the administrative process, the individual would be entered on the pay system and then the necessary documentation detailing the training requirements would be issued. The result was one new, fully paid-up member of the SANDF to be fed into the training machine. Wallmanstahl would have done its job.

However, before the clerks could use their sharpened pencils and dusty keyboards, we had to take the individual from inside the wire and assess his experience, training, education and potential to offer a rank and position. Today was the day that our system would be tested. It was, as ever, a delightful morning, each day getting gradually warmer as summer approached. The sky was becoming slightly hazy and a few white clouds speckled the otherwise flawless blue. The dust was flying. Across the complex were hundreds of people milling around the selection and assessment areas, and the camp seemed genuinely alive with a mass of people. There was a tangible sense of expectation.

We had our first draft of candidates. Xavier and Andre were keen to get a cross-section covering all the ranks so that we could prove our system and procedures. We were confident that if a candidate could answer a set number of questions, then he should automatically filter into the correct rank range. The interview process would iron out any outstanding issues, especially with those being considered for placement in the senior ranks. It would also be at the interview where a decision would be made about whether an individual could assume a full and active role at regimental duty; in other words, was he fit and able enough to be deployed on operations? If not, then there was a full career available either in the instructional world of the Artillery School or as a staff officer in an artillery role or on the general staff.

The candidates stood outside waiting. The first thing that struck me was that, although they were in a group, they did not seem to be particularly engaged with each other. There was not the normal interaction that you would expect from a group of soldiers. There was no bonding with this small group. Each had come from a different background, and in exile they had been scattered across the African continent or around the world. Although they had been brought together in Wallmanstahl, they had not yet formed a bond.

We went outside and chatted to them, trying to break the ice and spread reassurance. We made some impact, but decided that their nervousness was only natural as this was quite a leap into the unknown for them. The integration process was explained to them as a group and they were all given an individual time to report back. We had estimated that each candidate should be allotted an hour.

One potential challenge would be to maintain the integrity of the assessment and prevent a leaking of the details of the assessments getting back to future candidates, thereby providing them with an advantage. The option of delivering different tests, both practical and written, was discussed and rejected because we would thus lose the transparency and fairness of the system. We also reasoned that if there was any doubt as to the credibility of a candidate, then the interview would provide him with the opportunity to demonstrate his true credentials. Integrity was a requirement of any soldier; a cheat would not be welcomed. Our fall-back position was that we believed Xavier would be able to sniff out an unsuitable candidate. He had been placed as a major, which all of us agreed was a fair rank, and it was more than likely that he would be rigorous in the examination of anyone whom he felt was below his standard.

The most important issue for us was to ensure that each individual was placed in the correct rank to allow him to complete the Bridging Training successfully. We had all agreed that if an ex-MK officer failed a Bridging Training course because it was beyond his experience, then it would be our fault because we had placed him incorrectly.

Xavier and I followed the first candidates through the tests, more as a means of reassurance than anything else. The equipment display proved very interesting. It was clear that the number of pieces of equipment that a candidate identified was a very good indication of his practical experience and where he had received his training. There were hoots of recognition from some as they recognized equipment they had not seen for years, almost like coming across an old friend. Each person approached the tests in a different way. Some were studious, some rushed and some were dismissive. There were also those who were clearly worried. In the written tests, we were asking individuals to answer questions on subjects that they had last come across ten or maybe fifteen years previously. Some resorted to writing copious notes about what they remembered should be done but without the exact details – that was fine, because it demonstrated that they had covered this in the past. We could draw out some more of their understanding, and therefore their experience, at the interview. It was not the genuine or enthusiastic candidate who concerned us.

We were more worried about the candidates who seemed to resent the fact that they were being asked to prove their knowledge. They would try to pick fault in the equipment display or the written questions. There were some who would not bother once they realized that it was more complex than they anticipated, and would look to pick an argument. Xavier and I would correct them, but we knew that there was much more to it than just their bluster. There were some amongst them who could not write properly, and yet were still claiming that they were officer candidates. After the first couple of days we had seen a good selection of candidates and had relatively easily been able to place them into the right ranks. There had been one or two disagreements, but these had been resolved amicably.

The placement system in Wallsmannstahl was generally fair. If a candidate challenged a placement, then the arm or service board would review the decision and, if there was no change in the offer, it would then be referred to a neutral appeals board. At every stage of the process there were representatives from the ex-statutory forces,[1] former non-statutory forces and BMATT. The appeals board findings were binding. There had to be an extremely well-argued case to have an offer overturned. In the handful of disputes that I witnessed as the duty BMATT member of an appeals board none were overturned.

* * *

There were several interesting moments. Quite early in the procedure, there was one candidate who had an extraordinarily arrogant demeanour. He breezed in, claiming that he was a colonel who had been overlooked during the initial senior leadership cadre selection. He also claimed that he was a highly experienced artilleryman, and expected us to process him and place him in his rank. We explained that we could not place anyone above the rank of lieutenant colonel and referred him to the administrators in the main hangar. He soon returned, telling us that he had been told he needed to pass the artillery selection first.

Xavier had in the meantime begun to look quite uncomfortable. Out of his earshot, Xavier explained that he had heard of this man before, but he could not remember him from any of the artillery training and did not recognize him from anywhere in the camp here in Wallmannsthal. The longer this went on, the more suspicious Xavier became.

The candidate started on the assessment. He performed adequately in the equipment recognition and written tests, although he complained about the latter. What was most interesting was that he had not performed particularly well on the questions aimed towards the senior officers. Regardless of how long ago one did artillery training, the procedures are so drilled in that they can be performed whilst asleep. We became more concerned when he said that he was unhappy with the questions designed to assess a battery commander's knowledge. We had established that the battery commander's course was the highest-level artillery course that non-statutory force members could attend; any candidate purporting to be a senior officer with an artillery background would therefore have had to attend such a course. The candidate's complaint was that he found the assessment questions confusing because they were written in English. He sat there, almost preening himself, and said that as he was a member of the senior leader group, he had been educated in Russia and therefore was unable to deal with such questions unless they were in Russian. The fact that he was claiming he had attended the Soviet Artillery Academy was credible. After all, Xavier had attended that same three-year course.

Before we could say anything, Xavier smiled and, taking hold of the test paper, took it into the next tent. After about ten minutes, he returned. He passed the paper back across the table and invited our 'senior' candidate to have another go. Xavier had rewritten the questions and amended the diagrams, ensuring everything was now in the Russian language. He added, with a delightful intonation of genuine sarcasm, that he could amend it again into Spanish or German, if that was easier. Xavier's additional language skills were not needed, and a chastened candidate departed to have a second attempt.

The paper was marked, and our candidate was called forward for his interview. The interview, which was chaired by the Director, was difficult to say the least. On the one hand, there was a very aggrieved candidate who claimed that his seniority was being challenged. But there was also Xavier, who spent the whole interview glowering at the candidate, not bothering to hide his contempt. We had been placed in a difficult position. The paperwork stated that the candidate was seeking placement as a brigadier, but looking at the documents there seemed to be more than a few gaps in his 'service record'. The test results, be they in English or Russian, placed him fairly and squarely as a major. The interview was fractious and, even if nothing else came from it, there was a clear demonstration that this individual was not a team player. The offer to join the South African Artillery as a major was rebuffed with scorn, and we were then subject to a tirade of accusations of racism. The Director allowed him his say and to dig himself into a hole. Not only had his tests proved that he had only the knowledge of a middle-ranking field officer, but his behaviour did not demonstrate the qualities expected of a senior officer – especially one who would be key to the future of integration. The Director calmly stated that he had sought the opinions of all members of the panel and we were unanimous in our decision. Both the ex-MK and BMATT members of the panel had endorsed the decision. Therefore, if the candidate declined the offer, he had three options: he could appeal, which, of course, was his right; he could apply to another arm or service; or he could go back to the MK leadership and ask to be 'reinstated' on the senior leadership cadre. The candidate stormed out, and that was the last any of us heard from or about him. All we knew was that he never appeared on any of the senior leadership cadre lists. He was something of a mystery, and although the Director, Andre, Mr Boulter and I dismissed him as an enigma, Xavier was clearly quite troubled by the experience.

* * *

As the days moved on, so did the whole process, and it was not long before it was in full swing. There was a constant bustling crowd outside the marquees and a steady throughput into the artillery assessment. I was very happy that the system was running as well as it could; even with minor disruptions, I could confidently report to BMATT HQ that the artillery assessment and selection process was going smoothly and according to plan.

* * *

My responsibility extended to the air defence artillery, which in the South African Army was treated quite separately to the field artillery. In the British Army's Royal Regiment of Artillery, although field and air defence artillery are grouped into separate regiments, they come together under one cap badge and officers will often switch from one discipline to another. In South Africa, never the twain shall meet. The field artillery, which was the larger branch, was based at Potchefstroom with the Artillery School and 4th Artillery Regiment, whereas the air defence artillery was in Kimberley with the 10th Air Defence Regiment, which provided both the instructional and deployable elements. The officer leading the integration process for the air defence artillery was a tall man called Eric Botha, who was very serious and spoke with a booming voice. He gave the impression that he wanted to get the whole process right, and his plan was simple. The MK leadership had indicated there were only a few air defence candidates, and Eric had assessed that there would be few challenges in establishing each candidate's rank and training requirements. He had adopted a very sensible assessment test, similar in form to that of the field artillery. To further ease the integration, he sought to bring forward all the air defence candidates for selection so that they could go as a group to complete their Phase 1 Bridging Training, the basic training, at an infantry battalion in Kimberley. Upon completion of Phase 1 training, he would take them straight into the 10th Air Defence Regiment to start their special-to-arm Phase 2 training. The selection process took a couple of days, after which a line was drawn under the air defence artillery until the start of Phase 2 training. As with the field artillery, I had signed off the programme under the watchful eye of the White Rabbit, and I had no doubt that with Eric's dedication the line would remain drawn.

* * *

One day we came across a candidate about whom Xavier had been talking for quite a while. He had gone into exile a long time ago and had done the rounds of artillery and combined arms training in Russia and other communist countries. He had spent some time on the MK staff and was well regarded by everyone. We were all looking forward to meeting this candidate, and we were not disappointed. He entered wearing a uniform that was stretching quite obviously at the seams, and he had a broad smile on his face. The warmth of his character and his presence made an immediate impact. His pace through the practical and written test could not be described as a rush; it was more of a leisurely stroll. This was in part due to his demeanour, but also because he had not been at the practical end of artillery for many years. His answers were imprecise, but it was clear that he knew what was needed; he just could not quite remember all the sequences of calculations or orders. It was abundantly clear that he had been trained at a high level, and the contrast to the performance of the 'bluffing colonel' could not have been greater. This candidate charmed the panel, and we were all unanimous in awarding him the rank of lieutenant colonel. Abe had arrived.

The dilemma we faced with Abe was how he should be employed in the future. Unlike the others, all of whom were relatively young and therefore had a future at regimental duty, Abe had done enough service. He was not so old as to be considered for retirement, but he was not of an age to be running around the bush. We discussed this and agreed that the priority would be to get him into the system, when there would be plenty of time to see where he would be best suited. There would be plenty of appointments at the School or in the Directorate. Regardless, we had acquired a great asset. We all agreed that Abe would add tremendous value to the artillery and the integration process.

* * *

We had relatively few disputes in the artillery assessment and selection process, but as time went on, what disputes there were took on a more political flavour. The complaints we received were rarely about the process itself; they were regarding the perceived failure by the candidate to be placed in his expected rank. This was claimed to be because of obstructionism by the old regime, thereby preventing upward social mobility, a loosely worded accusation of racism. The complaints from those inside the wire were beginning to come in thick and fast, both from those who had been processed[2] and those still waiting; but they all followed the same lines. Trade unionism was creeping in, which was alien to the military and needed to be quashed as soon as possible. BMATT was not looking for an argument, but a discussion was needed, especially as we had observed that Xavier was becoming less of an officer in the SANDF and more of a trade union shop steward.

Chapter 7

Dis-Ease And Dad's Army

Life inside the wire continued. Although the process had started, the throughput was slow. To those who were waiting, it was painfully slow. The leader groups were being processed, but it soon became apparent that the 'foot soldiers', many of whom had done no military training whatsoever, were quite ignorant of the structure of the SANDF as a whole and of its constituent parts. They had no idea of the career structure or the trade training offered, and had little notion of military life. There was a large percentage who had only experienced the old SADF in its internal security role, either being stopped at checkpoints or seeing the military patrolling in support of the police in the townships in times of civil unrest. A sensible decision was taken to stage a military equipment demonstration just outside the wire and show the plethora of equipment that the SANDF operated.

A very interesting selection of vehicles and weapon systems had been developed by the South African arms industry during the embargo period. The armoured troop-carrying vehicles had been designed specifically to counter, or realistically mitigate, the effects of mine blasts, and the artillery system they had was world class. The G5 towed and G6 self-propelled howitzers had their ordnance designed by Gerald Bull, the renegade gun designer who was later connected to the production of the Iraqi super gun.

The equipment display was set up on the ample open ground surrounding the base, so each arm could display its wares. It was a useful exercise for all concerned. The ex-MK personnel could crawl all over the equipment and see the complexity of it. They could decide what took their fancy and then apply to join that arm when it became their turn to enter the process. In parallel, the serving personnel could explain the skills needed and what training to expect. Walking around the display was just the same as any army display anywhere in the world; it could very well be Aldershot Arena in the sun. The larger pieces of equipment drew the greatest interest, especially if there was a gun on top. The crowds would gather around the smaller pieces of infantry ordnance and then swell again as the larger calibre weapons were spotted. The more technical aspects drew the interest of those who were naturally that way inclined or who realized that they could get excellent trade training which would be useful later in their lives. It was also evident that there was much that still needed doing, and there continued to be a tremendous 'us and them' environment. The photographs taken that day show a series of large black-faced groups dressed in an assortment of overalls and tracksuits. The serving members were uniform in their dress and colour.

* * *

HIV and AIDS were at the time rampant throughout sub-Saharan Africa, and South Africa was no exception. It had spread with ease throughout the general population, but most especially amongst the black population, and there were many indigenous practices that exacerbated the situation. There were very hard-hitting documentaries broadcast on television which demonstrated the ease with which the disease could be spread. The traditions amongst some groups did not help, especially when a young woman needed to prove herself fertile before becoming an eligible bride. Although the public health initiatives in South Africa were far more advanced than in most, if not all, the other African countries, there was a concern that some of the non-statutory force personnel could well be HIV positive. There was clearly going to be an operational risk with a soldier being infected, and we in BMATT had assumed that there would be screening for HIV as part of the medical boarding. Our RAF doctor came back one day looking quite ashen, informing us that HIV testing was not to be part of the screening process; in fact it was expressly forbidden to ask a candidate anything about his or her HIV status. This was staggering news. We had assumed that if a non-statutory force member had been detected as HIV positive, or had any other disease or condition that would preclude military service, there would then be a procedure firstly to place the individual into the medical system and, if appropriate, to arrange a suitable discharge and pension programme. However, the twin subjects of HIV and AIDS were not to be discussed. These had been politicized, and Deputy President Thabo Mbeki, within whose portfolio lay the fight against AIDS, was establishing himself as an AIDS 'dissident'.

The official lines were quite staggering. It was said that Mbeki, of course later to become the second President of South Africa, had his view of HIV shaped by an obsession with race, the legacy of colonialism and sexual shame. Later, President Mbeki was to write that black people who accepted orthodox HIV treatments were self-repressed victims of a slave mentality. He described the HIV/AIDS thesis as entrenched in centuries-old white racist beliefs and concepts about Africans. With this uncompromising stance, all BMATT could do was to represent its opinion knowing that it would be acknowledged and ignored. It was obviously a mistake, and represented a disservice to many members of the non-statutory forces who suffered from the condition; without doubt, some later died of it. Sweeping this issue under the carpet and dressing up the reasons for doing so in anti-colonial rhetoric was destructive. It also did nothing more than delay the inevitable for the victims who would enter military service before anything could be done for them, and then only when they became sick. I must point out that I did not meet one South African who supported this view on HIV and AIDS, and all those within the integration process from any of the constituent parties thought it short-sighted and wasteful.

* * *

About a year later I was asked to go and see the new Commandant at the Artillery School, Colonel Theuns Coetzee. He and I had become good friends, so I realized as soon as I entered his office that all was not well. He seemed very upset and asked me to sit down. This was at the time when the first of the leader group intake were about to finish their final course, the Battery Commander's Course. There were a couple of ex-non-statutory force members on the course, and one in particular had been doing exceptionally well throughout. He had been continually scoring the highest of marks and had finished top of all the previous courses. There was no doubt he was going to finish top of the Battery Commander's Course. This was an excellent result, bearing in mind the course was made up of all the potential battery commanders, regardless of where they came from in the process. The great and the good of the South African Artillery had met the previous week to look at the next command list. This was, for the first time, to include ex-non-statutory forces officers. The outstanding results of this one officer had to be acknowledged, for not only was he technically excellent, he was a capable and popular leader as well; he was a natural.

The Command List was produced, and it had been decided to give him command of the parachute battery. This was 'right of the line' in the South African Artillery, and it was not only a great honour to the individual to be given this command but a huge commitment to the integration process. This was sending out a message in capital letters.

Theuns proceeded to tell me that this officer had just come to see him and had declined the offer of command. He had then asked to be excused, whilst also requesting a second interview to take place, with me being present, so that he could explain the reasons for his decision. We were both dumbstruck and tried to second-guess what was coming. Was there some political statement about to be made? What had we missed? The officer returned and entered the office with a very solemn demeanour. He saluted Theuns and me, and then shook our hands. The colonel asked him to be seated, summoned his adjutant to take a record of the proceedings, and asked the officer to explain his decision.

He started by saying how grateful he was to have been selected to command a battery, and that he fully understood the importance attached to this decision, especially considering the message that his appointment would send out not only to the Regiment but also to the whole Army. Then he added, quietly, that he must decline. It was like a thunderclap in the charged environment of the room; Theuns and I sat there dumbfounded, but before we could comment, the officer said his reason was that he had just found out that he was HIV positive.

He went on to explain that he had only recently been diagnosed HIV positive and had told his family the previous weekend. They were devastated. He said that he could not take on an active duty command if he would be a liability to his command. If he was to be wounded, then there was a risk he could infect others, and he felt he could not live with that responsibility. Theuns gathered his composure and asked where the officer's family were now, and whether they had been tested. When the officer replied that his family had not been tested, Theuns told him that he would arrange for this to happen as soon as possible and that the officer must receive the correct medical attention straight away. He continued to assure the officer not to worry about the battery; there would be many other opportunities for him to shine. I realized that I had been given an insight into a desperate personal plight, and at the same time had witnessed a warm bond between ex-enemies who were now, truly, comrades-in-arms.

Of course, if the officer had been screened for HIV at Wallmannsthal he might not have got to Potchefstroom; although he might have entered a medical programme earlier, he and his family may not have had the same 'regimental' support that he was about to receive. At the same time, he had displayed tremendous courage to have raised the issue, thus exposing a personal weakness, confidence in trusting his new comrades and integrity by putting not himself but his command first. After all, in the emotionally charged atmosphere surrounding AIDS, he could have just kept quiet. He could have commanded his battery spectacularly well and nobody would have been the wiser. He chose the difficult path, one which could well have gone badly wrong. What he did was to show the humble, selfless act of honesty, which is talked of in every military academy in the world but is so very rarely seen.

His family tested negative.

There were, I am sure, many others who had little idea that they were infected but who eventually became sick and died. To this day, I think the policy of not screening for HIV was a disgraceful decision.

In 2008, I returned for a short visit to Potchefstroom, where I met a lot of old friends, ate and drank far too much and swapped some hugely exaggerated stories. In checking up on who was doing what and where, I was delighted to hear that the officer was alive and well and was occupying a very important position in the South African Artillery. Sadly, he was on leave when I visited.

* * *

Africa is a wonderful continent; a land of staggering beauty, wonderful people and extraordinary culture. One experiences things there that are unique and cannot be explained using Western European logic. One of these is the power of the Sangoma, the traditional healer, or in derogatory terms, the witch doctor. The Sangoma has tremendous influence throughout South Africa. People will defer to the Sangoma, not through any form of ignorance but through tradition. The Sangoma provides different social roles in the community, including divination, healing physical, emotional and spiritual illnesses, directing birth or death rituals, finding lost cattle, protecting warriors, counteracting witches and narrating history, cosmology and myths. In addition to the Sangoma, who is a spiritual healer, there is the Inyanga, who produces various potions and remedies. There is little difference between Inyangas and the herbalists you find elsewhere in the world. There are some 200,000 traditional healers in South Africa, and they are regularly consulted in parallel with normal doctors. However, there is another side of this tradition which is far from pleasant and often practised by charlatans. It is well known that any Sangoma can have an unerring power over people, and although in the clear majority of cases the Sangoma is a force for good, some can use their teaching to the detriment of others.

One experience of the power of the Sangoma that I came across was with a young soldier going through his Phase 1 Bridging Training in Potchefstroom. He had been to see the doctor on several occasions, complaining about feeling unwell and saying that he was convinced he had worms inside his belly. This baffled the doctor; although he could see that his patient was unwell, he could find absolutely nothing wrong with him, and certainly no trace of worms or other form of parasite. Eventually he sat the patient down and tried to unravel the mystery. The problem then materialized. The soldier declared that he had had a spell placed upon him by a Sangoma because of a dispute in his home village. The Sangoma told the soldier that he had infected him with a worm that would eat him from the inside. The doctor reassured him that there was no credence in such a statement; he did not have a worm inside him and he should forget all about it.

Despite this reassurance, the young soldier became detached and weaker, and his performance was well below standard. He was admitted to the medical centre again and more tests were carried out, again with no result. The doctor was now convinced that this illness was psychosomatic; the young man was terrifying himself and this was causing his physical decline. The soldier got progressively worse until, after one weekend leave, he did not return to the unit. He had died – he had literally been frightened to death.

* * *

Meanwhile, complaints were increasing from within the wire. Xavier was in full shop-steward mode. He reported that the food was poor and served cold, and that no matter how many times complaints had been made there was no difference. Every soldier knows that Napoleon is credited with saying that an army marches on its stomach, and we had all heard experienced soldiers complaining about their food. I remember as a young officer receiving many complaints about the food. Once, when I was Regimental Orderly Officer standing behind the hotplate in the Regimental Restaurant, I was approached by a Jones – or an Evans, or maybe a Williams – and informed that the meat was raw and inedible. I looked at the meat in question and saw a perfectly presented joint of roast beef, slightly pink in the middle. Yet this was raw in my gunners' eyes, and it took more than a little persuasion and education to allay their complaints. Applying such experiences, two of us from BMATT agreed to go into the camp to visit one of the catering facilities and see the standard and quality of the food for ourselves. Our very own shop steward would accompany us.

The tent was partially open to the elements, but it provided an airy environment for the serving of hot food. A contractor had been employed to provide the catering and the company chosen was well accustomed to feeding hundreds of people. The food was adequate, in that it was hot and filling, but it was not to the same high standard as military catering in the UK. However, this was true across the whole of the SANDF. The food which we sampled was edible and, my taste aside, it was clear that the customers were eating what was provided. They may not have been eating with a great deal of relish, but the result was empty plates. A frequent comment was that the selection of food was boring, but when we pursued this with the caterers, they showed us that they produced a variety of main courses during the week, and always had mieliepap, the traditional maize porridge (like grits in the US), and other traditional dishes available.

If one recognized soldiers by their ability to complain, then those inside the wire were well on the way to being paid-up members of the SANDF!

* * *

Whilst the process of integration rumbled on and BMATT's focus was on the assessment process, the issue of what to do with those who could not be accepted into military service gathered steam. It was soon clear that there were two ways to deal with those of the non-statutory forces who were either unable or unwilling to join the SANDF. One option was demobilization, which would involve a cash payment and possible access to a pension. Alternatively, the idea of a Service Corps was suggested, the purpose of which was to create an organization to provide technical and trade training to those not able, or not wishing, to serve in the SANDF. It would provide the understanding of employment skills, employment-related attitudes and communication, social and behavioural skills, all of this done whilst being engaged on worthwhile projects.

* * *

Demobilization was politically charged. There would have to be thresholds and cut-off points, and regardless of where the line was drawn, there would be some discord. But what was unhelpful was that there was a delay in the announcement of the policy for the non-statutory force members. It was clear that whatever system was to be introduced, it would be different to that for the statutory force members looking towards redundancy. Those in the statutory force had extant Terms and Conditions of Service, and therefore knew what to expect in any redundancy package; they were just waiting for the details of how the process would be enacted. The issue for the non-statutory forces was different; it took until August 1995 to announce the final package, well over a year after the integration process had started. The process of demobilization involved, amongst other things, the provision of a demobilization gratuity to the member when he was demobilized. The size of the gratuity would depend on the number of years of service in the MK or APLA, and it was subdivided into five groups; for example, Group One would have served in the period 1 January 1961 to 31 September 1972 and would receive R42,058 (about US$11,500 in 1995). The process of demobilization started almost as soon as it was announced, and this applied to those in the PMORDs as well as to those who had yet to be called forward.

Most of those eligible for demobilization were classified as 'veterans' and 'vulnerables'. 'Veterans' referred to those who, due to their length of service in the MK and APLA and their age, were due for retirement. 'Vulnerables' was a collective term used to describe those who were medically unfit for integration into the SANDF. Both were older (aged 50–60) than the average non-statutory force member. Generally, 'veterans' and 'vulnerables' were not constructively employed after having reported at Wallmannsthal at an early stage in the integration process, and had in many cases been patiently awaiting the outcome of political decisions on the demob process.

Most of the 'veterans' and the 'vulnerables' also qualified for a pension, which was covered by the Special Pensions Act. This stated:

> 'Provision shall be made by an Act of Parliament for the payment of special pensions by the national government to: a) persons who made sacrifices or who have served the public interest in the establishment of a democratic constitutional order, including members of any armed or military force not established by or under any law and which is under the authority and control of, or associated

with and promotes the objectives of, a political organisation; or b) dependants of such persons.'[1]

As part of the demobilization process, there was an offer of a counselling period of two weeks, which would involve introductions to personnel matters, career guidance, social services and financial management. Most of the initial tranche for demobilization rejected this. This was a mistake on their part, as it soon became evident that many of those who had been in exile or operating within the shadows of South Africa had little grasp of what the real world had in store for them. Demobilization, like many other aspects of the greater integration process, lacked the intimate detail that was necessary to guarantee success. This was possibly because it was a non-military task which was forced upon the military, but mainly because it was mired in political wrangling and danced around what was politically correct in an era of affirmative action. The suggestion that many of the non-statutory force members were unprepared to enter normal civilian life, whilst quite probably true, was not articulated because it would have been considered racist and hark back to the Apartheid era. This lack of moral courage and failure to accept an unpalatable reality, fuelled by all parties having to play the game of hopscotch in a minefield of sensitivities, resulted in many people being very badly prepared for what was ahead of them.

The idea of the Service Corps was addressed by General Meiring at a conference in 1993, when he identified that there would be many in the planned integration process who would not be automatically accepted into the SANDF. It did not matter for what reason an individual would not be able to join; what did matter was that they were not just left on the streets without employment. He raised the concept of a Service Brigade, which would be used for non-military roles such as construction. Armed with new skills, the individual would then be able to leave after a set term of service and find gainful employment. This idea was appealing; it began to gather steam as people imagined a skilled labour force being able to tackle the shortfall in housing, schools and other capital projects. These projects were not only considered for South Africa; some enthusiasts even thought the deployment of the Service Brigade a possible means to address the regional challenges across southern Africa.

The Service Corps, which was launched on 31 January 1995, was to be the mechanism through which social integration would occur. The idea was to provide an eighteen-month package consisting of three months' literacy and life skill training, three months of vocational training and twelve months of practical experience. The members would be paid, and the labour would support the Reconstruction and Development Programme. The Service Corps was planned to have a strength of 1,800 by mid-1995, and to eventually rise to 10,000. The take-up was disappointing to say the least, as by September 1995 just over 300 trainees were in the Corps while almost 1,000 volunteers were still in Wallmannsthal. What appeared to be an excellent conduit shrivelled on the vine as a lack of enthusiasm took over. The hallmark lack of communications was telling, and trouble began to brew in Wallmannsthal.

* * *

I soon learned that trouble, when it comes in Africa, comes quickly and with passion, and almost certainly from a direction that one does not expect. The complaints were constant and the 'trade union' mentality was becoming quite wearing. Those applying to join the artillery were becoming more confident of their 'rights' as opposed to wanting to demonstrate their worth. The placement procedure was becoming more difficult, with more and more appeals, and many things began to suggest that we were entering a period of non-cooperation. The veneer was wearing thin.

One day we interviewed a charming candidate. He was senior in years and carried himself with the dignity befitting an elder. He knew his artillery, and was an articulate and witty candidate who combined intelligence with an inherent sharpness. He had a striking resemblance to Archbishop Desmond Tutu, which was quite disarming, and the interview process appeared to me more of a relaxed conversation in a tutor's study than part of a career placement process in a dusty tent. There was only one drawback; he was too old. We had recently been briefed about the aspirations of the Service Corps, although at this stage there was not any concrete information on the corps or the 'veterans' package – and our candidate was clearly in the veteran category. When we explained that we were unable to accommodate him in the artillery because of his age, we were subjected to a tirade that was like a breaking tropical storm. The pent-up frustration of years of sacrifice, exacerbated by being held for months in Wallmannsthal, exploded upon us. All we could do was accept his criticism, as we were not able to make or change policy that had not yet been promulgated. The irony was that he would still have to wait many months before he would have any confirmation of what his final

Nelson Mandela voting in the General Election 1994

South Armagh, Northern Ireland, 1993.

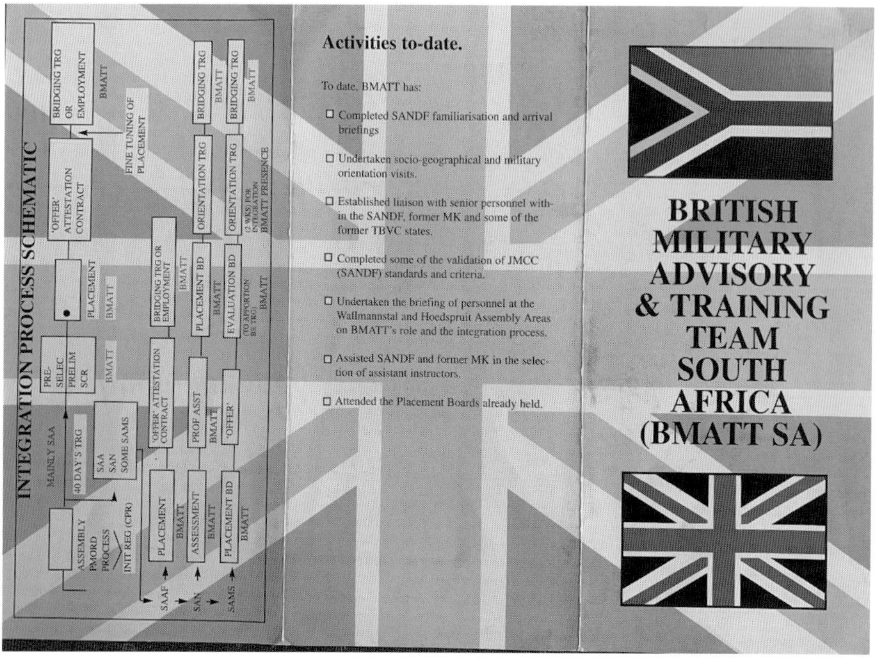

Activities to-date.

To date, BMATT has:

- ☐ Completed SANDF familiarisation and arrival briefings
- ☐ Undertaken socio-geographical and military orientation visits.
- ☐ Established liaison with senior personnel within the SANDF, former MK and some of the former TBVC states.
- ☐ Completed some of the validation of JMCC (SANDF) standards and criteria.
- ☐ Undertaken the briefing of personnel at the Wallmannstal and Hoedspruit Assembly Areas on BMATT's role and the integration process.
- ☐ Assisted SANDF and former MK in the selection of assistant instructors.
- ☐ Attended the Placement Boards already held.

BRITISH MILITARY ADVISORY & TRAINING TEAM SOUTH AFRICA (BMATT SA)

BMATT Flier 1, provided the most succinct schematic of the integration process.

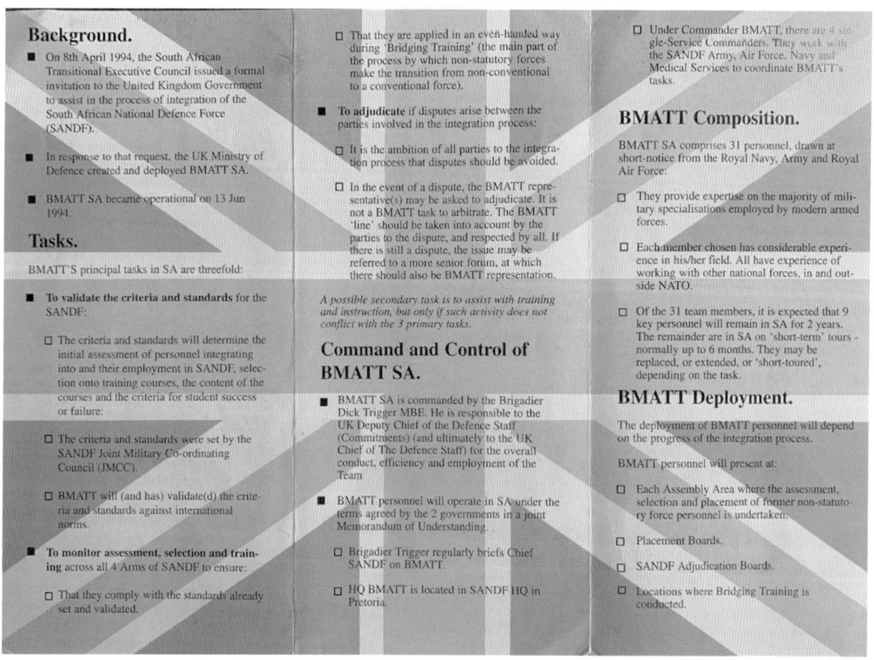

Background.

- On 8th April 1994, the South African Transitional Executive Council issued a formal invitation to the United Kingdom Government to assist in the process of integration of the South African National Defence Force (SANDF).
- In response to that request, the UK Ministry of Defence created and deployed BMATT SA.
- BMATT SA became operational on 13 Jun 1994.

Tasks.

BMATT'S principal tasks in SA are threefold:

- **To validate the criteria and standards** for the SANDF:
  - ☐ The criteria and standards will determine the initial assessment of personnel integrating into and their employment in SANDF, selection onto training courses, the content of the courses and the criteria for student success or failure:
  - ☐ The criteria and standards were set by the SANDF Joint Military Co-ordinating Council (JMCC).
  - ☐ BMATT will (and has) validate(d) the criteria and standards against international norms.
- **To monitor assessment, selection and training** across all 4 Arms of SANDF to ensure:
  - ☐ That they comply with the standards already set and validated.
  - ☐ That they are applied in an even-handed way during 'Bridging Training' (the main part of the process by which non-statutory forces make the transition from non-conventional to a conventional force).
- **To adjudicate** if disputes arise between the parties involved in the integration process:
  - ☐ It is the ambition of all parties to the integration process that disputes should be avoided.
  - ☐ In the event of a dispute, the BMATT representative(s) may be asked to adjudicate. It is not a BMATT task to arbitrate. The BMATT 'line' should be taken into account by the parties to the dispute, and respected by all. If there is still a dispute, the issue may be referred to a more senior forum, at which there should also be BMATT representation.

A possible secondary task is to assist with training and instruction, but only if such activity does not conflict with the 3 primary tasks.

Command and Control of BMATT SA.

- BMATT SA is commanded by the Brigadier Dick Trigger MBE. He is responsible to the UK Deputy Chief of the Defence Staff (Commitments) (and ultimately to the UK Chief of The Defence Staff) for the overall conduct, efficiency and employment of the Team
- BMATT personnel will operate in SA under the terms agreed by the 2 governments in a joint Memorandum of Understanding.
  - ☐ Brigadier Trigger regularly briefs Chief SANDF on BMATT.
  - ☐ HQ BMATT is located in SANDF HQ in Pretoria.
  - ☐ Under Commander BMATT, there are 4 single-Service Commanders. They work with the SANDF Army, Air Force, Navy and Medical Services to coordinate BMATT's tasks.

BMATT Composition.

BMATT SA comprises 31 personnel, drawn at short-notice from the Royal Navy, Army and Royal Air Force:

- ☐ They provide expertise on the majority of military specialisations employed by modern armed forces.
- ☐ Each member chosen has considerable experience in his/her field. All have experience of working with other national forces, in and outside NATO.
- ☐ Of the 31 team members, it is expected that 9 key personnel will remain in SA for 2 years. The remainder are in SA on 'short-term' tours - normally up to 6 months. They may be replaced, or extended, or 'short-toured', depending on the task.

BMATT Deployment.

The deployment of BMATT personnel will depend on the progress of the integration process.

BMATT personnel will present at:

- ☐ Each Assembly Area where the assessment, selection and placement of former non-statutory force personnel is undertaken.
- ☐ Placement Boards.
- ☐ SANDF Adjudication Boards.
- ☐ Locations where Bridging Training is conducted.

BMATT Flier 2, the intent was to explain who, why and what was BMATT.

Signing of the Memorandum of Understanding, Wallmannstahl

Prospective members of the new SANDF waiting to be accepted into the process.

Impatience showing. The buildings of Wallmannsthal PMORD in the background.

Potential recruits to the South African Artillery inspect the breech of a G-5 howitzer.

The potential recruits still dressed in boiler suits, old issue parkas and gum boots.

The Anti-aircraft stand at the Equipment Display at Wallmannsthal PMORD.

An ex-SADF officer briefing the potential recruits about the Anti-Aircraft Artillery.

Equipment display outside the wire. In the background is the tented camp 'inside the wire'.

On the first day of Assessment, the potential recruits wait patiently.

Two newly attested members of the SANDF.

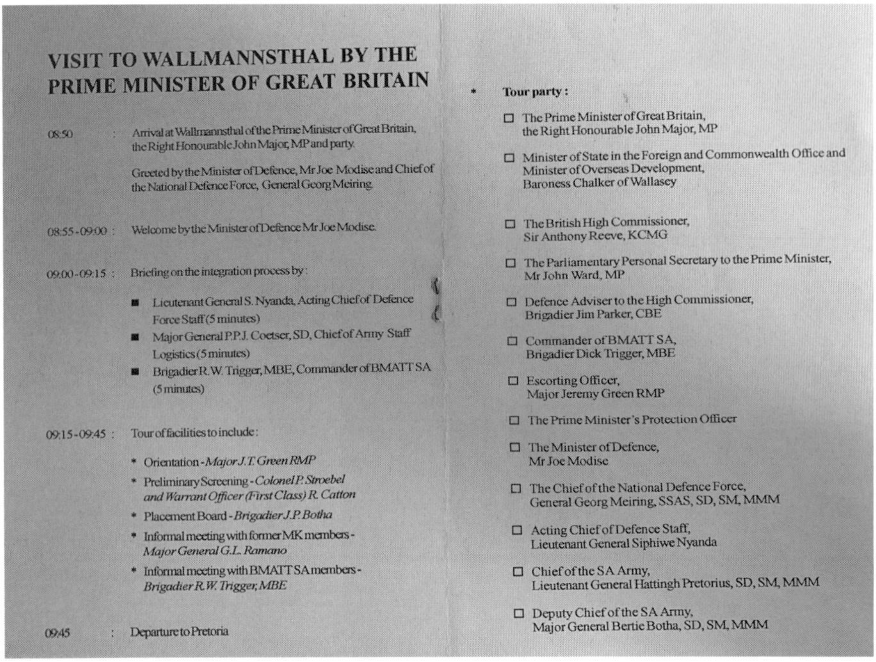

VISIT TO WALLMANNSTHAL BY THE PRIME MINISTER OF GREAT BRITAIN

08:50 : Arrival at Wallmannsthal of the Prime Minister of Great Britain, the Right Honourable John Major, MP and party.

Greeted by the Minister of Defence, Mr Joe Modise and Chief of the National Defence Force, General Georg Meiring.

08:55 - 09:00 : Welcome by the Minister of Defence Mr Joe Modise.

09:00 - 09:15 : Briefing on the integration process by:

- Lieutenant General S. Nyanda, Acting Chief of Defence Force Staff (5 minutes)
- Major General P.P.J. Coetser, SD, Chief of Army Staff Logistics (5 minutes)
- Brigadier R.W. Trigger, MBE, Commander of BMATT SA (5 minutes)

09:15 - 09:45 : Tour of facilities to include:

* Orientation - *Major J.T. Green RMP*
* Preliminary Screening - *Colonel P. Stroebel and Warrant Officer (First Class) R. Catton*
* Placement Board - *Brigadier J.P. Botha*
* Informal meeting with former MK members - *Major General G.L. Ramano*
* Informal meeting with BMATT SA members - *Brigadier R.W. Trigger, MBE*

09:45 : Departure to Pretoria

* **Tour party:**

- The Prime Minister of Great Britain, the Right Honourable John Major, MP
- Minister of State in the Foreign and Commonwealth Office and Minister of Overseas Development, Baroness Chalker of Wallasey
- The British High Commissioner, Sir Anthony Reeve, KCMG
- The Parliamentary Personal Secretary to the Prime Minister, Mr John Ward, MP
- Defence Adviser to the High Commissioner, Brigadier Jim Parker, CBE
- Commander of BMATT SA, Brigadier Dick Trigger, MBE
- Escorting Officer, Major Jeremy Green RMP
- The Prime Minister's Protection Officer
- The Minister of Defence, Mr Joe Modise
- The Chief of the National Defence Force, General Georg Meiring, SSAS, SD, SM, MMM
- Acting Chief of Defence Staff, Lieutenant General Siphiwe Nyanda
- Chief of the SA Army, Lieutenant General Hattingh Pretorius, SD, SM, MMM
- Deputy Chief of the SA Army, Major General Bertie Botha, SD, SM, MMM

Programme for the visit of the Prime Minister

Introducing the Prime Minister to member of BMATT (SA), September 1994.

Central Briefing. The ex-non-statutory force members in the foreground and the ex-SADF personnel to the right.

155mm G-5 Howitzer. Brought into service in 1982 and saw action from 1986-1989.

The first G-5 detachment comprising of fully trained and integrated ex-non-statutory forces.

Orders to the Tac (OP) parties. Note the mix of uniforms and the lack of full integration.

Proof of the Pudding. A good fall of shot during the live fire phase of the exercise.

Two captains completing the practical stage of the bridging training on Potchefstroom Ranges.

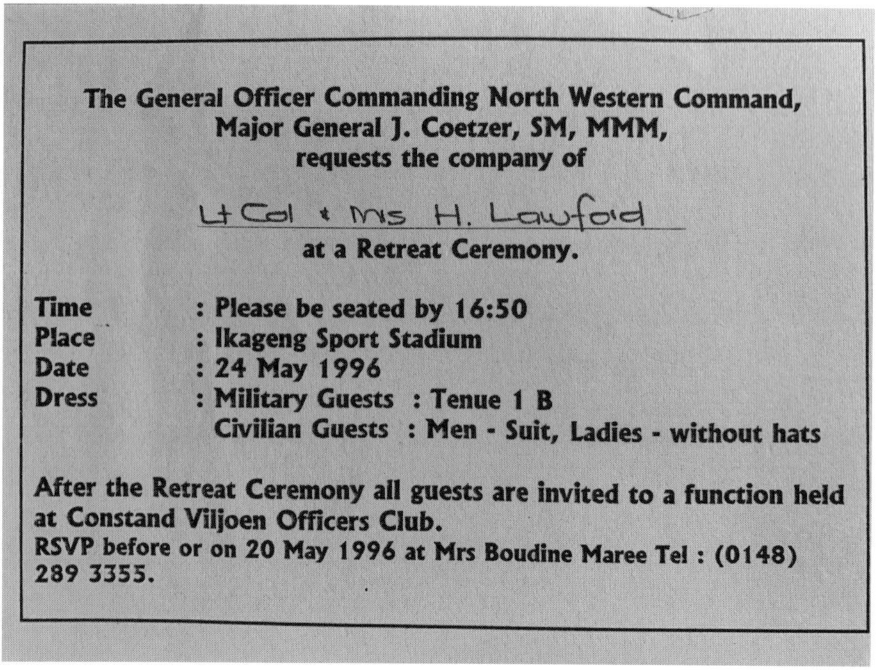

The General Officer Commanding North Western Command,
Major General J. Coetzer, SM, MMM,
requests the company of

Lt Col & Mrs H. Lawford

at a Retreat Ceremony.

Time : Please be seated by 16:50
Place : Ikageng Sport Stadium
Date : 24 May 1996
Dress : Military Guests : Tenue 1 B
Civilian Guests : Men - Suit, Ladies - without hats

After the Retreat Ceremony all guests are invited to a function held at Constand Viljoen Officers Club.
RSVP before or on 20 May 1996 at Mrs Boudine Maree Tel : (0148) 289 3355.

An invitation to a military parade in the black township of Ikageng near Potchefstroom.

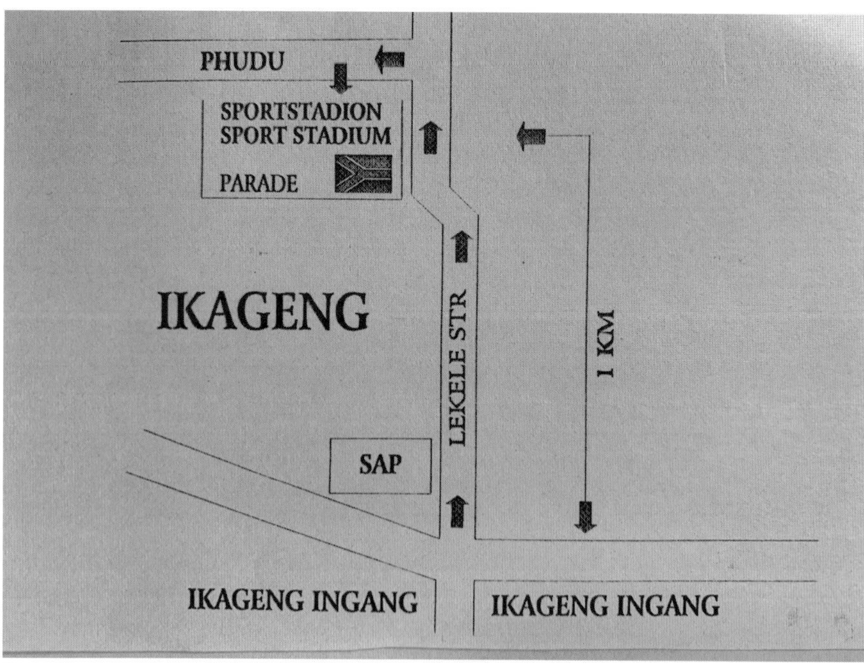

The map showing the location of the parade, previously the Army had only been there in the security role.

The girls at the wonderful Kruger National Park during one of their many visits.

The original signal was right, I needed my Mess Dress for the Potchefstroom Military Ball, October 1994.

A few years and a few medals later, NATO Defence College Ball, Rome 2009.

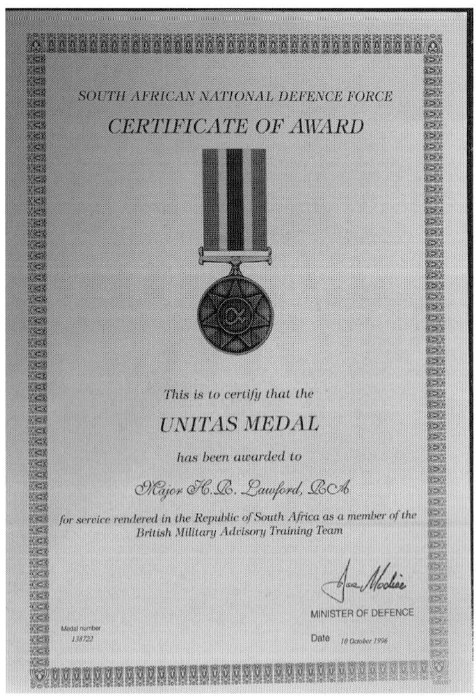

SOUTH AFRICAN NATIONAL DEFENCE FORCE

CERTIFICATE OF AWARD

This is to certify that the

UNITAS MEDAL

has been awarded to

Major H.R. Lawford, RA

for service rendered in the Republic of South Africa as a member of the British Military Advisory Training Team

MINISTER OF DEFENCE

Medal number *138722*

Date *10 October 1996*

The South African Unitas Medal certificate which was also awarded to the members of BMATT.

Trisha's first appointment as a qualified teacher: Mohadin Pre-Primary School, Potchefstroom.

Trisha getting ready for life in the new South Africa, in fact we weren't allowed to own a weapon.

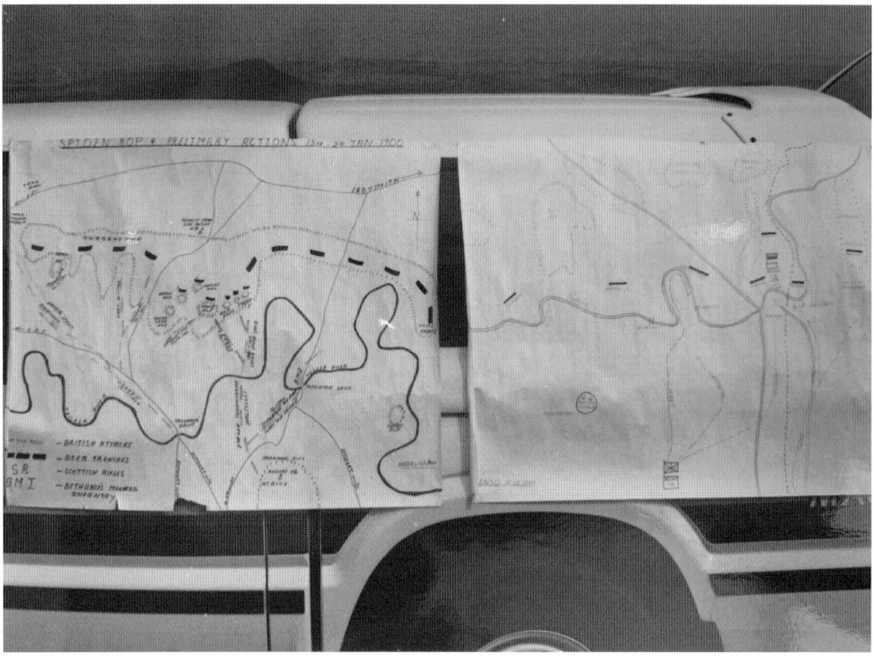

The family 'bakkie' being used as a map board at the Spion Kop battlefield tour.

Newly 'integrated' families enjoying the great South African tradition of the 'braai'.

package would be. We advised him to register with the appropriate cell in the hangar, supported by our documentation, and to return home to await the final decision. He stormed off, but I thought that would not be the last time we saw him.

I felt frustrated by this incident, as there was absolutely nothing any of us could do to assist him. The whole quagmire of demobilization and the Service Corps was a product of political expediency as well as poor military planning. It represented an almost selfish neglect by the ANC and MK leadership of the fellows left behind; a case of out of sight, out of mind. The only justice, I suppose, was that when details of the gratuity and pension package were announced, those non-statutory force members serving as elected representatives at national and regional government were precluded from receiving either gratuities or a pension.

* * *

Most of the BMATT team had reported similar incidents involving 'veterans' or 'vulnerables', and HQ BMATT had represented these at the various meetings of the Integration Committee at National Defence Headquarters, which was chaired by Lieutenant General Nyanda, but there was no response that we could see on the ground. African culture places a great deal of responsibility on the shoulders of the elders, who are awarded a great deal of respect by even the most hot-headed of young bucks. They are the group who will be approached to discuss problems and establish ways ahead, and they often communicate messages to allow progress to be made in whatever area is of concern. This was still true within the non-statutory forces and, although some of the veterans had been fast-tracked through because of their political or leadership status, the others were, uncharacteristically, left wallowing in the camps. When they became dissatisfied and angry, this anger would quickly spread. Towards the end of 1994, the logistic and administrative inadequacies of Wallmannsthal, together with the glacial progress of the integration process, began to result in verbal protests, disobedience and mass walkouts, not necessarily led by the 'veterans' but certainly with their tacit or other support. It must be remembered that the Integration Committee had originally envisaged that the whole process would be completed by the end of 1994, and it was quite a shock to them when they realized it would take several years. The elongation of the integration process had not been well managed at the strategic level, and with a poor communication plan, the resentment of those remaining in the camps rose. The resentment was aimed at the former MK commanders, the now Minister of Defence Joe Modise and Lieutenant General Nyanda. The anger was such that neither felt that they could safely enter Wallmannsthal.

Things came to a head and the 'veterans' went on strike. Refusing the pleas of their former commanders, the situation became ugly. The veterans were demanding intervention from the very top: a meeting with President Mandela, the Commander-in-Chief of the SANDF. It was very clear that this action by the 'veterans' had a far greater political impact than any strike or protest by the MK rank and file. Many of the 'veterans' were close to President Mandela and the MK hierarchy through their long years in exile or prison. Their protest could not be taken lightly because, unless they were brought back into the fold, the whole integration process could grind to a halt. Furthermore, there was the risk of the protest spreading to those already entering Bridging Training. The spectre of political disputes within the SANDF had to be prevented at all costs; failure to do so could lead to mutiny and a desperate crisis within the organization, which in turn could challenge the political process.

President Mandela did intervene, at two levels. Firstly, he admonished the SANDF command, demanding that they streamline and speed up the integration process. This was a political action at the strategic level, based on his understanding that there had to be action to avoid a political nightmare, but his second action was as a leader and a man determined to see political change succeed peacefully.

President Mandela was to come to Wallmannsthal to address the problems in person.

* * *

The instruction came from Pretoria like a lightning bolt: the President was coming! There were to be no fanfares, briefings or the normal paraphernalia associated with a VIP visit. The President was coming because he wanted to meet the 'veterans'. Staff officers began to run around like whirling dervishes, while cars screamed in from Pretoria, spewing out officials and senior officers of the Ministry of Defence and the SANDF. We witnessed the eternal military ballet of 'order, counter-order and disorder'. The chaotic atmosphere bred rumours aplenty. The SANDF was convinced that the President was coming, like an avenging angel, to sack SANDF personnel left, right and centre and make a huge political point to satiate the complaints of the 'veterans' and the MK as a whole. This was to be revenge on the SADF. The MK was similarly convinced that Madiba[2] was coming to hear their grievances and make decisions to punish those who had discriminated against them.

The latest instructions stated that the President wanted to address the 'veterans', and access to this meeting was to be limited. It was not to be an open session; there was to be only a token presence of other people. He was to be flown in, whisked to a large room within the hangar complex, and there he would listen to and address the 'veterans'. The aim of this meeting was to clear of the air. It was obvious that it would be in the interest of BMATT to find out what was happening, as this could well impact upon our future role.

* * *

President Mandela arrived in a helicopter and, as planned, was whisked into the hangar complex and into one of the large rooms. The room was full of brown-uniformed veterans, and the atmosphere was electric with anticipation and, to a large degree, expectation. I found out later that quite well to the front of the 'veterans' was the old fellow who had given me, and the others in the artillery team, such grief a few weeks previously.

The door was opened with a flourish and a phalanx of security men led in the President. He was characteristically dressed in dark slacks and a colourful long shirt. The room erupted in cheering, clapping and the enigmatic chanting that is quintessentially African; Madiba was welcomed as a hero. His grey-topped head towered over most of the people in the room as he made for the podium with the air of a man who had much to do and very little time to do it. He took his position at the podium and the room fell silent. Mandela had a presence; he filled a room. He was tall, surprisingly so, and spoke with a quiet voice, gesturing with his hands to emphasize a point and, in doing so, drew his audience to him. This manner of speaking required his audience to listen. Talking in this way, he was quite mesmeric.

President Mandela explained why he had come to Wallmannsthal. He said he was aware that the integration process had not been moving forward as quickly or as effectively as he and his government had wished, and that he had instructed the Minister of Defence and the Chief of the SANDF to ensure that progress was made. He also said he had been informed that the 'veterans' in front of him had grievances, and such severe grievances that they had decided to strike. He wanted to know what these grievances were. A couple of veterans stood up, including 'my' man, and highlighted some of their issues in typically African, long-winded fashion. They spoke in the manner that they would use to address a political rally, and as each point was made it was greeted with vociferous support. But this was not a political rally. Having made their points, the 'veterans' looked expectantly at the President, their political leader. What came next took everyone by surprise. Instead of supporting their grievances, the President made it quite clear that what they had highlighted was nothing new, and that he and the Minister of Defence and their old commander, Joe Modise, were aware of the issues and were in the process of addressing them. Many of these issues were complex and required time to introduce them fairly and through the proper channels, he said, while others were conjecture. He then rounded on the audience. What kind of example were they setting to the young people joining the SANDF? The days of political protest in all contexts were over, now they were part of an organization that was apolitical and they, the 'veterans', had a huge role to play in this by setting an example and being leaders. Their actions were damaging the MK, the ANC government and the whole integration and reconstruction process of South Africa. He followed this by saying that they had good leadership in the form of the Minister of Defence and Lieutenant General Nyanda, but these men were fully engaged in the business of maintaining the security of South Africa. There was a chain of command which must be used, and if they considered themselves soldiers then they should act accordingly. 'Go back out and get on with the process' was the message delivered loudly, clearly and quite unequivocally. With that, the President left.

The room was silent, and the stunned audience dispersed and went back to the camp. The strike was over, the 'veterans' chastened. The news spread quickly, and the air was cleared, at least for the time being.

* * *

A few weeks later, I arrived at Wallmannsthal to be met by my anti-aircraft colleague Eric Botha. He was looking concerned and said that I needed to speak to the ex-non-statutory force lieutenant colonel, who was far from pleased. He said that this lieutenant colonel had appointed himself as a spokesman and was threatening a strike because he and all the other integrated members had been lied to. Quite bemused, I followed

Eric into a marquee to be met by a clearly agitated man, pacing up and down like a caged lion. He was dressed in his new SANDF uniform and had clearly been one of the first of those to be integrated. I had seen him around, and I am sure we had spoken on a few occasions. He said that he wanted to speak to BMATT because there was a massive grievance with which we must assist him. He set out the background clearly.

His story was as follows. Once he had been processed, he had been fast-tracked through the system and was now waiting to start his detailed Bridging Training. He had been given a series of cash and bank payments to see him through the initial training period, but now that he was fully integrated into the SANDF, he had received his first pay statement the previous day. He claimed it was clear that the SADF had woven a web of lies as they processed him and his comrades. He had been told that he would be placed on a lieutenant colonel's salary and it had been agreed that he would enter as if on three years' seniority in that rank. He had been informed of his annual salary and had worked out his monthly package. He said it was clear that he had been lied to, because his monthly statement showed only half of what he was owed. He then launched into a diatribe which was anything but helpful, but the gist of it was that if it was the case that the non-statutory forces had been discriminated against, then this would provoke strikes and a most difficult political dilemma.

Between us, Eric and I calmed him down, assuring him that there had clearly been an error. We asked him whether he had any documents supporting his claims. He did, and he produced a very organized dossier with his contract, initial documentation and – most important of all – his pay statement. We looked at the contract and the statement, and then at our friend. His pay was exactly right, his gross salary was right, as were the monthly deductions, and the final figure of the net payment was also correct. It dawned upon us that, up until this point, this individual had never had to pay tax or any other form of state contribution. His pay statement duly listed all the stoppages of pay for tax, medical contributions, accommodation charges and indeed the initial repayment on the advance he had received. It was a short, sharp introduction to reality.

We explained to him what the deductions were and for what reason, and that these deductions were the same for any soldier around the world. Tax had to be paid, especially if you were a government employee, and if you were to receive the medical support that SAMS was to offer in service and in retirement a contribution had to be paid. Eric offered to bring in his own pay statement the following day as proof that he was similarly affected, and in the meantime I took this officer, who was now more confused and disappointed than angry, to one of the administrative offices to have the staff explain the deductions.

He eventually, and most reluctantly, accepted the new regime, but he and many of his colleagues were woefully ignorant of those simple facts that we took for granted. Naive it may be, but we were dealing with individuals, or a large part of a generation, who had in protest stepped out of normal society, had never had a salaried appointment and had not been briefed on these simple facts of life. This was a problem, and one that would not be addressed because it was considered not politically correct to do so.

Chapter 8

Yes, Prime Minister

There was great excitement – the BMATT team at Wallmannsthal was going to have some visitors! Having been ignored professionally by the Defence Section of the British High Commission, and with Colonel Paul Davis providing the only operational interaction with BMATT HQ, we were beginning to feel quite forgotten. It was a simple case of being out of sight and out of mind. Colonel Davis ensured we met on a weekly basis and used these sessions to pass down any policy issues whilst ensuring he received a thorough update from the ground. It is true that we had contact with the Chief of Staff, Ian Jenkins, and the Chief Clerk, both of whom were very efficient, but their remit was administration. The other person who seemed to be soundly ignoring us was the Commander. You could count the number of interactions with him on one hand. We were unanimous in regarding Colonel Davis as the de facto commander. It was he who announced that the Chief of the Defence Staff (CDS) was going to visit South Africa, and it would be more than likely that he would want to come and visit us at Wallmannsthal – that is, if he could manage to get the Defence Section to include BMATT on the visit programme. We had seen nothing of the Defence Advisor or his team, and it was clear that the relationship between the Defence Section and BMATT HQ was less than cordial. However, Field Marshal Sir Peter Inge, the CDS, was not one to be brushed off, and if he wanted to come and visit us, then he would. A visit by such a distinguished officer would be great, and it would put our work on the map.

That was the last we heard about it. The visit seemed to be very heavily under wraps, so we continued working as normal. The Army members of the team knew of Field Marshal Inge from his previous appointments, and some of us had even met him, although I had last seen him in 1987.

One morning we were gathered in our small BMATT annex to the hangar, making a brew and generally shaking off the dust before throwing ourselves back into the assessment and selection process. It was a time to catch up on any gossip and exchange stories and experiences from the previous day. I suppose it was a little 'British' island where we could relax. There would have been were about six of us chatting when the door opened and in walked a tall figure in an old-style combat jacket. He was not wearing a beret, had thinning grey hair and had an unusual rank insignia on his uniform. He had an imposing presence and had on his long face an air of expectation. We exchanged quizzical looks, and I was wondering whether his rank was an old-fashioned South African one, when the visitor barked, 'And who is in charge here?'

We quickly looked around at each other, not being used to having a gang leader. I discounted the younger captains, and when I looked back at the stranger I saw a look in his eye which prompted me to say, 'Well, sir' – the latter mark of respect seemed appropriate at the time – 'I suppose I am.'

There was no reason to suppose I was the senior, but my fellows were all hastily looking at their feet or the ceiling as I continued, 'Hello, my name is Major Huw Lawford, from the British Military Advisory and Training Team, and how can I help you?' He looked at me in a manner which simply stated 'if you speak then I know that you are stupid and if you keep quiet, I will continue to think that you are stupid'.

What he did actually reply was, 'I know who you bloody well are, and I have come from London to see what is going on, so brief me!' There are various times in your career when you know that you are damned if you do and damned if you don't. All the pennies had dropped at once and I realized that the CDS was in front of me, unannounced, unaccompanied and expectant!

Instinct took over. There was no need to start with the normal preamble of orientation; both he and I knew exactly that we were in a little metal annex to a large hangar in South Africa, and knowing where north was would not readily add value to the conversation. 'Field Marshal,' I began, 'may I firstly introduce you to the team and see if you want a brew?' He dutifully shook hands as one of the team scrambled around to find a clean mug to fill with coffee. I then proceeded to give him a potted history of our experience at Wallmannsthal thus far, illustrating this with a few stories. He seemed content at this and added some of his own observations from his visit, the itinerary of which we were unaware. Then he asked where the toilets were. One of the team stood up and offered to escort him there, and as soon as he left the annex I told one of those remaining to run to the Officer Commanding's office and tell him that a five-star ranking British officer was wandering around his establishment. At the same time, I had another member go and ring BMATT HQ and report that we had a VIP who they might be interested to know was roaming around meeting their team.

I was busy issuing instructions, as I now seemed to be the senior on the block, when the door was flung open and a highly flustered Ian Jenkins, BMATT Chief of Staff, burst in saying, 'For fuck's sake, Inge is coming. Clear this place up and get ready to brief him. The Commander will be here in a minute or two and will want to know what you are going to do.' Ian could not quite understand why we all just sat down and laughed at him. We broke the news that we had already made the acquaintance of Field Marshal Sir Peter Inge. He had been given a cup of coffee and would be returning shortly. Perhaps Ian would like to take it from here? Ian left, slightly open-mouthed, and scurried away to find the Commander, acquaint him with the latest news and take control of the roving CDS. We saw the union of the Commander and the Chief of the Defence Staff from the annex, and then saw our Field Marshal turn back towards us. He walked across, stuck his head in the door and thanked us all, said what a good job we were doing – and then he went off on his visit programme.

* * *

Our next important visitor was handled with the correct protocols. Whereas the visit of the CDS had been the responsibility of the Defence Section of the British High Commission, and had shown all the hallmarks of the lack of communication between the Defence Advisor and the Commander, our next visitor would be very much part of the international protocol that governs the visit of a British Prime Minister to another country. When John Major addressed the South African National Assembly in Cape Town on Tuesday, 20 September 1994, he mentioned that a fellowship had developed between the British and South African armed forces. He recognized the compliment that had been made in asking Britain to assist with the integration of the new South African National Defence Force. He considered it a task vital to the future stability of southern Africa. He also mentioned that he was looking forward to visiting the team that week.

This time we had our place in the visit programme. During his visit, the Prime Minister formally signed the Memorandum of Understanding between the UK and South Africa concerning the provision of UK Armed

Forces personnel to advise on the integration of the defence and other armed forces of South Africa.

The military are the same the world over. They like to be seen to get things right, and therefore every visit is thoroughly organized. They run like clockwork, with everyone properly coordinated, and in fine military style, it is rehearsed to death. The SANDF was no exception. A detailed programme was issued and we were brought into the planning process, albeit for information only. As in all visits, the military maxim of 'KISS' – Keep It Simple, Stupid – was applied. Since it was a political visit, any risk of embarrassment was to be eliminated. Demonstrations with placards and noise outside an official event are part of the political scene, but here in Wallmannsthal all was to run smoothly. The Prime Minister would fly in by helicopter, be met by MOD and military dignitaries and then escorted into the briefing room in the big hangar. He would see the tented camp and the selection and assessment areas, but not visit them, and anyway the process was to be suspended on that day. The Chief of the SANDF, General Georg Meiring, would brief the Prime Minister on the integration process and the progress to date. Mr Major would then meet and greet South African and British personnel before returning to Pretoria by helicopter. The visit would last about ninety minutes, but the rehearsals would take much longer because it was very important that a good impression was made.

* * *

The main event of the Prime Minister's visit to Wallmannsthal was the briefing, and that was the focus of the rehearsals. As the role of BMATT was to be in the audience, we had nothing to do. We were to be in during 'meet and greet' ceremony, and even then, we had been allocated just a little time during which Colonel Davis would act as host. Consequently, in the days leading up to the visit we were very much in the background, keeping ourselves to ourselves in and around our small annex. Once the rehearsals finished, we were back into our normal work cycle. The day of the dress rehearsal arrived, and everything was abuzz with activity. We were gathered outside our annex enjoying the warm weather and looking out for the arrival of General Meiring, when one of the SANDF generals came up to us and had a chat. He was a slim, sprightly officer who clearly kept himself fit. He had always made a point of talking to BMATT members whenever he met them. His interest was genuine, and his warm personality and quick sense of humour guaranteed him a welcome whenever he appeared. He came up and started chatting about the impending visit and then the latest sports news, the defeat of the Springboks by the All Blacks and the forthcoming tour of South Africa by the Argentine Pumas.

In the middle of philosophising about rugby, the Commander appeared in our midst. 'Hello Dick,' said the general in a warm greeting. 'How are you today? Tell me, you've been in South Africa now for three months, so what is your impression of the South African Army, eh?'

The Commander appeared preoccupied, and then in a very deliberate and dismissive tone said, 'What do I think? I think that you are generally overrated, overweight and over-paid. Frankly not much actually.'

There was an incredulous, collective drawing-in of breath. The general replied, joking, 'Well, thank you Dick. You're joking, right?'

'No' was the reply as the Commander, with not so much as a 'by your leave', walked away. None of us really knew what to do or say. The general spared us any more embarrassment by bidding us a good day and left – fortunately in a different direction to the Commander.

Regardless of what the Commander may have thought in a personal capacity, his opinion should have been reserved for an occasion behind doors. Such an outburst was embarrassing enough, but whilst being a guest in someone else's country, it was not only professionally misguided but also potentially damaging, especially when the remarks were made to a senior in front of juniors. It was not long before a concerned-looking Colonel Davis came up to us and asked what had happened, as a pretty irritated South African general had just collared him. From the way Paul received the brief, it was clear that this was not the first time he had heard a similar story. He said that there was a need for damage limitation and told us to lay on the charm and compliments with a shovel.

* * *

The day the Prime Minister visited was overcast, and perhaps gave a very clear indication that summer was around the corner. The flying conditions were touch and go, but the alternative 'wet-weather programme' was available and, of course, had been rehearsed. However, the air force avoided any embarrassment and made the short journey from Pretoria to Wallmannsthal without any drama. The Prime Minister, escorted by the

Minister of Defence, Joe Modise, arrived and stepped out of the Super Puma, followed closely by a slimmed-down entourage. There was no great press horde because the media coverage was to be provided by the SANDF. The visitors were formally welcomed and were then escorted to the briefing room.

We had been sitting in the briefing room for about fifteen minutes and I had managed to find a seat in the third row, just behind where the Prime Minister was due to sit. It was a smart and very modern briefing configuration, with the latest computer tools. A large screen dominated the stage behind the podium, and with the required wallpaper of camouflage netting it looked just the part. A cacophony of scraping back of chairs heralded the arrival of the visitors as they made their way briskly down the centre aisle and took up their seats. The thing that struck me about the Prime Minister was his height. Having only seen him on television, I had the impression that he was quite short, but no, he was at least 6ft tall. As an aside, I had the same impression of Tony Blair some eight years later; ironically, they are both the same height. John Major had a shock of grey hair and wore his tell-tale large glasses. He looked towards the lectern as the series of presentations began. Following the round of welcomes and introductions, General Meiring took to the podium to talk about the integration process. He gave an overview of the history and background as to how the process had progressed to the present day. He touched on the challenges, which were open and balanced, and then began to present the details of how many non-statutory forces had been processed. I was fascinated to see the Prime Minister making notes.

We were all lulled into a false sense of security, which comes with a programme running to time, when suddenly the mood changed. It was not because the PowerPoint failed or the general fluffed his lines, but because of a series of comments issued from the floor. At first it seemed to be a muttering or a muffled conversation which was a little too loud and therefore was interfering with the audience's concentration. People began to look around, and the general looked up on occasion from his notes. The interruptions, however, persisted, then my heart sank as I realised the noise was coming from the Commander. General Meiring was clearly irritated and, not without cause, embarrassed, but the inevitable intervention came from an unexpected member of the audience. The Prime Minister spoke up in his measured but authoritative tone and thanked the Commander for his comments, but suggested that this kind of discussion could be continued later and in a different setting. This was delivered with a smile enforced by a suitable and unequivocal level of steel. The room fell silent, including, thankfully, the Commander. General Meiring finished his brief without further interruption, and then the visiting party moved off to the next appointment on their programme and we prepared to move to our 'meet and greet' location.

Colonel Davis grabbed my arm, said simply, 'You host', and moved off.

* * *

We assembled in a room off the main briefing room and waited for the visitors. The conversation was muted, but everyone was concerned at what they had witnessed and, following the Commander's mutterings during the rehearsals, we were not sure how far BMATT stock could fall before our position in South Africa became untenable – a signed Memorandum of Understanding or not. Little time for speculation was needed because, almost exactly on time, the Prime Minister and his party came into the room. A few handshakes ensued before Mr Major moved away to meet one group, whilst the accompanying Lynda Chalker – then Baroness Chalker – who was Minister for Overseas Development in the Foreign and Commonwealth Office, met my group. She was in excellent form and possessed a fantastic knowledge of Africa. She was completely aware of the issues that we were facing and the need to show transparency as well to take the lead rather than accept failure. Baroness Chalker chatted with everyone with consummate ease and amused us immeasurably with her stories. She then excused herself with a characteristic quip, 'Well I suppose I had better move on so that you can speak to him', jerking her head towards the Prime Minister. She moved off, grabbed the Prime Minister by the elbow and led him across, saying that he must come and speak to us.

Mr Major was in ebullient form. He had clearly had a good visit thus far, and any issue with the Commander's intervention was clearly not on the agenda. He had been briefed well, and was keen to know about our experiences on the ground and what was going to happen with our families. I guided him through the group, and he chatted about everything under the sun, showing himself to be at ease with all ranks and backgrounds. He was even able to have a quick chat about the fortunes of Chelsea Football Club and the English cricket team, which we both supported with a passion. He was eventually pulled away to talk elsewhere, but I was pleased to note that we had taken up more than our allocated time.

It was then time for lunch and back to the integration process. I was still quite shocked by the Commander's interventions, and was sure that things could not possibly be left to fester. I was right; about a week later, I received a phone call requesting me to report to Colonel Davis in his office at Army Headquarters.

* * *

I was not the only one having problems. Apparently, the Commander was becoming more and more frustrated by the progress of integration and the administration in general. He appeared particularly vexed at the fact that the system would not pay for flights for his two maids, both of whom had worked for the family when he was serving in Hong Kong, to rejoin the family in Pretoria. This was the content of many of the dispatches that he was sending to London. Without any understatement, things were not going well for the Commander, and therefore for BMATT. The relationship with the High Commission was at a very low point.

As soon as I walked in to see Colonel Davis, I sensed that all was far from well. I was asked to sit down and was soon joined by senior representatives from the Royal Navy and the Royal Air Force, and the doctor. Paul then briefed us that London had become increasingly concerned about the behaviour and general wellbeing of the Commander. They had received reports from Brigadier Jim Parker, the Defence Advisor in the High Commission, about the upsets at Wallmannsthal both prior to and during the visit of the Prime Minister, and other incidents of unsubtle behaviour and inappropriate comments. He informed us that there was a complete breakdown of communication between the Commander and the Defence Advisor. The Ministry of Defence in London were very much in the dark as to what was going on in the assembly areas and the integration process itself. They had received reports from the single services, but there was no summary of the strategic-level actions and nothing to be gained from the Commander's comments, apart from his concerns over his two maids. The Defence Advisor was trying to fill in the gaps, but with difficulty. The bottom line was whether the Commander was fit for his appointment. Colonel Davis told us that he had been receiving regular calls from the Assistant Chief of the Defence Staff asking for an assessment, and now it had to be done. Paul went around the room before asking me to speak about the incidents which had happened at Wallmannsthal.

He then asked others for any additional reports, and received several. Finally, he summarized what had been reported and said that, as Deputy Commander, he was deeply aware of the damage which had already occurred to BMATT's reputation. By association, he continued, the reputation of the Ministry of Defence was becoming tarnished, which was the primary concern of the Defence Advisor and the High Commissioner. He stated that he was about to ask the senior officers and the doctor for their professional opinions on a sensitive subject. He asked each of them in turn whether, in their opinion, the Commander was fit to continue in his appointment. You could have heard a pin drop.

The Royal Naval representative wriggled like a worm on a line, answering that he had had very little dealings with the Commander so did not feel it appropriate to comment on such a serious issue. He was clearly deeply uncomfortable, but did not cover himself in glory by avoiding the subject. The Royal Air Force officer likewise was quite slippery, stating that he had also had few dealings with the Commander. He said that he did have some concerns about the Commander because of the rumours that were circulating in air force circles and from what he had heard in the room today. This was a criticism of sorts, but not a strong one. The doctor was the most slippery character of all, and you could see Paul getting more and more irritated before he interjected in a forthright manner. He informed the doctor that he was asking his professional opinion about the Commander's ability to carry on in his appointment. Did he, the doctor, think that there was something wrong? After more prevarication, Paul said that he wanted a simple yes or no. The doctor, cornered, stated that he was concerned the Commander seemed to be acting in an unusual way, and that perhaps he was demonstrating signs of mental stress, possibly exhaustion. Paul thanked everyone for their contribution and asked us to wait outside whilst he made a telephone call.

We were called back into the office about an hour later. Colonel Davis said that he had spoken to London and had reported our discussion. The Assistant Chief of the Defence Staff had consulted with the Deputy Chief of the Defence Staff, and a decision had been taken to remove the Commander. It would be done on medical grounds, as would appear to be the case; this would be more palatable to the South Africans and the High Commission than any other reason. The Commander would leave for London the next day and his family would join him as soon as possible, once BMATT HQ had made the necessary arrangements. Paul would assume command of BMATT in his stead. We were ordered to keep quiet about this arrangement as correct management of the whole situation was critical. We left feeling quite stunned.

Soon afterwards, we learnt that the Commander had indeed been an ill man, and had been for some considerable time. He had been diagnosed with a severe heart condition about eighteen months before coming to South Africa. How widely known this was, nobody knew. He hid his condition well, but it was clear that the severity of his illness had sadly begun to cloud his judgement. It was a shock to us all as he was undoubtedly an incredibly capable man who was destined for great things, but it had been obvious that there was something wrong. On his return to UK, he continued his service until his illness required him to retire. He died in 2000 at the shockingly young age of 49.

* * *

Everyone knows that when lovers have a tiff or when a child does not get his way, a sulk is just around the corner. It introduces itself with extended periods of silence, short answers, a lack of eye contact and occasional outbursts. It can last for either a short time, which is fine, or it can drag on – which just becomes frustrating for all concerned. In Xavier's case, the sulk came after the trade unionist phase. Unfortunately for the rest of us, it came without any pretext or as a consequence to any incident. He just arrived one morning in a sulk, and a major one at that. For a highly intelligent and articulate man, it really did seem out of place, and the longer it lasted the more concern it aroused. Each of us in turn tried to coax out of him what the problem was, but each received a terse rebuttal. Even his ex-MK colleagues noted that he was out of sorts. Maybe it was a problem at home, or had he had a fall out with his girlfriend? We knew that his family were in the Eastern Cape, but with all his time in exile a girlfriend could well be in the equation; to be fair, Xavier always gave the impression of being a 'ladies' man'. His sulk went on, and our concern began to turn into frustration and then more than a little irritation. However, as Xavier was a vital part of our team, we all decided that we needed to get him back on board and help him out of wherever the bad place was that he had landed.

Normally soldiers – or to be fair, men in general – sort out such situations by going to a pub or bar and thrashing things out over a few drinks. The logistics and sensitivities that still surrounded Wallmannsthal prevented this, so Andre came up with a great plan that would not only solve the Xavier sulk but, hopefully, demonstrate that he was part of the regimental family; one of the club. A friend of a friend had a game lodge in the bush, and it would be an excellent opportunity for all of us to head off, out of sight, and have what is now known as a 'bonding session'. We cajoled Xavier to join us, and eventually but reluctantly he agreed to come. All was set in place for the following Saturday, and four of us – two ex-SADF, one ex-MK and one BMATT – set off into the bush armed with plentiful supplies of beer, brandy and rum, and what seemed like several hundredweight of meat for the inevitable South African *braai* (or barbecue).

We arrived at the game lodge just before sunset. The lodge was in the middle of nowhere, which, whilst conducive to a bonding session, had the disadvantage of offering no easy escape if things did not work out. Having dumped our overnight kit in the bedrooms, Andre and Leon set about building up a fire and getting the *braai* ready. This was an art form in South Africa, and clearly one that I would have to learn. Xavier and I had the easier task of getting the drinks prepared.

We settled down and proceeded to break the ice. It took several attempts, as Xavier was definitely in a major sulk. He was unhappy generally, but after identifying that rum was his favourite tipple, we began to break down the barriers. Fuelled by rum and well fed with steak, it all began to come out. There were several issues that were wearing him down, but the most critical to us was the pressure that he felt under by being in the middle of the integration process. It was clear that he felt he was no longer part of the MK and that there were many inside the wire who resented him for being in both camps. He was expected to be a talent scout for us in the artillery, ensuring that we had the right candidates, but at the same time he had to be an unofficial trade union official representing the concerns and complaints of those inside the wire. He was a naturally open, likeable man who would be a natural magnet to those with issues. He was a conduit who was becoming overburdened with responsibility, unable to shake off his roots and adopt the standards and requisites of his new position. He was, in effect, neither one thing nor the other. His concern was that because he could not deliver change, he would be seen as more of a stool pigeon than an ambassador. He came from an irregular force and had spent years working in an organization riven by fear of infiltration. He had talked of what had happened to those suspected of being informers in the camps outside South Africa, how they had been placed into ISO shipping containers, sited in areas without shade, and had, in effect, been cooked alive. He knew from the violence which still haunted Wallmannsthal what retribution awaited those who fell under suspicion. It was a very difficult situation, but the tightrope that we needed him to walk was essential for the success of the integration process.

Xavier needed reassurance that we would not betray him, and this was exactly the purpose of our coming away for this trip. None of us could fully empathize as we had never been in a similar situation, but we could only reassure him that we were all on the same side. He was also concerned about how he would be treated once he entered into the Bridging Training, and we assured him that he would be treated as one of the regiment. His gunnery knowledge was first rate and he was expected to do very well. We were able to give him the reassurance he sought, despite our inability to place ourselves in his position inside the wire.

As the evening wore on, the conversation expanded; as with all soldiers, it inevitably ended up with the exchange of 'war stories'. Here I sat with three people who had spent the majority of their adult life on operations, be it conventional, as far as Andre and Leon were concerned, or very unconventional, with Xavier. What was interesting as an observer was how fascinated both were in hearing about how the two sides had operated against each other. I am sure that the truth was stretched in many cases, for the sake of the storytelling, but it was an eye-opener to say the least. Xavier kept us entertained with his experiences in Soviet Russia, East Germany and Cuba. Andre and Leon spoke about Angola and the campaign in South West Africa, or Namibia. I knew that Leon had received the Honoris Crux, an old South African decoration acknowledging bravery – the equivalent of the British Military Cross – and his story, which also involved fellow recipient Theuns Coetzee, kept us captivated.

The evening ended with all of us the worse for wear from just a few too many drinks, but much, much closer together. We were very confident that we had dragged Xavier out of his sulk. The next day we returned, slowly, to Pretoria and split up. I was to take a few days off to prepare the move to Potchefstroom, and Xavier was to take a long weekend to visit his family in the Eastern Cape.

* * *

A week later we gathered in Wallmannsthal to start the next tranche of the assessment process. It was a slow start because Xavier was nowhere to be seen. There again, transport from the Eastern Cape was quite unpredictable, especially with the beginning of the summer rains, so we assumed he had been held up on his journey. Monday became Tuesday and then Wednesday, but still no Xavier. We were now in a predicament because he was technically absent without leave, and none of us wanted to report it. We had no option but to make some enquiries as subtly as we could. However, we had no joy.

* * *

It turned out that Xavier had been shot dead on his leave weekend. Apparently, it was a revenge shooting. South Africa had lost another citizen and potentially a very fine officer.

* * *

Back in Wallmannsthal, the appointment of a successor to Xavier had to be made as a matter of urgency. It was essential that we had an ex-MK officer to use during the assessment process, and while the stand-ins were fine in the short-term, we needed an artilleryman to add credibility. A few names were put forward, and we considered using one of the officers we had already placed, but we felt that it was better to leave them in the glide path to Bridging Training than to call them back. So it was a question of interviewing the candidates and then rushing the chosen one through his assessment.

It was quite interesting that we settled on the first candidate straightaway. He was a short, compact man with a ready grin and a warm, engaging character. He had arrived recently in Wallmannsthal and knew Xavier. He sailed through the assessment and we were all happy to award him the same rank and seniority that Xavier had been given. They had both had very similar training and experience, and it was therefore appropriate that he should also be selected in the rank of major, and with hopes for him to complete all the required training up to the Battery Commanders Course. He was known as Stalin. Not that Stalin was his actual name; it was his combat name, and he was very proud of it. He would not be able to keep it when he joined the SANDF properly, but it would inevitably be his nickname. Stalin it was, and Stalin it would remain.

He set about his duties with vigour, and we looked forward to working with him in the coming months as we aimed to finish the artillery leader group selection.

Chapter 9

A Bridge Too Far?

The selection and appointment process for the artillery, both field and anti-aircraft branches, was proceeding well, even though the fractious atmosphere in Wallmannsthal continued with more strikes and protests. Whilst one could explain these by saying that it was just the venting of frustration at the slow progress of the overall integration process, the situation was definitely beginning to worsen. Accepting that the non-statutory forces were exactly as described – that is, irregular forces with a veneer of command and control – and with many of the leader group already embarked on their own Bridging Training, they were appearing more and more irregular. They were, after all, supposed to be soldiers and volunteers wishing to join a statutory force – a force that was based on all the personal and collective discipline that is not only mandatory but also essential in a regular armed force. But there was precious little of this being demonstrated at the various assembly areas.

* * *

The camp at De Brug, near Bloemfontein, was much smaller than Wallmannsthal. It was focused on the selection and integration of members of the Azanian People's Liberation Army (APLA), the military wing of the Pan African Congress (PAC). The camp was as dusty as Wallmannsthal, and even more isolated. The process here had the same frustrations as at Wallmannsthal, but, maybe because of its smaller size (by mid-1995, only 2,569 APLA personnel had reported), it didn't experience the same level of tension. A group of us went to visit to assess some of those wishing to join our specific arms and services.

It had been a pleasant trip down on the Sunday, and we gathered that evening in the Holiday Inn bar in Bloemfontein to watch the football World Cup final. It was good to catch up with some of the other members of the team, as we had not seen each other since our first week in Pretoria.

Monday arrived with (another) blue sky, and after breakfast we headed off to the camp, which was a ninety-minute drive to the west – seemingly in the middle of nowhere. The Free State, formally the Orange Free State, is on the flat plain in the heart of South Africa. It has superb soil and an excellent climate, and produces some 70 per cent of the country's wheat. It is generally flat and featureless, bordering on the Great Karoo semi-desert to its south. It is also a bastion of Afrikaanerdom. The journey from the relatively bustling metropolis of Bloemfontein to De Brug was a reminder of the size of South Africa. It was like driving through the endless prairie. I had originally thought that the north-west was flat and featureless, but it was a veritable paradise of topography in comparison to the Free State. To be stuck in De Brug must have been quite a challenge for the urbanite. We eventually arrived and were welcomed to the camp. After a quick orientation, we met up with our South African colleagues and got down to business.

I finished my tasks for the day and set off in search of a brew. No matter how hot, cold or wet a place is, the British Army always seeks a cup of tea. It has been forever thus, and will continue to be so. I met up with a friend, and was about to sit down and put the world to rights when an officer burst in and grabbed me. He said I was the senior BMATT officer present and there was a problem. I had already had the experience of being labelled the senior officer present when the CDS arrived unannounced into our little sanctuary in Wallmannsthal, so I was more than a little wary. I was bundled out of one tent and into another full of South African officers, all of whom were in a state of excitement. My arrival seemed to entice a feeling of relief, which further made me suspicious. I was assuming there had been a major mishap and I was needed to play the part of referee, but it was not that; it was worse: the BBC had arrived with a film crew and wanted to interview someone. The ex-SADF officers all played the '*Ek prat net Afrikaans*' ('I only speak Afrikaans') card, and as they did not want an APLA representative to speak, it boiled down to me.

Every soldier deals with the press with a great deal of caution. One is always more succinct, and a good deal more suspicious, than a civilian counterpart. The press is a vital part of democracy and has a huge role to play in holding governments and institutions to account. Consequently, the British Army has long recognized the need to provide media training to its personnel and to work alongside the media, giving them as much access and freedom as is tactically sensible. The media in turn generally respect the need for security. The BBC Head of News and Current Affairs had briefed the Army Staff College students during our visit to the BBC

Television Centre some four years previously that there is no story without an angle, and that the angle may change between recording and the editing for broadcast. Therefore, the golden rule is never to comment without the knowledge and authority of your headquarters, or your press officer, and to always stick to your 'lines to take'. Well, at De Brug there was no such staff support and BMATT did not have the luxury of a press officer. I rang the Chief of Staff in BMATT HQ. Ian was unaware of the presence of the press and had not been told by the High Commission that a visit was due, which was not a surprise bearing in mind the difficult relationship that still existed. We decided that not to engage with the BBC would only cause problems in the long term, and there was no point in waiting to get any lines to take from the High Commission. Our collective decision was to engage with the BBC but to keep to our normal story lines, and to ensure that we did not get drawn into any of the politics. At all costs, we must not blame any of the parties for delays or errors in the overall integration process. In other words, we were to occupy the interview time with non-committal pleasantries.

I met up with the young correspondent from the BBC, and I was very impressed with him. He knew that I had been 'volunteered for the Guardroom' and that I had been caught completely unprepared. What transpired was almost a brief masterclass in how to conduct a live interview on a complex subject. It did help that we bonded immediately, and I am now disappointed that I cannot recall his name. He talked about how he could approach the interview if he wanted to make me feel uncomfortable or appear reluctant to answer questions by simply conducting the interview with me facing the sun. He suggested how I should stand and where to put my hands; apparently, the military are liable to gesticulate wildly during an interview, as if describing ground or giving orders, and this is distracting to the viewers. His advice was to do the very un-military thing of shoving the excitable upper limbs into my trouser pockets, and to keep them there. He also mentioned how he could ask contorted questions, which could be edited out, and answers to Question A being superimposed on to the answer for Question B. He told me not to waffle, which was sound advice, because this could be edited to produce a different perspective. He also advised me how to ruin a take if I slipped up and gave an impolitic or incorrect answer – I just had to cough or pick my nose, which was guaranteed to force a retake. With these great tips, and a feeling that the correspondent was 'friendly forces', I continued with the interview.

Whether he took pity on me or not I will never know, but it was the easiest interview that I have ever given. He had talked through what he knew and what he wanted to report, and therefore we were able to agree a mutually acceptable way forward. He placed me so that I would not be facing the sun, with a backdrop of the tents and the dusty, flat terrain. The interview progressed smoothly, starting with the soft opening questions and then a discussion of the overall process and the role of BMATT. When asked about how the process was going, I responded with a straight answer, stating that it was a complicated process that had to be based on mutual trust and respect. This was coming slowly, but not without teething troubles; however, all parties were working together to make it work. It was a safe answer, and one that should not offend anyone. I declined to highlight specific issues and problems, and simply responded that we, BMATT, were there to assist and ensure that there was transparency and fair play. After about twenty minutes, the interview was terminated, and the correspondent and his cameraman were happy that it was good enough to be sent to London.

I never saw the finished item, and to be truthful, events were such that I had soon put it out of my mind. It was not until several weeks later that we started to hear from friends in the UK who had seen the interview, no doubt edited down to less than a minute's worth of stardom.

* * *

The South African Army had a different approach to rank structure than the British Army. This is not to say that they had extra ranks, although they had changed some of the names (for example, a lieutenant colonel was a commandant), but that they occupied some ranks at a different stage of their career than we did in the UK. Most notable was the rank of commandant. In the British Army, promotion to the rank of lieutenant colonel, announced on what is known as the 'Pink List', is very competitive and is generally recognized as the make or break point for a career officer. It is also the rank when the familiarity, which is quite peculiar to the British Army, of calling fellow officers by their Christian name, stops. A lieutenant colonel is called 'Sir' or 'Colonel'. Early promotion to lieutenant colonel should lead to command of a regular regiment, and then, if successful at both regimental duty and on the staff, further early promotion follows. Of course, despite the old saying that there is not a field marshal's baton in everyone's knapsack, if you were on a good track, then you should be a lieutenant colonel by your late 30s. It was therefore slightly awkward that our contemporaries in the South African Army, and indeed quite a few who were junior in age, were already commandants, or lieutenant colonel equivalents. We of course paid them the correct compliments, but it did make the possibility of any major disagreement over the integration process more problematical if rank became an issue.

It was established that part of the South African early promotion to commandant had its roots back in the war years, when the regular cadre were constantly deployed and gaining considerable operational experience. This resulted in the better individuals taking on more responsibility and the command of larger units early on in their career. As with all militaries, there was no bonus mechanism, so it was easier to promote as a reward than to try any other method. This also resulted in a knock-on effect to the next rank of colonel, but then seemed to level itself out again at the rank of brigadier, or brigadier-general in the South African system. A similar system of accelerated promotion, caused by war and achieved through success, happened in the British Army in the Second World War. Take the example of Lieutenant General Sir Brian Horrocks, a battalion commander at the age of 45 in France in 1940, but just over two years later a lieutenant general commanding a corps. However, the majority of career officers who were promoted early in wartime, and survived, had to relinquish their rank at the end of the war, when the British Army contracted in size. This did not happen in South Africa; the rank inflation had stayed. Because the wartime structure in South Africa had relied on a regular serving core reinforced by conscripts and citizen force soldiers, the rank inflation was passed onto the peacetime regiments. We visited regiments that were commanded by a colonel, with commandants in key regimental positions and with the sub-units commanded by majors. It was rank-heavy; the equivalent regiment in the British Army would only have one lieutenant colonel in command, with majors filling the key headquarter positions and commanding the sub-units.

After much deliberation, it was decided that we should receive local rank. This was a convenient means of 'promoting' us whilst not increasing the cost to the taxpayer. A local rank is just that. It is a rank for necessity and for a limited period of time, with no change in one's substantive rank and therefore no pay increase. If we were given acting rank, then this came with a pay increase and an associated change in pension entitlement. If, at the end of the tour in South Africa, one did not appear on the 'Pink List', then one would return to the UK as a major. It was decided that the local lieutenant colonels would be initially limited to those staying for two years in order to give a sense of credibility to the South Africans. A wholesale promotion would be out of place and probably negate any parity we were seeking to achieve and this parity was intended purely to create a level playing field in the event of a significant disagreement in the future. It was also important to give the impression that the promotions were genuine. A date was set, and it gave us time to slip into conversation that we were to be promoted. Was it deception? Yes, in theory, but there was no malice intended and it would pay dividends in the future. It was a means to rebalance the books.

I was invited to the Staff College during one of my visits to Pretoria. The invitation was to one of the regular artillery drinks parties, which were held throughout South Africa, but especially in the Potchefstroom–Pretoria–Johannesburg triangle. Sometimes they were sponsored by industry and sometimes by units or formations. They were very popular events, and it was good that, in the future, they were used as a way of introducing the ex-non-statutory forces officers to the wider military world. On this occasion, the drinks party was being sponsored by the Army Staff. We all gathered in the mess at the Staff College, the very same mess that we breakfasted in on our first day in the country – what seemed a very long six months ago. The guest of honour was the General of the Artillery, Major General Pretorius. Halfway through the evening, he made a speech, finishing with a long passage about me and how wonderful it was that I had been promoted. He managed to insinuate that it was the importance of my job in South Africa that had clearly caught the selectors' eyes. I had become a bit of a one-night celebrity, whose task now was to buy a lot of beer!

* * *

Another change that made life easier was the arrival of the new Commander, Brigadier Chris Elliott (late Royal Regiment of Wales). He was a breath of fresh air and had an immensely approachable character. He immediately took back many of the responsibilities that had been taken on by Colonel Davis, which allowed Paul to focus on the Army integration issues which were increasing by the day. The new Commander set about rebuilding the great number of bridges that had been burnt over the last months or so and re-establishing BMATT's reputation in the National Defence Headquarters. He was also clear that he wanted the BMATT team to make the best of their time in South Africa, appreciating that not only did we have an important and challenging job to do, but also had an unrepeatable opportunity to enjoy everything that South Africa had to offer.

* * *

Returning to Wallmannsthal the next day, I was saddened to hear that Stalin was dead. In the poorly disciplined environment that was becoming a mark of Wallmannsthal, Stalin had been killed; shot dead in a petty dispute. Following so soon after the death of Xavier, this did not bode well for the future.

* * *

Bridging Training was broken down into two distinct parts: Phase 1, the general military training, and Phase 2, the specific training required for an individual to qualify for his allocated arm or corps, known as special-to-arm training. The former had a clear intent, which was to bring all the ex-non-statutory force members up to the basic standard of military training so that they could receive the special-to-arm training, then progress to serve in the armed forces. The basic training was further split up to provide instruction for the leader group: the officers and SNCOs. Then there was a course for the JNCOs and private soldiers, most of whom had either limited or no recognized military service. Clearly the latter was relatively easy, as it equated to recruit training, but the leader group was more of a challenge. It was not just a case of rolling out a Sandhurst-style package, because the attendees had already received military training and so were not beginners. The course had to be a hybrid one that also considered the rank and age of those in the leader group, which was quite a range.

It was during these visits to units all over the North West Province that I appreciated the pressure placed on the various commanding officers. These officers, by dint of their length of service, had extensive operational experience in Angola and Namibia and on internal security duties during the years of unrest. They were also clearly career officers who had displayed the necessary military ability to be selected for command, and within their career had demonstrated the necessary political awareness to be considered reliable. I would say, as a general rule, that the commanders were intelligent and capable men who knew what needed to be done to set their country on the right track. They might not wholeheartedly embrace the political sea change that had occurred, but they were not fools. They had seen this monumental change coming and, as nobody wanted a civil war, they saw it as their duty to manage this change. They were under scrutiny, and it could not have been easy for them to have foreigners – especially those junior in rank and years – poking around their units, talking to officers, NCOs, soldiers and trainees alike and checking that they were doing their job properly.

It was also clear that the commanding officers had to have a much more direct involvement in the training than would otherwise have been the case. What they were being asked to deliver was relatively straightforward, and a unit would routinely have the number and quality of instructors required to deliver the task. It would normally have been a question of 'Second-in-Command carry on' and the commanding officer would only be required to show his face at the appropriate moments. But in this case, there were so many things that could go wrong. Infantry instructors have a reputation for being hard men, shouting and screaming and cajoling their wards through the physical and mental rigours of military training. Talk to any South African, especially an English-speaking South African, about their experiences of National Service and you will not hear many compliments. These same instructors now had to deliver to an audience who were their racial and political opposites. They could not use the same 'methods' that had been common in the past; if they did, then the recipient would complain, and the complaint would be referred all the way up the rank structure. The commander had to ensure that his staff treated the trainees with respect whilst all the time maintaining a very well-tuned political radar. It could be that, for some, this was not possible and then they were reassigned to await early release; but for the majority, this is what they had to, and did, deliver. Leadership was key and fell squarely upon the shoulders of the commanding officers. Needless to say, the first question I was asked by every commanding officer when I paid him a courtesy call at the end of a visit was, 'Are there any problems?'

Apart from ensuring their units delivered what was required of them in a professional and positive manner, the commanding officers had to establish an open and honest relationship with the BMATT officer. This took time because there was a natural suspicion of the role that BMATT was playing in the integration process. I realized that if I was to be granted freedom of access to all parties and was to be able to follow up any issue that might need adjudication, then I had to establish a personal relationship with the commanding officer. I believed that this was necessary to ensure transparency and to establish a trust that would allow problems to be either nipped in the bud or resolved in a mature and intelligent fashion. There was no need to display 'dirty washing', provided that a balanced and correct resolution was found, and that all parties were satisfied with the resolution and actions had been put in place to prevent a reoccurrence of the problem. To this end, I spent a long time getting to know the various commanding officers in North

West Province. After a while I was no longer viewed as the foreigner, or the '*rooinek*', but as part of the team.

I must also emphasize that the same relationship had to exist with the senior representatives of the ex-non-statutory forces. This was slightly more difficult, as in the beginning they were not only the representative but also one of the students of the group. This had advantages and disadvantages. The advantage was clearly that they were receiving the training themselves, so there was an element of the 'proof of the pudding was in the eating', but this also meant it was difficult to ensure that the necessary level of objectivity was maintained. I was very keen on getting an ex-non-statutory force senior officer through the Phase 1 Bridging Training and posted on the establishment of the Artillery School, in order that he and I could cover the province as a team and so that he would also establish a rapport with the commanding officers. The aim was to create an environment where he could be the initial point of contact with the commanding officers and only involve BMATT if they could not find an amicable solution – but that day was a long way off.

The majority of my days would be spent visiting the Bridging Training at the 12th South African Infantry Battalion, the Intelligence School, the 4th Artillery Regiment and eventually the Artillery School. Each commanding officer I dealt with was different, but each faced the same challenges.

* * *

Patrick Zwane was appointed as the new artillery ex-non-statutory forces representative. Unlike his predecessors, he was a quiet man who kept himself to himself. Although now a member of the SANDF, he still had the very characteristic gait of a civilian in uniform. He had a reasonable understanding of artillery from his many years in exile, and although his knowledge was predominantly Soviet-based, this would be addressed through the diverse courses which awaited him. These courses would be viewed more as a series of refreshers than as hard study to gain professional recognition. The fact that Patrick was going to be based in Potchefstroom and would therefore be an integral part of the whole integration system was looked upon as a huge advantage. Here was an opportunity for an ex-non-statutory force leader to be seen to be going through the courses – and seen by both the ex-SADF personnel and his former comrades.

When the leader group course began to assemble, the atmosphere was like treading on eggshells. Individuals manoeuvred around each other and conversation was quiet, almost hushed. The normal banter between officers gathering together on a course and catching up on each other's exploits since they last met was noticeably absent. Military courses usually have a party-like environment, but this atmosphere was serious and heavy with suspicion. The young ex-SADF officers were as suspicious of the ex-non-statutory forces officers as the former non-statutory forces officers were of them. This was the first time that they had come together as SANDF officers and as comrades-in-arms. The young ex-SADF officers had been the product of the Apartheid regime, albeit the younger ones in the period of its demise, and here they were rubbing shoulders and sharing the mess with those whom they had been trained to fight. The ex-non-statutory forces officers felt the same tensions, having come from the other side of the fence. Neither group seemed keen to embrace the opportunity of advancing as equals towards a new future. There was no overt hostility, but neither was there even a modicum of brotherly love. Although these were early days, there was clearly a very long way to go.

The instructors, however, treated all the students the same; they considered them all to be ignorant and in need of education. The South African military training techniques were many years behind those of the UK, not in content or the end product, but in the manner in which instruction was delivered. I put this down to the sausage-machine style that had been necessary during the period of National Service and the need to churn out officers and soldiers to take part in the various external South African military campaigns. It was not the relaxed, rather university-style training which I had received. This was a more basic training delivery. Learning by rote was the method, and testing was a regular event. It would be unfair of me to suggest that the students came out just regurgitating facts with no fundamental understanding – but they certainly knew their facts.

I was looking forward to seeing how the students approached the course. Some of the young Afrikaners were clearly going to serve a few years and then leave, akin to the Short Service Commission officers in the UK, but the others were signed up to be career soldiers. The ex-non-statutory forces students were an unknown quantity. They were attending the training course because that was part of the contract they had signed at Wallmannsthal. At this stage I could not tell if there was any intent on their part to make a career of the Army, or if the plan was to stay in as long as necessary to allow them to leave with a pension, medical care and all the benefits of a military retiree. Naturally, no former non-statutory forces officer would declare his or her hand at this stage. The leader group in the artillery knew that it was essential to retain the best officers, regardless of where they had come from. This aspiration, however, whilst correct, would be difficult to deliver as we were about to embark upon a journey of perceptions.

The preferred end state would be to achieve a multiracial fully integrated defence force that maintained and improved upon the standards of the SADF. It would be a fully professional force and able to serve as a shining example to all other African nations, to be '*primus inter pares*' on the continent and stand shoulder-to-shoulder with other Commonwealth military forces. To deliver on this perception, the students would have to share those aspirations too. But whilst self-segregation existed, there was little chance of this happening; the challenge would now be in the classroom. Nobody in their wildest dreams would have expected everyone to fraternize from day one, but perhaps within the year the possibility would arise. To that end there was a major leadership challenge for the senior officers at the Artillery School. Amongst them I would include myself and, perhaps most importantly, Patrick, who was present not only as the senior ex-non-statutory forces representative, but as a student himself.

* * *

The classrooms at the Artillery School were quite basic. The absence of fancy technology meant that the instructors instructed, as opposed to hiding behind PowerPoint presentations as they do today. The students would sit at their desks, normally in a hollow 'C' formation, and follow the instructor attentively. One challenge was that all the instruction was in English. For some who had been delivering the same lessons for years, but in Afrikaans, and could deliver the lesson thus with their eyes shut, this did cause a headache. Everything had to be changed. I was ambivalent about some existing material being used that had been printed in both English and Afrikaans, but I made it clear that all new products should only be in English. All oral instruction was to be in English, and if an instructor was unable to stick to that simple rule then the message was 'get me a new instructor'. There were, needless to say, a few hiccoughs, but after one instructor had been removed all went smoothly. I said on several occasions that I did not mind how much the instructors muttered in Afrikaans, provided they spoke in English. I knew that if there was a transgression, then it would come straight to Patrick's ears, and he would be complaining to me in seconds.

Of course, all this may seem one-sided, but it was not. In order for the process of integration to be successful, it was beholden upon all parties to commit themselves to the courses. These were not attendance courses; they were part of an individual's professional training, and once qualified these individuals were deemed to be suitably qualified to operate artillery systems. This was a significant gauntlet being thrown down, a 'put your money where your mouth is moment' for all concerned.

But it was not long before it became clear that things were not going to go smoothly.

Chapter 10

The Truth, the Whole Truth and Nothing but the Truth

It had been a long while since we started the integration process, and all parties had been required to take many deep breaths and bite collective tongues. Now that we had all travelled so far down the road, we were at the stage of phasing out the PMORDs and pensioning-off the veterans. South Africa had not collapsed into civil war and the government seemed to be moving in a moderate direction, steered by the omnipresent Nelson Mandela. But there was a need to keep up the vigilance. It is at times of complacency that the greatest threat can materialize. At the strategic level, there were issues beginning to emerge that were likely to interfere with national unity through integration. One big issue was looming on the horizon that was guaranteed to raise emotions and open old wounds: the Truth and Reconciliation Commission.

* * *

The Truth and Reconciliation Commission (TRC) was established under the terms of the Promotion of National Unity and Reconciliation Act in 1995. The mandate was to bear witness to, record and in some cases give amnesty to those accused of human rights violations. The commission also had powers of reparation and rehabilitation. With this mandate, the TRC was entering into very emotive and potentially explosive areas. The chairman was Archbishop Desmond Tutu who, although hugely respected outside South Africa for his peaceful campaigns against Apartheid, was viewed with suspicion by others for having been too closely involved in the 'struggle'. This was a typical myopic, introspective attitude shared by many of the Afrikaner community, but to be fair, it could be justified when viewed through the prism of an Afrikaner family in the more remote locations of South Africa. They saw the TRC as a government-endorsed means for the subjugated to have their revenge on the subjugator. These people were concerned that, as Chairman,

Archbishop Tutu would look to punish those who had acted to preserve the old regime and protect their opponents. Many of them hysterically drew parallels to the Nuremberg Trials.

Regardless of how far Apartheid ideology could be used to justify decades of racial suppression, it could not remove the fact that racist suppression, segregation and formalized discrimination did take place. Within that state regime there had been elements that had used excessive force, either in the guise of law enforcement, protection of the state or as a means to extract information. This had been done in the name of the government, but as a white-only electorate had elected the government, it was also done in the name of the white population. As in Nazi Germany, the population could not deny the activities of the state; when the going was good, the white minority benefited at the expense of the black majority. When each regime came to an end, there were very few who admitted that they had supported the ideology that had been promulgated, but in both cases the number of votes cast in the elections tell a different story. Elections in Germany may not have given Hitler a clear majority, but the millions who voted for him had a fair idea where the Nazi Party was heading. Similarly, in South Africa from 1949 onwards, the National Party was elected on each occasion with Apartheid being its core policy. The big difference between the two was that the National Party had lost power in an election, and not because of an unconditional surrender after a world war.

Racism was a primary component of Apartheid, and in his foreword to the TRC Report, Archbishop Tutu said the period being considered by the TRC was dominated by Apartheid and racism, and this must be understood. He stated that racism arrived with a Dutch fleet in 1652, since when it had become a fundamental part of South African society.

This difference explains why the Nuremberg Trials were established as an international process for the prosecution of prominent members of the political, military and economic leadership of Nazi Germany who had allegedly planned, carried out and participated in war crimes. In Nuremberg, this was a criminal trial, through the means of military tribunals, to exact revenge. Nothing could be further removed from the intent and spirit of the TRC. President Mandela stated that 'we were expected to destroy one another and ourselves collectively in the worst racial conflagration. Instead, we as a people chose the path of negotiation, compromise and peaceful settlement. Instead of hatred and revenge we chose reconciliation and nation-building.' The Truth and Reconciliation Commission was a means of reconciliation, not revenge.

Because the liberal elite and the media were centred in the cities of Pretoria, Johannesburg, Cape Town and Durban, there was very much an 'inside and outside the bubble' view of the realpolitik as represented by the TRC. There was considerable fear in the farmsteads and the hard-line Afrikaner centres, such as Potchefstroom, which was balanced by an equally myopic, misguided and almost belligerent feeling within the various townships. Some of the white population saw the TRC as the new Nuremberg; the means of revenge. Meanwhile, the more radical members of the ANC actively encouraged the view that the TRC was a tool to wreak vengeance. It came as a surprise to many in the townships that the activities of their own freedom fighters would be subject to review by the commission. No side was exempt from being called to account. The TRC had the power to grant amnesty to those who had committed human rights abuses during the period of the Apartheid regime, regardless of which side of the struggle the perpetrator might have been on. This was dependent on three key principles: firstly, that the abuses were politically motivated; secondly, that the abuses were proportionate; and finally, that the individual was prepared to enter full disclosure. This would allow the TRC to avoid being seen to be meting out a victor's justice. The Truth and Reconciliation Commission was about restorative justice, not retributive justice.

The work of the TRC was done through three committees: the Human Rights Violations Committee, the Reparation and Rehabilitation Committee and the Amnesty Committee. Each had a clearly defined task. The Human Rights Violations Committee looked at human rights abuses which occurred between 1960 and 1994, based on statements made to the TRC. The committee established the identity of the victims, their fate or where they now lived, the nature and extent of the harm they had suffered, and also whether the violations were the result of deliberate planning by the state or any other organization, group or individual. Once victims of gross human rights violations were identified, they were referred to the Reparation and Rehabilitation Committee. This committee aimed to provide victim support to ensure that the TRC process restored a victim's dignity, and to formulate policy proposals and recommendations on rehabilitation and healing of survivors, their families and communities at large. The envisaged overall function of all recommendations was to ensure that there would be no repetition of the crime and that there would be a healing process, which would lead to future healthy co-existence. The Amnesty Committee, meanwhile, considered applications for amnesty provided that any applicant had met the principles mentioned in the preceding paragraph. Applicants could apply for amnesty for any act, omission or offence associated with a political objective committed between 1 March 1960 and 6 December 1993. The cut-off date was later extended to 11 May 1994. The final date for the submission of applications was 30 September 1997. Being granted amnesty for an act meant that the perpetrator was free from prosecution for that particular act. The fact that 7,112 amnesty applications were heard and only 849 were granted certainly did not satisfy everyone.

The records of all 7,112 amnesty applications are available in the public domain, and can be accessed on the South African Ministry of Justice website. I was struck by one example of an ex-MK member who had been sentenced to twenty-five years' imprisonment for murder and a further eight years for attempted robbery associated with the incident. He maintained his innocence about the attempted robbery and did not seek amnesty for this. He had left South Africa and joined the MK, and had been trained in Tanzania, Angola and Cuba, returning to South Africa in 1992. The incident occurred on 3 November 1993. He had left his home in KwaZulu Natal and travelled to the town of Mount Aycliff in Transkei, where he was going to work as an ANC activist. He reported to the Chairperson of the ANC Youth League, who gave him his tasks. These included canvassing and educating people on voting, and also a survey of the social and political conditions of the area. Whilst he was doing this, he was constantly told about a man called Baxter who was insulting people regularly and calling them 'kaffirs'. This individual, was also encouraging people to place their mark against the picture of President de Klerk, so to vote for the National Party rather than the ANC. His story was that a cross against a candidate meant that the candidate was wrong; a simple trick on people who had never voted before. Baxter was deliberately misleading voters in the guise of an ANC supporter. The issue was discussed at the next committee meeting, and having decided that Baxter was a government agent or spy, the ex-MK member decided to kill him. He met him by the side of the road, where Baxter was selling milk, and coolly shot him five times. The former MK member stated that he had acted alone and had not received orders to kill Baxter.

As there was no evidence to the contrary, the Amnesty Committee ruled that the applicant satisfied the requirements for amnesty in that the offence was considered to be an act associated with a political objective. The committee adjudged that the end-state of the liberation struggle was peaceful elections, and that people were prepared to die in order to secure such elections. The ex-MK member, by being a member of the MK, was also prepared to die for the cause, and at the time of the killing he believed that the deceased was actively preventing the rural people from taking part in the elections. In order to safeguard the local peoples' right to vote, he killed Baxter. This was a simple case of an MK operative killing a person whom he had concluded was a political enemy. Although one may argue that it was an extreme measure, it was an act that was politically driven.

The same could not be said about another amnesty hearing, which was held in Potchefstroom in September 1996.[1] The importance of this case was that it distinguished between a racial crime and a political crime. The four van Straaten brothers had been convicted of the murder of two black security guards and the theft of a vehicle in Vereeniging in June 1989. They had been sentenced to thirteen years' imprisonment. The brothers based their amnesty application on the grounds that their crime was racially, and therefore politically, motivated. They had had a strict Afrikaner Christian upbringing in a climate which taught them to hate black people. They had all done National Service, and stated that the South African Army had taught them that 'blacks were the enemy'. They also stated that they were members of the Afrikaaner Weerstandsbewiging (AWB). Adriaan van Straaten said that he had been approached by an AWB activist and asked to set up a cell to engage in terrorist activities in order to destabilize the National Party government, with the ultimate aim of establishing a *volkstaat*.[2]

The brothers embarked on their first terrorist act by planning to tie up the two black security guards and to steal a truck, thereby, in their minds, demonstrating that blacks were unable to carry out such jobs as security guards. However, the two security guards proved they were able to do their jobs and put up a stiff resistance. The four brothers overpowered them and went on to kill them, using chisels and rocks that were on the premises. The van Straaten brothers' defence unravelled when it was made clear that none of them were members of the AWB; in fact, the AWB made great pains to distance themselves from these men. It was clear that the robbery was a criminal action, not a politically motivated one, and that the subsequent murders were also criminal. Their amnesty application was rejected, and they all returned to prison to carry out their sentences. This case was an important milestone for the TRC as it distinguished between what were politically motivated attacks by members of ascribed political organizations and those carried out by individuals purely motivated by racism.[3]

As part of the conscious effort for the work of the TRC to be seen as being as inclusive as possible, the hearings were held in various locations throughout the country.

It was quite extraordinary to witness the scepticism expressed by so many of the people that we had come to know. Outside of a handful of the more liberal thinkers, the vast majority of the Army and the civilian population in Potchefstroom saw the TRC as a thinly veiled show trial. They were not prepared to open their eyes and ears to witness that justice was being applied to all. They did not want to recognize the closure that such a commission could offer. I suppose there were some things which did not help the cause, such as the delay in starting and the fact that some of the earliest cases, which received media attention, were against white members of the old State apparatus. As is the case in most protracted activities, after the initial excitement and intrigue the media tired of the proceedings, as did the general public. Instead of being in the headlines daily, news of the proceedings soon faded from the papers and was replaced by infrequent reporting. In the beginning, the sessions were heard in camera, but after extensive lobbying the media were allowed to broadcast live the first two hours of the first human rights violation committee. Subsequently, the SABC broadcast weekly updates under the title of 'Truth Commission Special Report'. These were broadcast from 21 April 1996 until 29 March 1998; the eighty-seven episodes covered the first two of the five years of the TRC.

It is important to remember that the TRC was not just about the amnesty process, although clearly this was the most politically potent area; indeed it was that which attracted the most interest and comment. The TRC also gave an opportunity for individuals to tell their own story of loss, pain or violence. The stories are harrowing, but in some cases the individual, by exposing their grief in public, was able to achieve closure. In other cases, it was a means to put their version of events on record.

One particular session of the Human Rights Violations Committee was held in Klerksdorp, a town very close to Potchefstroom, where Mrs Susan van der Merwe gave evidence[4] about the disappearance of her husband. Whilst this was but one of thousands of such submissions, this case is poignant because it reflected the fear felt by many of the farmers and those living or working in the remote areas. In the court extract, Mrs van der Merwe states that the South African Police Service had determined, with the assistance of one of the assailants, Mr X, that her husband had stopped to give four men a lift. The group then pulled guns on him, forcing him to turn around and help them load some items. Two of the group then shot him in the back, and when he had fallen face-down, they turned him over and shot him in the face.

The police investigation was aided by the testimony of Mr X, who would appear to have turned police informant, allowing the Supreme Court to pronounce the husband dead. For the previous four years, Mr van der Merwe was recorded as having simply disappeared, his car having been found abandoned near the Botswana border. Mrs van der Merwe told the committee of the pain and suffering that the disappearance of her husband had caused, and the impact it had had upon the family, especially as his body had never been found.

* * *

Both sets of sceptics were ultimately proved to be wrong, and the TRC did much to lance the multitude of boils that had been becoming more septic as the years passed. But its very nature was seen to be too liberal for some and too protective for others. The Centre for the Study of Violence and Reconciliation considered that the TRC had not achieved reconciliation between the white and black communities. It felt that justice was still needed and that there was no alternative. However, using justice would have been against the mandate of the TRC and would have been politically more explosive. The purpose of the TRC was to find out the truth, not to pass judgement. One of the loudest voices of criticism was from the family of anti-Apartheid activist Steve Biko, who had died whilst in the hands of the security police. They labelled the TRC a vehicle for political expediency, and his son, Nkosinathi, having met face-to-face with the alleged killer, Colonel Gideon Niewoudt, said that Niewoudt and his 'cronies' had 'evaded justice'. This criticism has been repeated many times by the lawyer Sir Sydney Kentridge, who represented the Biko family at the inquest into the death of Steve Biko. At the end of the day, the TRC, with its flaws and critics, still managed to do a tremendous task. It was a very difficult task, which tried hard to address wrongs, but most importantly let the truth be heard. That truth is still both unpalatable to many and denied by others.

* * *

Were emotions raised within the integration process? I think without doubt that they were, but as in most areas of the process, the feelings were suppressed openly whilst remaining fertile in private. If I was talking to the ex-SADF personnel, the TRC was declared a witch-hunt and a blame game. Because the South African Army had been involved in the townships and on the periphery of some of the terrorist incidents, feelings ran high when members of the security forces appeared in front of the various committees, but then there was a uniform stepping back when some of the police and security police were called forward. Mutterings of 'law unto themselves' and 'we knew nothing about this' abounded. It was clear that brutal methods against unarmed civilians were not endorsed by the military, but whether the military leadership knew about what really happened one will never know. I am sure that the same suspicions could be levelled against the British Army from their time in Northern Ireland. Nobody is completely 'squeaky-clean', as has also been seen from recent incidents in Iraq.

As far as the ex-non-statutory forces personnel were concerned, they generally commented less. The screening process in the Assembly Areas had identified those who had blood on their hands, and generally I would have said that, although some of the ex-non-statutory forces personnel we had in Potchefstroom had been deployed within South Africa, they were not the major players. One common thread was that neither party would discuss the TRC and its activities with the other. At the end of the day, the TRC had not been able to increase trust and reconciliation between the parties integrating within the SANDF.

There have been various studies conducted about how effective the TRC was. The general consensus was that the Afrikaners did not believe the commission was effective or efficient, the English South Africans were more positive, but nowhere near as positive as the black South Africans.

Chapter 11

Scales Of Justice

In the early days of the SANDF, BMATT members were frequently asked to attend courts martial or boards of inquiry to ensure transparency. It made a good deal of sense, and although we were only observers it did provide reassurance. I had become used to attending courts martial and various boards of inquiry; a complete *volte-face* to when I was in the UK or Germany, where I had consciously avoided them, almost at any cost. When I was requested to attend a Board of Inquiry in Mmabatho, I just went with the flow. It seemed as if it would be interesting this time, dealing with the mutiny of the Bophutaswana Defence Force in 1994 prior to the elections. A hearing was arranged under the Presidency of a brigadier general and was scheduled to last for two days, beginning on 22 June, a Thursday morning, and ending on the Friday afternoon. I was quite happy with the timings, as it was concluding on the afternoon before the Rugby World Cup final on Saturday 24 June. This was hugely important as I had a ticket for the match. That gave me heaps of time to leave early on the Saturday morning and travel the three-and-a-half hours to meet Andre for a late breakfast before leaving for Ellis Park, the venue for the final.

Mmabatho was two-and-a-half hours' drive from Potchefstroom, so I left for the Board of Inquiry in plenty of time and met up with the general and his staff bright and early. The board was to hear evidence surrounding the circumstances of the mutiny and rule on the legal way forward. This was not a court martial, but it was still a solemn affair that had to be conducted in the strictest of administrative and legal parameters. There was an ex-non-statutory force representative present too. Our role was explained to us clearly; we were there just to observe the proceedings, which were a *de facto* military tribunal. If we had any concerns, then they must be brought to the attention of the President of the board. At the end of the proceedings, we would be requested to sign a document stating that we considered the process to have been conducted in a fair and transparent manner. We felt ourselves to be more touch judges than referees, and we settled down for what we expected to be a pretty serious couple of days.

We were not to be disappointed. The tribunal was serious, meticulous and, frankly, as dull as ditch water. It was a case of having sharpened pencils close to hand as an aid to keeping awake. However, it was also quite clear that the process was deliberate and fair, with ample opportunities for representatives to discuss points of order with the President. It was run in a very professional manner and according to the guidelines which had been issued to us.

By the afternoon break on the first day, we had almost lost the will to live. However, it was important that fair play was seen to be done, so we returned for the final session of the day with highly sharpened pencils. Never mind, I told myself; the day after tomorrow I would be heading south to Johannesburg and the Rugby World Cup final. At the close of the day's proceedings, we retired to a very pleasant hotel and spent the evening talking about anything – anything but the Board of Inquiry. The President was not a mad rugby fan, which was surprising, but his deputy – a large and jovial lieutenant colonel – was, so much time was spent discussing the match to be played on the Saturday. I kept quiet about my ticket, as this seemed politic. The ex-non-statutory force representative was not a follower of rugby – he was much more a football man – but as a proud South African, he was rooting for the Boks as much as the next man. He, like so many black South Africans, had been swept up by the World Cup fever, and although to many the Springboks were a glaring testament to the racial policies of Apartheid, he was supporting what the *Sowetan* newspaper had christened the 'Amabokoboko'. We had a good evening together, but were all quite drained, so we headed off for our beds at a very sensible time.

* * *

Mmabatho was created in 1977 as the capital of the Bophuthatswana. It was built as an adjunct of Mafikeng, which was in the old province of Western Transvaal. After the elections in 1994, the homelands ceased to exist, and it was decided that Mmabatho would be the capital of the new North West Province. It is not the most exciting of places; it is very much a local capital, with many government buildings, a huge sports stadium and the mandatory casino, which was one of the main *raisons d'être* of the homelands.

Mafikeng is older than Mmabatho; dusty, and not the most picturesque of towns. It was the scene of one of the sieges during the Second Boer War, when Mafikeng (or Mafeking to the British), Kimberley and Ladysmith were all besieged by the Boers (farmers). The Boers were well organized and brave, and had no problem in conducting both irregular and regular warfare. What made Mafikeng stand out from the other sieges was the brilliant use of the media through pictures, cartoons and newspaper copy. Although as sieges go it was a pretty average affair (and there is much evidence that it could have been broken earlier), it was skilfully turned into a celebrity action in which Colonel Robert Baden-Powell, the British commander, became the hero. He became a household name in Britain, and in 1901 was personally invested as a Companion of the Order of the Bath by the new King Edward VII. He later achieved even greater fame with the foundation of the Boy Scouts movement. Nevertheless, Mafikeng soon reverted to a sleepy border town within months of the siege being lifted.

The conglomeration that is Mmabatho-Mafikeng had another more recent and chilling episode in its history that reflected the underlying distrust that still openly existed within some elements of South African society, especially in the North West Province. The Province was home to many of the more radical right-wing white political groupings, especially the Afrikaaner Weerstandsbeweging (AWB). The AWB was formed in 1973 in Heidelberg in the Transvaal as a protest against what was considered the National Party's policy of appeasement and forfeiture. The new party wanted to create a '*volkstaat*', and their policies were based on the ideal that Afrikaners did not share the same destiny as others.

The AWB reached its heyday in the 1980s, but then steadily declined as the politics of the far-right fragmented. By 1995, any major overt threat, no matter how unrealistic, had passed, but there was still a lingering presence, demonstrably from graffiti and the occasional parade with troops of horsemen. The AWB had to many become an almost comical parody of a neo-Nazi organization. The height of contempt for the organization came when its bearded leader, Eugene Terre'Blanche, fell off his horse whilst leading a parade of the AWB. The media had a field day. The death throes of the party continued, but its unpleasant aftertaste remained. There were rallies organized in the towns of the North West Province on several occasions, when groups of men dressed in khaki bush jackets and shorts would swagger around chanting right-wing slogans. It was very much out of the bullyboy mould of the early days of the Nazi Party: lots of bluster but nonetheless carrying the menace of violence. Friends sometimes warned us to avoid the centre of Potchefstroom because the AWB were holding a parade. We watched from a discreet distance as this rapidly declining and wholly irrelevant bunch of thugs strutted around the high street with their flags flying. The similarity to the Nazi Party was sobering, with the AWB flag being similar to that of the Nazis, but with the swastika replaced by three black sevens forming a triskelion and the addition of the motto '*God, Volk, Vaderland*' ('God, People, Fatherland'). During these demonstrations, it was felt that a car with a Union Flag prominently displayed could well have provoked some of their supporters. With a young family, it was not worth the risk.

The episode that did reflect the unhappy status quo was the killing of three wounded AWB supporters in front of the media by a Bophuthatswana police constable, Ontlametse Bernstein Menyatsoe. The three AWB men were in a column of AWB vehicles that was ordered to leave Mmabatho at the height of the Bophuthatswana coup d'état in March 1994. This column, which was nothing more than a collection of vehicles containing armed irregulars, drove through the town and fired indiscriminately at the local population. The Bophuthatswana Defence Force returned fire and a blue Mercedes in the AWB column was hit, with its three occupants wounded. What happened next was appalling. A Bophuthatswanan policeman walked up to the vehicle, disarmed one of the passengers who had staggered out of the car brandishing a handgun, and then promptly shot all three dead. All this was conducted in front of the media. It was a sickening sight. I do not wish to enter into the rights and wrongs of the matter, but I cannot condone the shooting of unarmed civilians and disarmed combatants, especially as the perpetrator was later granted amnesty by the Truth and Reconciliation Committee. This action, however, was part of the backdrop of the North West Province and one of the cases of a simmering disquiet that fed the insecurities of many.

Although this act happened just before we arrived in South Africa, it had been broadcast widely in the UK, along with 'necklacing' (an execution carried out by forcing a rubber tyre filled with petrol around a victim, and setting it on fire) in the townships. Tensions were building in the lead-up to the April 1994 election, including the death of famous South African news photographer Ken Oosterbroek in the East Rand. The situation was not rosy. North West Province, which was formed from the merger of Bophuthatswana and Western Transvaal, whilst less populous, was still tense. The AWB carried out a series of bomb attacks in the province to disrupt the election. Local Afrikaner friends of ours commented that there had been a bomb attack planned at the local power distribution plant which was intended to cut off the power to demonstrate what life would be like with a black majority government. The impact and influence of these attacks was as insignificant as the body that had carried it out had become. However, the North West Province was where the radical white political class met the '*Swart Gevaar*',[1] along with others deemed to be a threat to their white supremacist world. We British, especially the military working with the ANC government, were deemed to be a threat.

* * *

The Board of Inquiry hearing continued at a steady pace on the Friday, and I was gradually ticking off the minutes and hours. It was not exciting stuff; I realized how grateful I was for discounting the law as a possible career option. This was the grit and gristle of legal work, and it clearly was not for me. But I was quite convinced that progress was being made and was looking forward to a few quiet drinks that evening before a good sleep and an early departure. At around four o'clock in the afternoon, the President of the board called a break and suggested that we have some tea, during which he summoned us together, announcing that he was pleased with the progress of the hearings and that we had almost finished. I was delighted to hear this. He added, however, that he wanted to run over some issues in more detail, which he considered gave him three choices: continue today and finish at about 8 o'clock that evening, (perfectly acceptable); adjourn until Monday (perfectly acceptable, but logistically painful); or continue tomorrow morning (surely, I could not be hearing this?). He then sent his deputy to check diaries. I kept quiet at this stage, trusting that common sense would prevail and that surely someone else had an interest in the World Cup final?

His deputy returned about fifteen minutes later, after having consulted with the others and made some telephone calls to Pretoria, and he took the President aside. After a minute or so, he called us together and announced that in his opinion, we had done enough for the day. As the remaining issues were primarily administrative and legal technicalities, it would benefit from fresh minds. Therefore, because there were diary conflicts, it was clear that we should adjourn now and reconvene the next morning at eight o'clock. He believed that we should be finished by midday. My jaw dropped as the others seemed to take the news in their stride and continued chatting away, finishing their tea. I grabbed the ex-non-statutory force representative and said to him that I could not do the Saturday morning because I was off to Ellis Park. He laughed, but appreciated my dilemma. When I asked him whether he had any issues with the hearing or the recommendation made by the President, he said that he was perfectly happy with the way it was being run and as far as he was concerned, our role was over. He reckoned we could sign the papers and leave now. If the President was only going to deal with legal and technical issues in the morning, then we would add no value. I was really growing to like this guy! I looked around for the President, but he had already left, so I decided that I would tackle him in the bar where we would gather before dinner. My new best friend said that he would be there as my wingman.

Armed with a cold beer, I approached the President, who was chatting to his deputy. He looked up and smiled, and I commented that I had been impressed with the proceedings and that both the ex-non-statutory force representative and I were very content that the proceedings had been carried out in a fair and transparent way. He thanked me, but clearly was expecting more. I obliged by saying that, unfortunately, I would not be able to be present on the Saturday morning. He was somewhat taken aback, saying that the proceedings were not complete and that I was required to sign a statement that everything had been conducted correctly. I agreed, but replied that the business the following day was about technicalities. The hearings concerning the mutiny were completed, and satisfactorily so, therefore neither the ex-non-statutory force representative nor I could add anything to the following day's activities. He then said, 'Well, what if I said that I order you to attend?'

This was not the way I wanted the conversation to go, but I decided to take a chance. I said, 'Well, Sir, should you do that then I might have to disobey your order and that would be a difficult call which would lead to some very difficult questions being asked in Pretoria between Army and Defence HQs and the Commander of BMATT – but I would be prepared to take the risk.' I took a deep breath.

He looked me straight in the eyes and, after what seemed a very long time, said, 'Well, we would not want anything like that to occur. I suppose you want to watch the Rugby. Why can't you watch it here?' I pulled an envelope out of my jacket pocket and showed him the ticket for the final.

He smiled and said, 'I may not be a Rugby man, but I am a South African, and I would love to be there, and I would not wish to stand in any man's way if he has a ticket to Ellis Park tomorrow. Go then, enjoy it, and tell your ex-non-statutory force friend that the papers will be ready to sign after dinner.'

He chuckled, and as he was about to take a sip out of his beer, his deputy started, 'You know, Sir, that I was hoping to watch the game …' 'Here,' said the President, 'you work for me and you're going nowhere!'

I did feel a bit guilty! Next morning, I set off at sunrise and the guilt faded as I headed east towards Pretoria. In the early morning, in winter, the bush looks fabulous. The fiery ball that is the sun emerges against a weak blue sky and lights up the vast plains of the North West Province, and as the the scrub is low you can see for miles. Everything seemed to be rising and shaking the night away, and as I headed towards the sunrise, little did I know what momentous events I was to see the next day. Colonel Davis had rung me to ask who I thought would win, and I had said the Boks. His reply was that I must be soft in the head as the All Blacks were odds-on favourites. I couldn't really explain my reasoning, but I said that if I was a betting man, then I would be betting on Green and Gold, not All Black; but there again, I am not a betting man.

Chapter 12

Affirmative Distraction

The one great advantage of not being tied to Wallmannsthal was that it gave me a great deal of freedom to travel around North West Province and to visit the complete range of training activities. There was a growing sense of satisfaction that the process was beginning to work. I was starting to see genuine integration within the units, and those ex-non-statutory forces members having completed their basic training were now quite properly part of their new unit. The integration was most apparent at the lower level of the military strata, where the soldiers had completed their short course and the young officers had undergone their special-to-arm training following their initial leadership cadre. The full integration of qualified members across all ranks was a long way down the road, but happily there were signs that integration was emerging.

The role of the BMATT team was very much in the monitoring mode, with the occasional adjudication task. It was important for us to be seen. After all, we had agreed and signed off the training regimes and been involved in the screening and selection of the candidates, so we were becoming much more a presence in the background. I felt it was important that I let everyone know I was available and could visit whenever there was a need.

I spent a lot of time around the Potchefstroom garrison to show that I was part of the team. I was keen to be involved in all areas, and because Potchefstroom had always been a military town, this meant that we, as a family, became a greater part of the scene. We were gradually overcoming the natural resentment about my role, although occasionally some people would still exclude us. They were not part of the change, and never would be. There was nothing I could do or say that would change their minds, and changing their minds was not part of my remit.

* * *

I began to notice a 'them and us' feeling creeping in between BMATT HQ staff in Pretoria and those of us deployed in the provinces, and this began to show in the routine of our roles. Because Wallmannsthal and the other assembly areas were collapsing inward, BMATT presence was reducing correspondingly. With most of the leader group having already been processed through the system, those left were generally foot soldiers. Any leader group members who appeared were more than likely senior members who had been fully engaged on ANC or MK business since the election. They were processed individually at either the Army or Defence Headquarters. Accordingly, BMATT split into two camps: those in Pretoria and those not. This was a natural consequence, but it did mean those of us outside Pretoria became fundamentally self-sufficient. These were the days before the internet. Mobile phones were still quite rudimentary, and were certainly not provided for BMATT staff. Communication was based on landline phone calls and faxes. A weekly report was requested by BMATT HQ in Pretoria that covered the number of individuals involved in Basic and Bridging Training by location, the number who had successfully completed their training and were now part of a unit, and any issues that we had dealt with on the ground or we thought should be brought to the attention of the Commander. The latter varied tremendously, and could be anything from the report of a complaint that had been resolved to information that we had picked up needing to be investigated further. It was a reasonable way to share best practice. I also reported on the broader aspects of life in the North West Province; if nothing else, it reminded those in Pretoria that life in the province was somewhat different to that to which they were accustomed. Sadly, there was little feedback and I soon realized that to all extents and purposes we were on our own.

Clearly, a commander needs to be at the most critical point of any engagement. If your area is under control and you have demonstrated that you are able to deal with issues on your own and within your own resources, then there is no need for the commander to sit on your shoulder. You know what to do, you know your part in his plan, and therefore it is the epitome of mission command. There is a little element of disappointment in this when you and your family are alone in a location that is not necessarily supportive of your activities, but every cloud has a silver lining and we therefore gave ourselves carte blanche to go native.

* * *

It was a dark, very dark, still night, with the only light coming from the spectacular southern night sky – and it was quite cold. It takes a while to adjust to the fact that it might be so hot during the day that you can literally fry an egg on the armour plate of your vehicle, but several hours later you can be shivering like a lunatic. The dry-stone Kalahari Desert of the Northern Cape is unforgiving, but it does offer an excellent area for all forms of military training. There are huge tracts of bush on a stony carpet, with stark *kopjes* (small hills) breaking up the horizon. We were in the South African Army Combat Training Centre[1] for a major exercise and the chance for the newly integrated artillery officers and men to earn their spurs. Lohatlha is about 200km from the Botswanan border and 200km north-east of Kimberley.

Perhaps the two major differences between Lohatlha and the other training centres that I have known are the itinerant wildlife and the nomads, both of whom can cause challenges to the military freedom of manoeuvre. I had seen wildlife cause chaos on the local ranges in Potchefstroom because the ranges offered sanctuary to many species of wildlife, so the aim was to have a managed co-existence. The most effective method to reduce the disruption to training caused by wildlife could be described as a policy of 'gentle movement encouragement'. Wild animals are very alert and will automatically move away from danger, be it fire, a predator or man-made distractions such as loud noise. I saw on regular occasions a large herd of bok happily munching their way across the impact area which needed to be cleared for use. The solution would be a loud bang from a well-placed artillery round, well way from the animals, and as a result the impact area would be clear for use. However, there was one old fellow in Potchefstroom who was a bit more difficult to shift. This was an old bull wildebeest who knew the range better than any South African gunner. He had his favourite pasture, and inevitably this was exactly where one wanted to fire. There was absolutely no question of killing him or even hurting him, but this old boy knew the calibre of the guns and how far away the rounds were landing; he was an expert in judging what was 'danger close'.[2] On one afternoon, I watched as the Forward Observer painfully fired one round after another, creeping slowly towards the old wildebeest. Each round landed exactly where it was calculated to land, but there was no reaction from the old bull, not even a shake of his head. Eventually, when we were all expecting that the next round would surely dispatch him to his maker, the round landed within about 150m of him, causing shrapnel to go skitting through the nearby grass. His only reaction was to look up with a clearly disgruntled expression, shake his scraggy tail vigorously and then trot off into the distance.

A similar process was required in Lohatlha, but this time to move on the nomads who had a habit of moving into the several deserted villages that were dotted around the training area. The homesteads had been compulsorily purchased in 1978, and although not used for training, they were situated in the middle of the training area and deemed dangerous to occupy. But no matter how many times these people had been told of the danger, they would still drift back in. Consequently, the policy of 'gentle movement encouragement' was applied again. It would have taken a very long period to clear every homestead, and if any of the people were in occupation, it would take even longer to bring in the translators and officials to formally evict them. A simpler solution was used, one that all parties understood and which required no translators. The nomads knew that they were occupying the homesteads illegally, but they were doing it for convenience, with no political agenda, and were not interested in any form of standoff. There had almost been a tacit agreement that the authorities would turn a blind eye to any illegal occupation during a non-training period, but would not tolerate occupation when the area was required. Therefore, a simple demonstration was required. The first part of the procedure was to see if any of the homesteads were occupied, and this was achieved first thing in the morning by looking for the tell-tale signs of cooking smoke. If there was no smoke, then the homesteads were empty; if there was, then another of those well-placed artillery rounds landed on the opposite side of the village to the road. Within minutes, a trickle of people moved out and went on their way again. They would return when the exercise had finished, so it became a constant game of ping-pong in which, fortunately, no one got hurt.

* * *

Lohatlha was an excellent opportunity to shake out the students and see them put their new skills into practice. We would conduct straightforward live artillery practice and then look to join in with other units to conduct integrated dry training and some live firing exercises. All went well, and after several days of dry fire and movement, in which the guns would be brought into action, and the sequence of fire missions and fire planning practised without firing live ammunition, the crews in the command posts and the guns were ticking along nicely. Sharing the training area was the 8th South African Infantry Battalion from Upington, who were regulars at Lohatlha. They were planning to do a live night attack onto a *kopje* and were very pleased to be able to have artillery in support. It was agreed that the artillery would provide co-ordinated illumination for the battalion attack. Co-ordinated illumination is perhaps the most technically complicated mission for artillery. It is controlled by the observer, who needs to make the calculations needed to allow the illuminating shell to burn for just enough time to see the fall of shot of the high-explosive shell and then order the necessary correction. The command post feeds the data into the fire control computer and issues orders to the guns; all the pressure is on the observer. If he gets the co-ordination wrong, then he will miss the fall of shot and illuminate the advancing infantry, giving the enemy an open goal.

I sat in on the orders group delivered by the CO of the battalion, and it was a very slick set of instructions. The battery commander was to co-ordinate the fire from the artillery, mortars, recoilless rifles and heavy machine guns, but the key to everything was the co-ordinated illumination, which was to be conducted by one of the young Forward Observation Officers (FOO). I decided that I would like to watch the attack from the FOO's position. The FOO would have been one of the students from the recent courses, and I thought I could add a little moral support. After the battery commander's orders, I jumped into the back of the FOO's Ratel[3] and set off for his position on a *kopje* overlooking the objective. We approached from dead ground and left the vehicle on the reverse slope, continuing towards the selected position on foot, and waited short of the position until dusk began to settle on the desert. I made myself comfortable whilst the FOO party went about their business silently marking the objective and making sure they were all prepared for the attack, which was scheduled for a couple of hours later. I was quite looking forward to seeing the local wildlife at night, and was scanning the near and far ground – the near ground especially for snakes, which I loathe. But no wildlife of any significance appeared as the temperature began to drop and the incredible blanket of stars that are the southern night sky started to appear.

The FOO was one of the Afrikaner officers who had done well on the course, and I walked over to him and had a chat. He was clearly anxious about the shoot, as one would expect, so I asked to see his calculations. They seemed correct from the data at the head of his crib sheet, and matched those that I had written onto my old crib which I had found in my day-sack, but I was slightly concerned that his crib sheet was in Afrikaans rather than in English. English was the agreed and official language of the SANDF, but I assumed that he had done this out of habit or a form of comfort. I asked him to confirm that he would be giving his orders in English, and he nodded positively. I then left him alone, as the last thing he needed was me staring over his shoulder.

The time seemed to pass slowly, especially as it was now getting quite cold. I worked out that there must have been an almost 20°C drop in the temperature from the afternoon. Acclimatized or not, this was quite a temperature drop. It was whilst I was contemplating how to keep warm that I saw a staggering sight pass overhead: a fireball streaked across the sky like a blazing football trailing a fiery tail. It appeared to pass almost directly to our front; no noise, just an extraordinary vision. It was breathtaking. I assumed that it was a tiny meteorite, or part of a meteorite, burning up in the atmosphere. I half expected to hear a huge explosion as it made impact, but this was not to be. I assume a small, very hot pebble landed somewhere in the Kalahari that night. Nonetheless, it was a spectacular sight and certainly shook me out of my hibernation.

It was almost time for the fire orders to be passed to the guns. I moved across to the FOO party, and it was clear that tension was growing by the second. This was a complicated mission, but there were procedures and drills to be followed to allow the process to be conducted successfully and, most importantly, safely. Fire discipline, the language of fire control for the artillery, is set in stone and follows a very pedantic procedure to ensure, as far as humanly possible, that the right information in the right sequence is passed from the observer to the command post. Everything is repeated back to ensure accuracy. Of course, mistakes can be made, but there are assistants who check the data and any instruction can be corrected. There are many factors that have an influence on a projectile in flight and where it will land. These include ambient temperature at various altitudes, wind speed and direction, the rotation of the Earth, charge temperature and muzzle velocity but careful calculations and computer programmes reduce the errors potentially caused by these factors. The strictness of fire discipline reduces any error from mis-communication to a minimum.

All seemed to be going well. The orders came down from the battery commander to his FOOs confirming the extant fire plan and the time for H-hour. The scene was set, and shortly afterwards the battalion began moving up from its assembly area and deliberately approached the line of departure. The noise of the engines was covered by the deafening sound of artillery fire directed well away from the objective as a means of deception. Very shortly, my FOO would start his co-ordinated illumination that would allow the artillery to be brought on top of the objective. As soon as the co-ordinated illumination begins, there is no doubt that an attack is coming, so this needs to be done as quickly as possible. As soon as the FOO is happy that the rounds are landing on target, he can order 'Fire for effect' and the bombardment can begin and be in concert with the other indirect and direct fire.

What happened next was quite surprising. The FOO took hold of his radio handset and gave his orders, in English, and the command post duly repeated back the orders. So far so good. The guns reported ready and the illuminating round was fired, followed a few seconds later by the high-explosive round. This is where the FOO earns his money. His assistant will say 'Splash', indicating that the illuminating round will burst in five seconds. Shortly afterwards, the high-explosive round will land, and the FOO must be able to observe the fall of shot and calculate the necessary adjustment whilst the illuminating round is still burning. It is a question of quick thinking and speedy calculations followed by brisk orders back down the radio net. The illuminating round burst and the *kopje* was bathed in bright light, but the high-explosive round burst short and well to the left of the objective. A correction was needed to bring the next round closer to or on the target. Without going into too much detail, the correction is ordered from the perspective of the target to the FOO. The command post knows the location of the guns and the target, and the FOO and trigonometry take over. The correction ordered over the radio should have been 'Right 100 add 200, over', but instead the FOO started speaking in Afrikaans. He was nervous and had completely forgotten the protocol. The command post, manned by some of the ex-non-statutory force personnel, either genuinely or deliberately, did not understand what he was saying. The call 'Say again, over' came across the net. Again, the FOO blurted out the correction in Afrikaans. The battalion was advancing steadily, and nothing was happening with the artillery. Again, the command post replied, 'Say again, over.' The FOO froze. I said to him, 'Say it in English. You are speaking in Afrikaans.' He looked like a rabbit in the headlights – his mind had obviously gone blank. I realized that there was a major problem in the making, so I grabbed his radio set and ordered the correction. The rounds landed safely and, after one more correction, he ordered 'Fire for effect'.

There was no point in me ripping into him; that would be done much more effectively by his battery commander, and was not my role. But I was staggered that he could be so set in his ways. I began to realize that all the focus had been on the ex-non-statutory force personnel, expecting them to be slow and make mistakes. We had, rightly or wrongly, chosen to see only one side of the coin. It was clear that there would be both able and less able people at the end of the integration process, but no longer could I allow myself to presume that the less able would be from just one of the integrating parties. It was becoming obvious that we needed to create a level playing field so that, in the future, there would be fair competition and the previous advantages of colour could be whittled away. We were a long way from achieving this environment, but what I saw on the *kopje* that night – and having observed the developing confidence of some of the ex-non-statutory force officers – I was convinced that it could be achieved. As Napoleon said, 'you cannot make an omelette without breaking eggs'; therefore, an integrated, professional army could not be created without some individuals failing along the way. Failure was now possible on both sides.

The rest of the exercise proceeded without incident, and there was genuine progress on all fronts. The instructors were happy with the professional ability of the students, but they were more than a little concerned about the capacity of many of the ex-non-statutory force personnel to live comfortably and hygienically in the bush. This was understandable when considering the very limited amount of training that they had received in Phase 1 training and when set against the years of experience a professional soldier had had to perfect his skills. It was a concern, but one that could be addressed over time.

* * *

About a year later, I was on exercise for a couple of days on the training area in Potchefstroom, observing the culmination training of the latest group of courses. It was winter, so the days were warm, the nights cold, but the real bonus was that it was always dry – rain is a summer phenomenon in the High Veldt. I was particularly interested in the gun group as it was some of the ex-non-statutory force officers that had qualified on the previous course who were in the senior positions. It would be good to see how they were progressing and how they handled the students.

The exercise was straightforward and involved a lot of movement and bringing the guns into and out of action. It was hard work. I was working closely with Warrant Officer Bennie van Zyl, a very capable professional soldier who was hugely respected across the South African Artillery. We shared a small tent at night which he called a 'chopper tent'. I eventually found out what he meant – it was a tent issued to helicopter aircrew as part as their survival pack. It could be pulled out of its bag, which was about the size of a small thermos flask, and literally thrown to the ground. The pre-stressed lightweight ribs would spring out, and in front of your eyes a comfortable two-man tent would appear – perfect. That evening we made a final tour of the gun lines and, content that everything was in good order, retired to our 'chopper tent' for a few hours' sleep. It was to be only for a few hours because we were going to move the guns just before first light.

I woke at the appointed hour and walked to the command post to observe the action when the order to move was received. Warrant Officer van Zyl said he would pack away the tent. The next thing I knew I was almost knocked over by the said warrant officer, who hurtled into the command post, barrelling into me and whoever else had the misfortune to be in his way, grabbed something and exited equally unceremoniously. Shortly afterwards, there were two loud reports, which could only be gunfire. We burst out of the command post to see him standing over a punctured 'chopper tent', which looked worse for wear after a couple of shotgun rounds had gone through it. Having made the judgement that he had not completely lost his mind, I still approached somewhat cautiously – man, sudden outburst of unusual behaviour, shotgun and dead tent didn't necessarily add up to situation normal.

'Did it upset you?' I asked quizzically.

'No Sir,' he replied, 'but they did.' He gingerly pulled back the ruptured tent, and there were a couple of puff adders, or dead puff adders to be precise. They had been quite happily hibernating when we had decided to sleep on top of them. Our body warmth had told them it must be summer again, so they had begun to wake up. They were clearly none too impressed with the fact that their new warmth had been whisked away.

* * *

The progress of the Phase 2 artillery training for the leader group was progressing well and their performance in the field was satisfactory, accepting all the limitations placed on the newly integrated ex-non-statutory force personnel. In their game of catch-up rugby, they were generally on form. Another group that was coming on well was the young soldiers who had undergone the Phase 1 Bridging Training with the 4th Artillery Regiment. These were the 'foot-soldiers' with no previous military experience. Their Phase 1 training was completed, and they were embarking on their gunner trade training within Phase 2 training. There was nothing particularly difficult with this; it was the same as the 'sausage machine' of National Service training that used to be the routine of the old SADF. Of course there were differences, but with clear direction and good leadership the result should have been more than satisfactory; and this certainly appeared the case with the 4th Artillery Regiment. One day, during a visit, the Commanding Officer mentioned that he was required to have a battery trained to assist the police in its operations in some of the more difficult townships in North West Province. I was further intrigued when he said that he was going to use the battery that had just received the largest intake of ex-non-statutory force soldiers. Although technically out of my remit, I visited their preparatory training on a couple of occasions and it reminded me of the training we used to conduct prior to deploying to Northern Ireland, although with one or two more robust aspects!

The training was soon completed, and a couple of weeks later I visited the regiment during one of my routine trips to find that the battery had already been deployed on a couple of occasions, and very successfully too. The Commanding Officer was very pleased, and told me that the new gunners had won the admiration of the police for two main reasons. Firstly, they could identify and assist in the arrest of the top ten wanted men within a couple of days, a task the police had failed at for the last two years. This was because they knew where to look – simple really. Secondly, they knew instinctively the locations of all the shebeens.[4] I suppose it is the same as having a poacher as a gamekeeper. As I have said before, Africa is a continent full of surprises.

Chapter 13

I'm Sorry I'll Read that Again

The instruction to attend a court martial came somewhat out of the blue. As the integration process continued and had become an accepted progression, the focus was shifting to ensure that all the staff functions required of the SANDF – from human resource management through to operations – were transparent and able to give reassurance to all parties. With the potential abuses that could result from a misuse of summary justice, it was understandable that BMATT should be asked to observe various cases and inquiries, almost to add some form of endorsement. This was especially the case in any event that could become controversial, particularly in the political context, and it was also important to monitor a sample of activities that, by their nature, would be undertaken behind closed doors. This is not to suggest that the old SADF would use the traditional, some would say anachronistic, methods of summary justice to protect their own. Neither is it to suggest that there was the opportunity for the ex-non-statutory forces officers, especially those who had been commissars, to wield undue influence in the military legal environment. By this stage of proceedings, most of the bad apples – on all sides – had been removed.

The case that Patrick Zwane and I were asked to attend was more of an extended Commanding Officer's Orders session; not quite a court martial, more a Board of Inquiry with powers of punishment. The decision to open the proceedings to BMATT and ex-non-statutory forces representatives clearly meant that there was something potentially awkward going on and the SANDF needed to demonstrate that it could act in a fair manner. Patrick was very interested in the proceedings, as he had heard that it was all to do with racist insults. Even though we did not know the full facts, we were both intrigued. We simply had to be there.

The court martial was to be held in North West Province, but close to the border with Botswana in the town of Zeerust. This was the home of the 2nd Battalion of the South African Infantry (2 SAI), and they were playing their part in the training of the private soldiers. As with the 4th Artillery Regiment, the training regime was like that which had been done in the past, with obvious additional sensitivities.

* * *

Patrick was not the most enthusiastic of officers, but he was certainly fired up about this case. A Corporal van de Merwe had been accused of using racist language against a couple of the recruits undergoing one of the last courses of basic training from the Assembly Area in Wallmannsthal. So on the face of it, and certainly as Patrick interpreted it, here was an unreconstructed Boere calling black soldiers 'kaffir', or some other colourful name. And here in the North West Province, where the conservative white population had not changed their attitude in private, let alone publicly, this could be quite a feisty case. It was clear in Patrick's mind what the scenario was; to him it was an open and shut case. Patrick was determined that justice must be seen to be done for both the legal and political benefit of the defendants and the freedom movement. To be fair, it would seem to be so. I felt it was imperative that I should attend the court martial to ensure that the trial was conducted fairly and transparently for the sake of the new SANDF – but also to ensure that there was no undue pressure placed on proceedings by Patrick. Ironically, I had reasonable faith in the summary justice system, as it was very like that which we used in the British Army. However, the pressure for a verdict would come not from the circumstances or the manual of military law, but from years of alleged abuse and years of a desire for revenge.

* * *

As part of the new South Africa there were many changes, not just the new national anthem and the new flag, but a host of measures intended to bring together what President Mandela had termed the 'Rainbow Nation'. The Apartheid regime had refined division, whereas the new government wanted to develop harmony, and part of this included legally, or by a process of understanding, removing from the language such emotive words as 'kaffir'.

'Kaffir' is derived from the Arabic word *kafir* and is usually translated into English as 'infidel', or a similar word *kafara*, 'non-believer', i.e. a non-Muslim. The word was originally applied to non-Muslim black peoples encountered by Arab traders and then to other European settlers and explorers by the black population. Other sources suggest that it was used by the early British missionaries when referring to the Bantus. Bantus in this context referred to the group of Niger-Congo languages spoken in central and southern Africa, including Swahili, Xhosa and Zulu. I was also assured that the term was used by the Boer Trekkers to describe anyone who was not a Christian. Regardless of its etymological background, during the Apartheid era all such terms became deeply offensive to the black population. To call someone a 'kaffir' in South Africa post-Apartheid was asking for more than a little trouble!

* * *

The camp at Zeerust was a hive of activity. Squads of recruits were being doubled around the barracks from classroom to rifle range, from rifle range to gymnasium, and from everywhere to the drill square. It was a mixture of colours, and the appearance of the place – from the guard at the gate to the look of the camp – was 'professional'. If first impressions were anything to go by, then this was a good unit. Later in my career, when I was travelling to all the gunner regiments, I realised that my first impressions of a unit were rarely wrong. If you were well received by a smartly turned out member of the guard, who knew his or her business, directed to the right building and then met by an informed member of staff, then the chances were that the rest of the unit was equally proficient. The opposite is also sadly true. But in this case, 2 SAI looked the part.

We were met at the door of the building in which the hearing would take place by the adjutant, who introduced us to those present in the room, including an ex-MK captain who was on the staff. He was slightly in awe of two lieutenant colonels arriving on what he would have considered his patch, but he was nonetheless welcoming. He declined to discuss the case with us – which I thought was interesting, although absolutely correct – and said that he would not stay for the proceedings as it was felt that it was better that 'outside neutrals', such as Patrick and me, were there to deliver and maintain neutrality within the unit. The room in which the hearing was to take place was poorly lit but cool. There were a series of tables opposite the door, which were clearly where the President of the Board and his team would be seated, facing into the room. On either side were a couple of desks, which I assumed were there for anyone representing the accused and witnesses. Ample tea and coffee were available to one side, and we settled down to make small talk whilst we waited for the proceedings to commence.

It was not long before the President of the Board arrived. An infantry colonel, he was a tall, well-built man with a tanned face and square jaw; an almost typecast infantry commander. He was very friendly, explaining that he was keen that we were here because of the sensitive nature of the case. He gave us the background, which was as we expected. There were a series of allegations against the accused, Corporal van de Merwe, one of the section commanders in the basic training company. The accusations ranged from making his section work excessively hard to verbal abuse, including calling two members of his training section 'kaffirs'. None of us were taken in by the notion of the section being worked too hard, as we had all been through basic training; regardless of where you are in the world, the training is always challenging and you feel as though your section or platoon is always being worked harder than everyone else's. I remember my own days at Sandhurst, when the platoon colour sergeant was a member of the Parachute Regiment. He was not keen on drill. He was good at it, but he did not share the same fanatical devotion to the subject as did the other colour sergeants. So rather than 'beasting' us on the drill square whenever we did not perform as expected, he thrashed us around the training area for several miles instead. We certainly felt hard done by. Whether Corporal van der Merwe was guilty of anything excessive would come out during the hearing.

The President of the Board called the room to order and introduced Patrick and me to those present. He explained that he would conduct the proceedings by the book, and ensured that everyone understood the process. He made a point of emphasizing that the nature of the allegations against Corporal van de Merwe were highly sensitive in the current circumstances, and that they could not be treated as a case of simple name-calling. If these allegations were not addressed swiftly, then they could impact directly on the discipline and good order of the unit and its role within the integration process could be undermined. The nature of the allegations was known widely, and this board would be setting a precedent. It was clear from the mood in the room that everyone understood the potential impact of the case.

The President announced that he was ready to start and asked for the accused to be marched in. With a very familiar series of shouted orders and a mad flurry of stamping boots, the accused was brought in and came rigidly, and thunderously, to attention at his required place. If the room had not already been silenced by the cacophony of shouted orders and boots being smashed into the floor, it happened when everyone had a chance to have a good look at the accused. Corporal van der Merwe of the South African Infantry had a long and distinguished service. He had served for many years on operations and was a thorough professional; a man you wanted next to you when the proverbial hit the fan. He was tall, athletic and exceptionally smartly turned out. He just was not quite what we expected. Corporal van der Merwe, in our collective minds' eyes, was supposed to be a tall, sun-bleached blond, moustached Afrikaner, straight out of the bush. But he was not. Corporal van der Merwe was black. If not audible, there was a collective intake of breath as a significant mental recalibration took place. The script had been ripped up; to use a military analogy, no plan survives first contact – this one had not even lasted a minute. The whole room was immediately held captive by the events which were about to unfold.

The President, maintaining his composure, read out the allegations to Corporal van der Merwe. He then asked if van der Merwe understood the allegations, to which he answered, or rather replied in a sharp parade-ground volume, that he did. He was asked how he pleaded, and the response was a crisp, loud, 'Sir, Not Guilty, Sir.'

Corporal van der Merwe was informed that the witnesses would be summoned to explain their grievances, and then he would be questioned and allowed to make a statement of mitigation. He again responded in a manner which guaranteed nobody would fall asleep. I sneaked a look at Patrick, who was sitting with his mouth slightly open and with a look of utter confusion on his face. This was clearly not what he had been expecting.

* * *

There were two witnesses who were called to give evidence. They were summoned and entered, but even though they did so with the same associated drill orders being yelled out at parade square volume, their entrance could not have been more different to that of van der Merwe if it had been staged. The best description was that they shambled in. There were a few arms waved around and a shuffling of boots, but it could not be described as a sharp demonstration of drill; bearing in mind that they were nearing the end of their training it was not a good demonstration at all. The two witnesses stood there, slightly slouched and looking uncomfortable in their surroundings. Indeed, it would be fair to say that they also looked uncomfortable in their uniforms. These two soldiers could not have been more than in their early 20s. They were certainly not members of the MK who had gone into exile.

These were typical examples of youths who had been radical in the period after the release of Nelson Mandela and had no doubt been heavily involved in the rioting in the townships. They had a very loose affiliation with the MK and had received no military training prior to being processed through Wallmannsthal. They were clearly not well educated and had most probably been involved at the end of the school boycotts, which ended in 1987 but had left the education system in places like Soweto in chaos. There had been a major boycott of education, starting with the Soweto protests in 1976, which became fully fledged in the mid-1980s. The schools were the centre of revolt, with many young people embracing the destructive slogan 'liberation before education'. Unfortunately, all it did was to produce a generation that was not educated and had little respect for school or qualifications. The ANC, like all progressive political parties, embraced the notion that education could lead one out of poverty. The consequence of the protests was a lost generation, and although the protests formally ended in 1987, the results are still seen today. Nearly half of South Africa's 18–24-year-olds are neither in employment nor the education system.

The witnesses gave their evidence, recounting the type of training they had received under Corporal van der Merwe. The training they described seemed hard, but not overly so. Their evidence seemed to be based on their assumption that the military was a nine-to-five job and that they could decide which instructions to obey and to question things that did not appeal to them. Throughout their evidence, there was an underlying thread of naivety. These were two young men who had stumbled into the military, most probably to escape from the townships. It was quite clear that they did not enjoy the military environment and that they were not really suited to it, so they had reverted to their default setting, one of protest. In the questioning from the President, it soon became quite clear that the idea that these two individuals had been subjected to harsh and undue treatment was not sustainable. They had not been physically abused, nor had they been singled out for punishment. They had been subjected to rigorous training, of the type that one would expect to be given to any infantry recruit. An infantryman must be robust, and the transition from civilian to soldier starts at basic training.

With those allegations having been stated, the proceedings moved onto the subject of the racist language. The witnesses were again asked to state their allegations. They claimed that Corporal van der Merwe had frequently used offensive language, both to them as individuals and to the whole squad. When questioned, while the language quoted could be described as 'fruity', it was nothing that had not been used to recruits the world over. The witnesses were gently encouraged to get to the point and describe the actual instance of racist abuse; that is, when van der Merwe had allegedly called them 'kaffirs'. On each occasion it had been during a run or forced march. The defendants said they had found this language offensive in the extreme, and that they considered the corporal to be a racist who should not be part of the SANDF. The room was still. Here was the accusation. The witnesses were thanked for their testimony and told to remain where they were.

The President of the Board asked Corporal van der Merwe directly whether he had or had not called the defendants 'kaffirs'. There was no pause in the reply. Corporal van der Merwe just said, 'Yes, I did call them kaffirs Sir.' He then went on to deliver what can only be described as a show-stopping statement, which I will paraphrase.

Corporal van der Merwe said that he did indeed call them 'kaffirs', because he felt that was exactly what they were. He said that neither the President nor any of the white officers and soldiers had a right to call them 'kaffirs', because that was a racist term that a white man would use; but he, van der Merwe, was not white. In fact, some whites would call him a 'kaffir'. Corporal van der Merwe continued by saying that his understanding of the word 'kaffir' was an 'idle black'. It was a derogatory term, but not a racist term for a black man to use against another black man. He further said that, whilst he was a black man, he was not a 'kaffir'. He then turned to the witnesses and stated that these two were the idlest recruits he had ever experienced. They were lazy, untidy, slow and – worst of all – were disrupting the cohesion of the squad by undermining the authority of the instructing staff. They did not fit in with the other recruits and were bringing his squad into disrepute. They were bad people and a disgrace to the new South Africa. Finally, Corporal van de Merwe said that, if he had caused offence to his battalion and fellow instructors, then he was sorry, but the President must understand that these men were 'kaffirs' by his own definition.

The room was silent. Everyone was stunned by the explanation and the utter honesty of the statement. After a long pause, the President asked the witnesses if they had anything to say. They both looked stunned and, with their shoulders slumped forward, appeared humbled. They had nothing to say, so were asked to leave the room and remain in one of the waiting rooms until summoned. The President then turned to Corporal van der Merwe, telling him to also leave and wait in another room until recalled to hear the verdict. Finally, he asked that everybody apart from the Board members vacate the room and wait to be recalled. The time of deliberation had come.

The President told us that he intended to proceed by giving us his considerations on the case and then to ask us to express our opinions. He would then conclude and announce his verdict to the Board before recalling the others. He started in a very deliberate manner to run over the accusations made in the first allegations, setting them into the context of the current training regime. He identified those facts that had been presented which were irrelevant to the case and focused on the core of each. He said that he considered the witnesses were of poor character and clearly were not suited for an army career. Concluding, he said he was content that the first allegation of excessive treatment had no grounds and he would dismiss it forthwith.

The President then moved onto the second offence, that of using racist language. This clearly was a difficult conundrum. He said that, by his own admission, Corporal van der Merwe had used the term 'kaffir' on several occasions when referring to the witnesses. Although the word 'kaffir' was considered inappropriate and was discouraged, it was not technically illegal, unless used deliberately in a racially offensive context. In that case it was actionable under the offence of *crimes injuria*, which is where such language is the unlawful, intentional and serious violation of the dignity of another. As both the witnesses and the accused were Tswana, could the term be deemed to be used in a racial context? The question that had to be answered was whether, by his actions, van der Merwe had acted in a racial manner. The President wanted to hear the opinion of the Board on this matter, but he did caveat this with the statement that, regardless of the opinion of the Board members, van der Merwe had been indiscreet and he must have known that the use of the 'K-word' was against the policy of the SANDF. Corporal van der Merwe was clearly guilty of the use of inappropriate language, but whether it was used in a racist manner was going to be the crux of the matter.

With one exception, the four members of the Board considered that the action of Corporal van der Merwe was inappropriate but could not be termed as racist. The President turned to Patrick and me. Patrick squirmed a bit, so I volunteered to give my opinion first. I said that I had seen a lot of the basic training on different sites around the country, and what we were seeing here was the last of the Wallmannsthal intake. They were not the best recruits, and without doubt there were several who were not suited to military service. I had witnessed the frustration of the instructors, but I had not heard of any white instructor using such language; if there had been such an incident, then it would have been an open and shut case. It was not so here. I believed that van der Merwe should have been more aware, but I did not consider his actions to have been racist. Patrick nodded, and could not or would not justify any other conclusion.

The President then referred to the records of the defendant and witnesses, which were like chalk and cheese. Corporal van der Merwe was a good soldier with an excellent record of service and destined for further promotion. The defendants, on the other hand, had very poor progress reports. They were poor recruits and would need to have a very close eye kept on them, if they even completed training. The President had made up his mind and called everyone back into the room.

In his summing up, the President was brief. He said that he had dismissed the first count, as there was no evidence that the treatment of this squad had been different to any others. As for the second count, he found that Corporal van der Merwe was guilty. There was an audible intake of breath from the room. He turned to van der Merwe and said that, considering his experience and service, he should have understood the use of the word 'kaffir' was wrong and that such behaviour was not acceptable to the SANDF. However, he said he appreciated the frustrations of dealing with some recruits, adding that language which was not considered appropriate in polite society would be used on occasion and as a means of reprimand or exhortation in difficult and extreme conditions. He said the Army was not a primary school. In the circumstances, he did not consider that the word 'kaffir' had been used in a racial context. It was, however, completely inappropriate. He stated that as a punishment, Corporal van der Merwe would receive a formal reprimand.

He then turned to the witnesses and, in a very avuncular manner, proceeded to tell them what was and was not expected of a recruit and soldier in the infantry. He told them that their progress was poor and that, if they had any intention whatsoever of finishing their training, then they needed to think long and hard and to change their attitude. They were to be reassigned to another company.

With that, the Board concluded and the protagonists were marched out. Justice had been done, and fortunately in this case, common sense had prevailed. As we walked away, I asked Patrick why he had not said anything. He mused, then replied that he was glad he was a gunner because our recruits were so much better. This was a clever way of avoiding the issue.

* * *

As a footnote, the government in South Africa introduced legislation in 2000 dealing with hate speech.[1] Clause 10 of the legislation states: 'Subject to the proviso in Section 12 no person may publish, propagate, advocate or communicate words based on one or more of the prohibited grounds, against any person, that could reasonably be construed to demonstrate a clear intention to: (a) be hurtful; (b) be harmful or to incite harm; (c) promote or propagate hatred.' It is ironic that the words it intended to ban – such as 'kaffir', 'koelie', 'hotnot' and 'Boesman' – were not listed.

Chapter 14

Facing Reality

As time moved on, Potchefstroom, as with the whole of South Africa, was changing. There was a lot of development taking place: a new shopping mall was built and the area around the university, very close to where we lived, was being rejuvenated, with new restaurants opening on a regular basis. Over time, we noticed that the number of black people seen in the town was increasing; not just more workers, but people shopping and families enjoying themselves. If it was happening in Potchefstroom, it would be happening elsewhere in South Africa. Without doubt, there was still an endemic reluctance amongst the older people to accept change, but amongst the youngsters the change was very noticeable and freely accepted. At the same time, however, the number of poor whites was on the increase. No longer was the beggar the preserve of the black population.

There was also, of course, a change in local politics, with the ANC now having a majority on the provincial government and the local council. There were plenty of snide comments about affirmative action and mismanagement, but at the same time I heard many say that all that had happened was that a corrupt and inefficient National Party had been replaced by a corrupt and inefficient ANC. There was no real difference between the ways in which people were being governed; the only difference was the colour of the skin of the provincial leadership. This was not affirmative action but the realization of democracy.

However, real affirmative action was present in every niche of society, with a structured rebalancing of society based on representation, itself based on ethnic grouping. In the same way that Apartheid had ensured that the white population enjoyed the lion's share of appointments and opportunity, now, post-election, affirmative action was associated with white people being replaced by black people to fulfil quotas. This rebalancing was not based on merit, merely on skin colour. This was undoubtedly beginning to rankle with the middle-class white population, especially those of more liberal thinking, who saw doors being slammed shut in their children's faces. Soon there was a steady exodus of professionals to the UK, Australia and the US, and a flight of young white people to find work and education abroad. They joined the thousands who had sold up and fled South Africa in the lead-up to the elections, fearing a meltdown in society. The term 'affirmative action' soon became quite toxic in certain circles, being a catchall phrase for anything that was not working as it should. It was also beginning to be the mantra of many serving and retired ex-SADF officers and soldiers.

It was easy to nod one's head and agree. Things were not what they used to be, and things were certainly not better, but one had to stand back and start by asking the question – why? The integration of the SANDF was a political imperative, and politically the end state was to have a defence force that was no longer a threat to most of the population. These are harsh words, but they are true; the SADF was an organ of the Apartheid state and could have been used to fight against its own people. This was not an expressed intent of anyone I worked with, but a defence force is charged to protect its nation from external and internal threats. The SADF had been used for internal security duties throughout South Africa, including intervening robustly in township troubles when the police had lost control. Consequently, the SADF was considered a threat by the majority black population. It was for this reason above all others that BMATT had such a critical role. It was able to work with the new government, the new South Africa, to create the SANDF, which regardless of its final state or composition would be acceptable to the majority of South Africans. This concept, which really lay at the strategic/political level, was essential if there was to be any real chance of a successful end to the integration process. At every level, integration had proceeded along its course and resulted in members of the ex-statutory and ex-non-statutory forces working together, alongside each other, but still there was not a homogenous body. At all levels, as in the larger civilian society itself, there was very little harmonization, no merger and no real unity. So alongside integration there had to be a clear policy of affirmative action to get to the desired result, which was a defence force that reflected the society that it was charged to protect. If integration was the process by which two or more different armed forces were merged, then affirmative action was the process by which the historical imbalances were to be redressed. It was becoming apparent that BMATT would have to take a role – no matter how uncomfortable it would be – in this process of rebalancing, because once integration and affirmative action had created a new structure and composition within the SANDF, there would still be a need to encourage reconciliation and, through that, harmony. Once that had been achieved, then the SANDF would truly be ready to move forward and fulfil its mission.

One thing that was clear was that the military standards of the SADF were unlikely to be maintained, no matter how hard people tried to put a brave face on things. Once the various military forces had been integrated, and the SANDF was at the size and composition that the government had prescribed in its Defence Review, then it would be a different organization in every respect. Its composition would be more reflective of the country. But even though the transition was managed, you cannot replace like with like. The departing members of the SADF were leaving, having spent their whole career being trained, and were being replaced by ex-non-statutory force personnel who had demonstrated their ability and potential but had missed out on all those years of progressive training. The net worth of the SANDF would fall until a stage was reached in the future when there was equal opportunity, which would then take over from affirmative action. In other words, a level playing field would be created, and candidates – regardless of background or colour – would compete for appointments and promotions as equals, with the best candidate being selected. The full effect of this level playing field would only really be cemented once these equal candidates had been able to progress through the graduated training required of any professional modern military.

The maintenance of standards was seen by some as a block to proper integration and affirmative action. I would not support that premise totally, as striving for high standards at regimental level can be achieved; the South African Artillery were clear on their intent and, to a large extent, achieved it. A defence force is a sum of all its parts, and its effectiveness is judged by how well it can achieve synergy. This is achieved by the staff officers. Young soldiers and officers always start from scratch; they start with nothing but enthusiasm and then gradually gain experience. The senior staff and commanders have years of both training and experience, and this is what allows the working parts of any military organization to perform effectively. Replacing an experienced ex-SADF officer with an ex-non-statutory force officer, who has a fraction of his training and a wholly different type of experience, is not an equal or fair substitution. It is, however, a substitution that must be made, as otherwise it would still be a white SANDF; appointments based on merit would preclude the majority of black personnel because they would still be somewhere in their career training.

The figures for affirmative action are quite stark. Before any integration took place, all officers in the top five salary bands in 1991 were white, and officer ranks up to and including the rank of colonel were filled by twenty-five Africans, fourteen Indians, 123 coloureds and 7,191 white officers. By 1995, Vice Admiral Loedolff, Chief of Staff Personnel, reported that the situation in respect of the representation of non-white members had improved from 0 per cent to 19.6 per cent in the case of general officers, and from 1.6 per cent to 9.26 per cent in the case of senior officers. As these figures suggest, it was easier to be integrated as a general officer than as a senior officer. The rationale was that general officer appointments require a mixture of military and political skill, which the ex-non-statutory force candidates possessed because they made up for their lack of formal military training with huge political experience. These general officer appointments, especially within Defence Headquarters, would not necessarily impact immediately on the operational effectiveness of the SANDF.

One of the major differences between the SADF/SANDF and the British Army is political allegiance. The British Army is apolitical; it serves its civilian political masters regardless of the party in power. In South Africa, the SADF had a very strong link to the National Party, which could be seen in the benefits of patronage. This was replaced by an association with the ANC, with an ANC government having to find posts for certain people who played a strategic role in helping them to win the election. The move of General Nyanda into the government once he retired from the SANDF was testament to this intimate relationship. In fact, it has been observed that the MK lost many of its higher-calibre members to politics before the integration process started.

Has the integration process and affirmative action worked? This is a difficult question to answer, and I may suggest the answer is both yes and no!

I could say that yes, the integration of the non-statutory forces with the SADF has worked. The process was successful in general, and by 2003 the composition of the SANDF was 64 per cent Black, 25 per cent White, 10 per cent Coloured and 1 per cent Asian. When you compare this to the South African population at the time – 64.6 per cent Black, 24.4 per cent White, 10.2 per cent Coloured and 0.75 per cent Asian – then it is a pretty fine match. So yes, the integration process did work, although it took longer than estimated; it was eventually declared complete in 2003. The peaceful integration of statutory and non-statutory forces happened, so it was a success. The SANDF is now under civilian control, has a composition to reflect the nation, and its leadership is predominantly black. The transformation happened in a unique set of circumstances; in fact South Africa coined the term Security Sector Reform before it had been recognized anywhere else. In addition, when one considers that in an ideal world a new defence structure and mission would be in place before integration was attempted, in South Africa the transformation and downsizing took place during integration. It was a bold venture, but it worked, at least in theory.

I could also, however, answer that no, the process has not worked, as there have been legacy problems which are yet to be resolved. The major issue is that the new South Africa is a reluctant hegemony and seems to avoid playing its regional role as many would wish. This problem is primarily political, a reluctance of one black government to exert undue influence over or to criticize a fellow black government – Zimbabwe being the classic case in point. Furthermore, the overwhelming military supremacy and technical superiority that South Africa used to have is no longer present. The South African intervention into Lesotho, Operation *Boleas*, in September 1998 highlighted how far the SANDF has fallen back from its peak of regional prowess.

As mentioned above, it was easier to appoint ex-NSF officers to general rank positions, but this soon resulted in an inflation in ranks – which, to be fair, had started in the SADF during the period of the wars in Angola and Namibia. In 2001 there were 193 general officers, and by 2003 there were 206, with one general for every 291 defence force members (in the US, it is one general to every 2,428 personnel). As the SANDF continued to reduce in number, the general officers increased; by 2009, there were 218. There was also a reduction in the effectiveness of the South African Air Force. Between 2001 and 2009, 298 pilots resigned, leaving only twenty fighter pilots in the whole Air Force. In 2009, it could fill only 237 out of 369 pilot posts, but even in this dire situation not all suitable white candidates were accepted into training as there was a need to maintain the racial quotas. The problems were not only within the Air Force, as the Army was only able to properly deploy four out of its eleven infantry battalions. The disorganized performance of the SANDF in Operation *Boleas* in 1988 and the poor standard of some units on peacekeeping operations in the Democratic Republic of the Congo called into question the capability of the force and begged the question of how long it would take to get to the position where equal opportunities could overcome political affirmative action.

The suggestion that BMATT could be utilized in a policy of reconciliation was an interesting one, but one that was outside our remit. We were there to assist with the integration and help to resolve disputes within our own areas of responsibility, but enabling or assisting in the act of reconciliation at a formal level was very different. The BMATT's emphasis shifted as the weight of effort of the SANDF moved from the assessment and selection processes at the PMORDs to the Bridging Training. On the ground, we were monitoring the training and became immersed in the minutiae of daily life of the units within our areas of responsibility. The senior staff at BMATT HQ became more involved in addressing the issues of the inequalities and contradictions of the integration process at Defence Headquarters and the various service headquarters and within the realm of the Army Headquarters, which was bearing the brunt of the integration within the SANDF. BMATT was therefore operating at two different levels of effect. Without doubt, we on the ground were dealing with the realpolitik of daily issues, of personality and dogma, whilst those in Pretoria were becoming rapidly involved in national and service politics. If there was to be a reconciliation impact from BMATT, it was to be delivered on the ground as opposed to along the corridors in Pretoria or Cape Town.[1]

There was no remit for BMATT to deliver reconciliation, so there was no clear direction from BMATT HQ as to how to approach reconciliation; as each of us on the ground was dealing with totally unique circumstances, there was little we could be given as a doctrinal steer. It was up to us to make judgement calls as to whether we could or should become involved. One factor we had to consider on each occasion, as we did with every other aspect of our role, was whether the transparency, neutrality and integrity of BMATT would be threatened by any individual action. It was not as simple as weighing up whether to act if there were issues of unfairness or discrimination – in these areas, our remit was clear. Reconciliation was complicated, potentially fraught with difficulties, and could only be approached if all parties were prepared to engage in it, and most importantly if one's involvement would do no harm. I also found that in many cases, the ongoing Truth and Reconciliation Committee was looked at to provide the panacea, but what this really meant was that individuals either did not recognize that there was a problem or simply did not want to see a problem.

It is no surprise that only once was I asked to help in finding some form of roadmap for reconciliation.

As I mentioned before, I was very fortunate to be working with the South African Artillery. They had approached the integration process objectively from the start. By being open and relatively flexible, they had been able to move well ahead of the pack as far as Bridging Training and integration were concerned. They were aided in this by being relatively small, so there was much more control of change and in many respects it was easier to bring ex-non-statutory force personnel up to the designated standards. There had been an attempt at affirmative action, although I would suggest that nobody would have labelled it as such, with the appointment of an ex-non-statutory force officer to command the prestigious P Battery. As I mentioned in a previous chapter, this appointment was declined for personal reasons. It did, however, demonstrate very openly the intent. Even with a progressive leadership and a clear end state, the ability to achieve a sense of 'family' that is the lifeblood of a fighting regiment was still missing. The 'us and them' was still present.

The Commandant of the Artillery School discussed this dilemma with Patrick and me. We all knew that, as far as the overall integration process was concerned, the artillery was a success; but we also knew that this division was going to be a millstone to any further progress. The question was simple: how were we going to encourage or force this final merger? It was a case of 'you can take a horse to water, but you can't make it drink'. We all agreed that it was a clear example of the necessity of reconciliation; we needed to bring the two groups together, talk over the grievances and get on with life together. But it was so much easier said than done, and we just went around and around in circles. Eventually we decided that, as the staff worked well together in the classroom, in the gun sheds and in the field, it clearly was not a professional issue. The one thing they did not do was socialize together. This, we decided, was the weakness but also the key. During morning coffee, each group kept to themselves, and the same happened at mealtimes. There was no social interaction, and at the end of the day everyone went their own way. Our solution was to organize a team-building drinks party as an icebreaker. We started with the young officers – majors and below – and had a three-line whip the following week to attend the Rhino Bar at the Artillery School after work. What the invitees did not know was that they were not going to leave until they were mates. It was quite a gamble, but we decided that everyone concerned could look after themselves and were quite able to say what they thought. The secret was to get them talking while making sure that no fighting broke out.

The evening came around, and we watched as the junior officers trooped into the Rhino Bar. It was like witnessing a high school dance, with the girls on one side and the boys on the other. Our intention was to get all sides to mix, with the Commandant delivering a 'State of the Nation' address, after which the senior officers, with Patrick and me, would break out, grab small groups and bring them together. At first it was as painful as drawing teeth, but after a few drinks, one of the ex-NSF captains in my group remarked how funny it was that he had been taught the vehicle check point (or VCP) drills in his Phase 1 Bridging Training and that they were the same that he had been briefed on when he was infiltrating into South Africa many years ago. He joked that it was no wonder infiltration had been so easy. A moderately heated discussion ensued, with pieces of paper being grabbed and sketches drawn, fingers being pointed forcibly at a sketched piece of road and old campaigns retold. This went on for about twenty minutes before the first laugh was heard, after which it was a case of swapping vastly exaggerated 'war stories'. The ice was broken, and suddenly the men began to realize – whether subliminally or not – that they were just young men who wanted to be soldiers and serve their country, and that perhaps most important of all, none of them had wanted a civil war.

There had been doubters amongst the leadership as to whether this strategy would work, but there was a huge dent in the beer stocks by the end of the night and everyone went home happy. Although these men might not have become the best of friends that evening, they had moved on from being the best of enemies. Progress, they say, is generally measured in small steps – but this was quite a major leap in the right direction.

Chapter 15

We Will Be Back

In Potchefstroom, we were measuring progress in mostly every area, but in Pretoria it was not so. It was in Pretoria, with the oversight provided through the National Defence Headquarters, where trends, bottlenecks and problems could be identified across the whole of the SANDF and within each of the armed services. It was here that the stress points in the integration process had to be acknowledged and rectified.

On the ground, we were operating at very much the tactical level. We were seeing snapshots. These incidents and occurrences, whilst impacting immediately upon the local process, were just a few statistics for the National Defence HQ staff to analyze and assess. The individual BMATT representatives were blissfully isolated; whilst fully aware of the issues within their own area of responsibility, each was unaware of what else was happening across the country. Weekly reports summarizing activity in our areas of responsibility were sent to BMATT HQ in Pretoria. The reports involved filling in tables detailing the number of personnel undergoing the various phases of training and highlighting any significant issues, observations or concerns. I would also add a 'Court and Social' section just to make sure that BMATT HQ knew that the Lawford family was still alive. All the reports would be collated and used as grist for the mill for the Commander and his staff to use where they saw fit. It would also provide a means of checks and balances to cross-reference against the reports coming through the SANDF chain of command. It was a sensible way of doing business in an era where the fax machine was the most effective means of communication; using the post was lengthy and unreliable, and it was well before the age of the internet.

I always showed a copy of my report to the Commandant at the Artillery School to underline my transparency and neutrality. I worked on the theory that anything I put in my report would have already been discussed with the Commandant, and regardless of the outcome would not be a surprise to him. This worked well. However, I was equally conscious that for BMATT to operate effectively there had to be a series of relationships. I knew that in some locations there was not a harmonious relationship between BMATT staff and SANDF officers. This was generally because BMATT staff had identified fundamental flaws in the integration process or the conduct of individuals, and this neutral criticism was not welcome. I was fortunate in that I had a good relationship with all the parties; this allowed issues to be discussed openly and frankly, and then rectified. In other locations, however, the personalities of the individuals hindered the creation of a harmonious and objective working environment. This was especially so for the some of the six-month rotational staff who had very little time to acclimatize, to get to know the procedures and forge a working relationship with the numerous people directly – or indirectly – involved in the integration process. Added to this, there was the inevitable percentage on all sides who were not blessed with a diplomatic personality, and the consequence of this was that suspicion could easily overcome transparency.

Although reports went up the chain of command, very little came back down. The only way to get a feel of the larger picture was to visit Pretoria, which I tried to do at least once a month, or to receive a back-brief whenever Brigadier Chris Elliott, the new Commander, or his deputy, Colonel Paul Davis, came to or through Potchefstroom. This was quite sensible, because the faxes we used were unclassified, and without doubt the collated data and some of the observations were now becoming sensitive. This was especially the case when the same issues were being reported and there was no remedial action taken. In addition, flaws in the process were being identified. This was especially so in the training of those ex-non-statutory forces officers being fast-tracked through the system. Not only were they having to crash their way through the routine career courses expected of their rank within their arm or service, but they were also having to go through the staff and combined-arms training appropriate to their rank and future appointment. Without doubt, too much was being asked of these individuals in too short a time. They were attending these courses, not in isolation, but with their 'new contemporaries'. The latter had received regular and progressive training throughout their service to date,, unlike the ex-non-statutory force officers who had galloped through the whole of the professional training in just a couple of years.

The system was not designed to generate failure, but the challenges faced by the individuals, and the blatant political pressure to effect change now, was creating a catastrophe waiting to happen. Much of this was coming to the fore at the South African Army Combat Training Centre in Lohatlha. The ex-non-statutory force personnel were struggling and simply did not have the experience to be able to perform to anywhere near the same standard as the former SADF personnel. There was a difficult atmosphere and all parties were dissatisfied; it was becoming almost a regular occurrence that ex-non-statutory force personnel complained about being unfairly treated, whilst ex-statutory force personnel would claim that the ex-non-statutory force personnel were incompetent and not good enough to assume command of sub-units or units. The opinion of BMATT staff in attendance was that expectations were too high and that the instruction at Lohatlha had to be amended both in content and the manner of its delivery. This was very badly received and caused a good deal of discussion and indeed argument. When it was not addressed, the Commander took the case to the appropriate service chief. He was aided in this by the weekly reports that documented observations and the lack of action. These observations gave justice to the weekly reports. The reports in themselves provided a very accurate, neutral picture of how the integration process was proceeding, and perhaps most importantly, a regular record of what and where progress was not being made.

Whereas at the local level it was acceptable for me to share my observations with the Commandant, it was not appropriate, or indeed sensible, for these to be shared with all the team. When issues became intractable and there was an unwillingness to either address issues or recognize that there were issues in the first place, then the report would become politically sensitive, especially if individuals had to be named. In this case, the report had to be delivered in person to the Commander. I was aware that in some areas there were very heated discussions between BMATT and senior members of the SANDF, especially in the South African Army, which was a result of issues being escalated from the local to the national level. There was a simple method of dealing with incidents that BMATT assessed were contrary to the spirit, or process, of integration: the BMATT representative at the location in question worked with the local commanders and the ex-non-statutory force representative to resolve the issue. If this was unsuccessful, and if either the nature of the incident was sufficiently severe or there were repetitions, then the BMATT service commander would take this up with the appropriate division within the service headquarters. If there was still no satisfactory conclusion, then the service commander had access to the chief of that service. And if there was still no resolution then the Commander would raise the issue with the senior staff in SANDF HQ. As we learned right at the beginning, it was all about creating an environment of trust and transparency. Pivotal to this was communication. At my level, I had regular meetings with all the commanding officers and their training staff, and at least once a month I would meet with the Commander at North West Command. At the higher level, Colonel Davis tried to have regular meetings with the Chief of the Army. These meetings were often seen by members of the SANDF as a means for BMATT to complain. In some cases, if units were not delivering on their mission, then there might be some truth in that impression. However, most saw it as a means to communicate face to face, to bring out the positives and to comment on where more work was needed. Most important of all was that communication channels had to be kept open. Of course, at all levels, it also provided the SANDF with a reciprocal channel of communication. I should emphasize that in most meetings, I tried to ensure my ex-non-statutory force representative was present.

I must admit I assumed that a similar SANDF reporting system was in place informing the chain of command about integration, including reporting dialogue with BMATT.

* * *

The military oversight of the integration process at the national level was through the Integration Committee, on which BMATT had a seat. The Integration Committee had two sub-committees: the Integration Working Group, which was responsible for the day-to-day work of the Integration Committee, and the Personnel Working Group, which dealt with personnel matters on behalf of the committee and the Integration Working Group. The political oversight was provided by the Joint Parliamentary Committee on Defence, while its Standing Committee provided members of the Integration Oversight Committee. The Integration Oversight Committee ensured that any matter referred to Parliament and the Joint Parliamentary Committee was properly handled and that the subject matter was vested in the spirit of the original intent of the Joint Military Co-ordination Council.

BMATT was charged with reporting to the Joint Standing Committee on Defence in Parliament that sat as the Parliamentary Integration Oversight Committee. It was at these committee meetings that the Commander would report his observations and concerns, with the unique and protected position of a neutral observer appointed by the South African government. The Commander could express what he observed and understood the situation to be, and on occasions it was not good news for certain individuals. But regardless of the message that was delivered, it was the presence of BMATT that ultimately gave credibility to the integration process. This is not to say that the BMATT team ensured the success of the integration process, but it gave credibility to the process that had been drafted and agreed upon in the heady atmosphere of 1994. Of course, hindsight is a wonderful thing, and without doubt if one had to start again then many aspects of the integration process would have to be done differently. However, a plan had had to be developed and implemented to deliver a unique political solution to a military problem, and the credibility of the process – for both internal and external consumption – was critical to its success.

Right from the start, transparency was BMATT mantra. Every member of the team had to be neutral and work within the parameters of the integration process; one did not and could not take sides. Throughout the process, everyone had to be objective; if any of the integrating parties were out of line, the team was required to inform them as such. This applied to us on the ground as much as it did to the Commander in Pretoria. Whereas most of those involved in the integration process were content with BMATT's impartiality and its ability to adjudicate fairly, there were some who did not agree. Colonel Lucas Sigela, who had been a member of the APLA, stated that BMATT was not a neutral observer but served to protect the interests of the SADF at the expense of APLA and MK members.

With its neutrality, BMATT could report incidents to the National Defence Headquarters to ensure that they were in the public domain and not hidden in either a military or political wasteland. As mentioned earlier, we could warn about the problems at the South African Army Combat Training Centre in Lohatlha. The team was also able to report about the growing racial tensions in the 1st Battalion of the South African Infantry (1 SAI) in Bloemfontein, which needed to be addressed immediately by all parties. Matters were only raised at the highest military or political levels when the Commander deemed it necessary and all other means of addressing the issue had been tried without success. At the end of the day, BMATT was physically located in South Africa and it needed to ensure good relations with all parties, but this relationship required the moral courage to inform both bad and good news. It also needed the moral courage of the receiving parties to take criticism and act to address the issues in the spirit of the integration process.

There was one explosive example of the need for BMATT to be prepared to confront issues, deliver bad news and take a stand on a matter of principle. This occurred with the delivery of a BMATT report to the Joint Standing Committee on Defence in 1988. The report had been dated 1 October 1997 and had followed the standard format of 'Introduction', 'Reports on Assembly Area Activity', 'Bridging Training', 'Demobilization', 'Rationalization', 'Special Issues', 'Administration' and 'Outlook'. The report noted that, during the period in question, the SANDF had been grappling with a Defence Review, a transformation process and the management of a significant cut in the Defence Budget. BMATT had considered that, because of these activities, integration had moved down the SANDF order of priority. In the 'Introduction', Colonel Davis, as the acting Commander, also noted that there had been 'a marked change in attitude towards integration. On reflection BMATT believes that this hardening of attitudes towards ex Non-Statutory Force (NSF) integratees mostly seen in the South African Army (SAA) and South Africa Medical Service (SAMS) can be traced back to the first quarter of the year.' He continued: 'Despite these developments the processes of integration, demobilization and voluntary rationalization have continued despite some disputes which have increased in number during this period.' It was clear that all was not well, and the BMATT team assessed that this was as a direct result of integration falling down the order of priority.

The report went on to detail the perceived progress in the areas of 'Assembly Area Activity', 'Bridging Training', 'Demobilization' and 'Rationalization', which was routine. The controversy came in the section on 'Special Issues'. Having reported on the progress of the integration of the Former Statutory Forces (FSF), encompassing ex-SADF and ex-TBVC Forces, and the establishment of the Equal Opportunities Directorate, the report then highlighted the changing attitudes towards integration in paragraph 18:

> 'We have formed a clear impression that the attitudes of some top-level management in the SAA (South African Army) and SAMS (South African Medical Services) has hardened noticeably towards ex NSF integration since our last report. Since then we have had to raise 'yellow cards' and a 'red card' on a number of integration issues where we have identified foul play. 'Yellow cards' have been raised on APLA Placement Board Appeals (now resolved). The Special Course for former NSF

> Senior Officers (in the process of being resolved), the Army's postponement of Phase 1 BT (Bridging Training) (not yet resolved) and others. A 'red card' has been raised after SAMS refused to accept BMATT adjudication on 2 officers at Placement Boards on 16 and 17 Jul. This was unprecedented and has caused much acrimony. On 1 Oct the Chairman of the IC has stated that if SAMS still wanted to overturn the adjudications that they should refer the matter back to the original Placement Board. Since the beginning of the year we have noted that there are an increasing number of ex NSF personnel who are now joined by a number of ex SADF officers who feel that the former NSF members are not being fairly treated. After nearly 3½ years of integration no one, including ourselves, can help but notice little in the physical structure of Army training institutions to show any ex NSF ownership. Very few room names, street names, flags, symbols, pictures or traditions come from the NSF. Thus, many of the ex NSF firmly feel they are being absorbed rather than integrated. The implications of this are far reaching.'

No matter which way one looks at the above paragraph, it was explosive, especially in the political environment in which the integration process sat. But it was not a shot fired from a loose cannon; it was a statement that had to be made. If it had been issued without consultation, then it would have been dangerous, but every fact stated was backed up by previous reports and recorded in minutes of the Integration Committee and the Integration Working Group. It should have been a wake-up call. But it was not, and the ensuing fight ended up with the resignation of Lieutenant General Reginald Otto, Chief of the South African Army.

There had been a growing perception that attitudes had been hardening, and without doubt there had been pockets of resistance to change, especially in locations far from the gaze of National Defence Headquarters. BMATT itself had a part to play in this because, as the team had become progressively smaller, its ability to cover all the Bridging Training locations became less. This was exacerbated as the process of integration had become larger in that Bridging Training was being conducted in many more locations. I was responsible for all the units within the whole of the North West Province. It was fortunate that four of the major units were in Potchefstroom, but my area of responsibility was still just under 105,000km², almost five times bigger than Wales! Regardless of the presence of BMATT, it was the SANDF that was delivering the integration process. It was therefore the SANDF chain of command that had to ensure that the transition was being managed correctly and any instances of ill-discipline or racism were stamped out vigorously. In fact, the final paragraph in the BMATT report states:

> 'As the international monitors of SANDF it is tempting for BMATT to become totally immersed on integration matters and oblivious to enormous chan[g]e occurring elsewhere within the SANDF. As much momentum has moved to other areas it would seem that integration has become a lower SANDF priority. Firm leadership is required to stem the present trend and to put the whole process firmly back on course.'

Lieutenant General Otto did not accept the report and had several bad-tempered exchanges with the Commander, at one stage claiming that Colonel Davis had a personal vendetta against him. By the time of the Joint Standing Committee on Defence meeting in May 1998, Lieutenant General Otto still had not discussed the report with either the Minister or Deputy Minister of Defence. Although he had talked it through with the Chief of Defence and his own Army Staff, he believed that the report reflected BMATT not following the normal means of communication with his staff at Army HQ, as well as BMATT personnel on the ground not dealing with the local provincial chains of command. It was surprising that he should take this line, as in one of the other papers published by the committee in May 1998 was the formal BMATT letter to Lieutenant General Otto dated 18 November 1997, almost six months prior to the committee meeting. The opening paragraph of the BMATT letter clearly indicates the tension that existed at the time:

> 'It is against my better judgement, and I believe not wholly in the interest of integration, that I submit to your request (made on the telephone at 1015 hrs on Wed 12 Nov 97) for further information concerning the recent BMATT PIOC report. I had hoped to brief you in the way traditionally adopted for Ministers and Chief SANDF which consisted of a verbal briefing. You have rejected this. Furthermore, you have asked me to be precise and give you all the facts, stating occurrences, names and dates.'

Two further extracts highlight that matters were becoming serious:

> 'If adhering to the requirements of the MOU involves us questioning the competence of certain officers involved in the integration process, so be it.'
>
> 'You also told me on the telephone that you intend to carry out a full inquiry, once I have furnished you with the details that you requested. Earlier this year a similar exercise was done by the Army Inspector General (IG). While carrying out his investigation he did not, at any time approach the source of the information: the Comd or DComd of BMATT. The IG produced a report which contained a number of factual errors and some mis-perceptions which Brigadier C H Elliott brought to your attention in writing. While carrying out the inquiry the IG met a BMATT officer in the OFS Command. The outcome of this meeting was a letter of complaint from BMATT officer. Brigadier C H Elliott did not act upon this complaint then in the interests of integration but, as you want all the facts, I now enclose the letter at Flag 0. I sincerely hope that if there is to be another investigation, that the investigating officer follows normal internationally recognised norms, and during his inquiry questions the source of the criticism, which in this case is Comd BMATT.'

By pursuing the issue, Lieutenant General Otto unintentionally drew attention to two major problems that the BMATT reports had been highlighting to the Integration Committee and the Integration Working Group: the hardening of racial tensions, especially in the Free State, and the extraordinary lack of consistency of courts martial sentencing. From being issues supposedly being addressed within the SANDF chain of command, they were catapulted into the political arena and right on to the desk of the Minister of Defence, Joe Modise.

The result was quite revealing and not only justified BMATT's role but also emphasized the need to keep open lines of communication and to have open, frank and honest reporting. The BMATT officer in the Free State had been reporting his concerns about the hardening of attitudes, especially in the 1 SAI in Tempe. This had been staffed through the correct channels and, as the paragraph above states, an inquiry was held, but with no reference to BMATT, which had highlighted the concerns in the first place. The BMATT officer concerned had written formally to the Commander about the way he had been treated by the inquiry, but the Commander had not pursued the issue at the time 'in the interests of integration'. Now the letter was in the public domain. In effect, complaints about 'stonewalling and bureaucratic blockage of integration and transformation by elements in the highest echelons of the SANDF … [and] actions by old-guard elements in the Army attempting to retard transformation and integration' were shown to have been ignored by the Chief of the Army. Lieutenant General Otto went on to say that BMATT was 'sabotaging' the integration process and was involved in 'formatting trouble between the former statutory (SF) and non-statutory forces'. The Minister of Defence rejected these quite outrageous claims.

Further concerns were highlighted over the differences between courts martial sentences awarded to ex-SADF and ex-non-statutory forces personnel. Two cases were quoted; firstly, the case of 187 ex-non-statutory forces soldiers who had refused to report for training at Tempe and had been found guilty of mutiny. Sentences varied from demotion to dishonourable discharge. The other case involved a white ex-SADF soldier who had assaulted three ex-non-statutory forces superiors; the sentence was a reprimand. The Minister of Defence commented on the latter:

> 'The SA army cannot afford incidents which appear to result from racism … one wonders about the message that this slap on the wrist has sent to other members of the army.'

This would have been difficult for BMATT members, but it was a necessary engagement that proved the team's transparency and commitment to the integration process. It may not have won the team many friends with the 'old-guard', but it reminded everyone why they were there. BMATT stayed on but Lieutenant General Otto resigned.

* * *

The following year, on 16 September 1999, Lieutenant Sibusiso Madubela shot dead six white military colleagues and a white female civilian at the Tempe base of 1 SAI. Madubela was shot dead by one of those he had also shot and wounded. It was clear that this was a racially motivated attack. What followed was a wide-ranging inquiry into the incident and the related issues within the SANDF, ordered by the new Minister of Defence, Patrick Lekota. After the murders, there was a break-in at the barracks and a minibus was stolen; the suspects were members of the Afrikaner Weerstandsbeweging (AWB), who painted on the wall, 'We will be back'.

Chapter 16

Farewell and Adieu

They do say that all good things must come to an end, and our stay in South Africa was no exception. A career in the British Army is structured; it is deemed essential that you have a regular series of postings, some of which are in command of soldiers, but mostly they are a series of staff appointments in headquarters or in the Ministry of Defence. These postings are generally for two years, as was my posting to South Africa. However, at that moment in my career, I was looking at promotion to lieutenant colonel, which would normally require an absolute minimum of one posting on the staff and one at command. If you were lucky enough to be picked up having just had one posting for two years on the staff and one at command, then you were destined for stardom. My aspirations were humbler, without being unduly pessimistic. I believed that I had the potential for command at the rank of lieutenant colonel, and whereas I would love to command a regiment, I was realistic enough to understand that our posting to South Africa – no matter how exciting it had been – was not one that had necessarily kept me in the eyes of the selectors. It was therefore quite important that I had a career review before I decided on my next step, or before a decision was made for me, so I asked Colonel Davis, as my line manager, for advice. He agreed that I should have proper advice from the personnel staff in the Military Secretary's department; not just from those managing my regiment's affairs, but also from the staff branch that was responsible for the selection of officers for promotion to lieutenant colonel, their subsequent postings and selection for command. They would know where I stood on the promotion ladder. Colonel Davis discussed this with the Commander, who, as it happened, had been considering getting proper career counselling for all of BMATT's permanent Army staff.

The solution came a few weeks later. A good friend of the Commander was highly placed in the Military Secretary's staff. It just so happened that he was coming to South Africa on holiday, and the Commander convinced him to combine a little work with pleasure. He obliged and agreed to interview everybody. This was the ideal solution for me, as my posting was due to end in about six months' time.

I went along to the interview with a certain degree of confidence, based on my personal assessment of where I stood alongside my peers. However, I left the interview stunned and more than a little bemused. The Commander was in his office and, seeing me leave the interview room, called me over and then shut the door. He asked me to sit down and tell him how it had gone. I said it had not gone exactly as I had expected; in fact it had been disappointing. I had been told that because of having had this job in South Africa, I would not get a chance of promotion for at least five years. This would place me out of contention for any kind of command opportunity in my regiment. He had in effect told me that my time spent in South Africa had ended my career. To be fair to the Commander, he was somewhat taken aback. He said that this had not been his impression. In his opinion, I had performed well – very well – and he had rated me as the most effective major on his staff. He had recommended me for promotion as soon as possible and had strongly recommended me for command of a regular artillery regiment. Now we were faced with a quandary; here was a high-flying brigadier who was having his judgement questioned. Brigadier Elliott then took the only option available to him, an option that I was to use in similar situations later in my career when faced with such peculiarities in the personnel system. He said, 'Leave it to me, I will find out what is going on and then I'll get back to you as soon as possible.'

I left his office with the clear impression that he would do exactly this, but I was also aware that while we were in South Africa, many of my contemporaries were busy earning their spurs in the civil war in Bosnia. I realized that I could eventually end up as a victim of someone else's war. Leaving conjecture behind, I reflected on the conversation that I had just had. If the reading of my tea leaves was correct, then there were two options available to me. Firstly, I could throw all the teddy bears out of my cot, resign my commission and find a job in civvy street; on the other hand, I could look on the bright side of life and plan the rest of my career in the sunshine. I drove back to Potchefstroom that afternoon, mulling over the conversations and the options available to me. It was clear that there was no point rushing into anything, or certainly not until the Commander had spoken to the Military Secretary's staff.

I was back in Pretoria about a fortnight later, and Colonel Davis asked me to go to Army Headquarters to see him. Earlier that morning, the

Commander had spoken to him and briefed him on the conversation that he had with the Military Secretary's staff about my future. He had asked Colonel Davis to discuss it with me as the Commander had to fly back to the UK that night. Apparently, there had been a mix up of messages. I was in fact in line for promotion either that coming year or the year after, and yes, I was in contention for command. It had been suggested that, in order to minimize the disruption to my family, my posting would be extended for a further year in South Africa. Both the Commander and Colonel Davis were happy with the proposal, as it meant being able to retain an experienced member of the team whilst BMATT was reducing in size.

* * *

After a further year had passed and I had only six months left on my posting, I asked Colonel Davis what my next move should be. The promotions board to lieutenant colonel had sat and the results were not to be released for another couple of weeks. The Military Secretary's staff were quite clear that there was an embargo until the release date. Colonel Davis agreed that it was worthwhile exploring options, and he would speak to the postings branch the next day. The message he received back suggested that I was being considered for a technical staff appointment in the procurement area in Bristol, very close to Trisha's parents. This was exciting as it suggested that I was to be promoted, and was also geographically convenient with the turmoil necessarily associated with returning to the UK. It was now just a question of sitting back and waiting. However, it was not long before I received a telephone call from my regimental postings branch. I was, with a certain amount of expectation and gently suppressed excitement, waiting to hear that I had been promoted. Therefore, when my desk officer told me that the Director Royal Artillery[1] was keen that I should go as second-in-command to one of two regiments, both of which were commanded by people I knew very well, I was somewhat taken aback. This was not promotion – this was another major's job. Apparently, I had done very well on the board, but had just missed out on a promotion. The Director had a new policy whereby people knocking on the promotion door could usefully fill a year as a second-in-command. To be the second-in-command is a thankless job at the best of times, and I decided this was just not for me and told the desk officer as such. The conversation ended, and I was quite clear that he had gathered that I was far from pleased – a prime example of British understatement.

They often say that good things come to those who wait, and about a fortnight later my desk officer rang back and said that he had spoken to the Director Royal Artillery, who had understood my decision. The Director had then selected me to be sent as a company commander to the Royal Military Academy, Sandhurst. This is a very high-profile job, as all my regiment's previous incumbents had been promoted after a year and subsequently gone off to command regiments. I said I would get back to him as soon as I had discussed the matter with Trisha. The following day, I returned his call and accepted the Sandhurst appointment. The downside was that I learnt the appointment had to be filled in six weeks' time. It would appear that my exit from South Africa was going to be as speedy as my entrance.

It was a great sadness to leave South Africa. As a family, we had fallen in love with the wonderful country and its people. We genuinely felt as though we had been witnesses to a part of history, and so fortunate to see world-changing events at first-hand.

But it would be wrong of me to conclude this story without Africa having its last say.

As I stated above, when I had had my first career interview and was told my career was over, my first instinct was to throw all my teddy bears out of my cot. I did not do that. However, it would be fair to say that I did just that, in a spectacular fashion, after the final phone call about becoming a second-in-command. Trisha and I had agreed that enough was enough. I was furious – and made the decision to resign my commission the next morning. The next morning came along, accompanied by quite a thick head as I drove to the Artillery School with the single-minded intention of ringing the Commander and informing him that I was resigning. I had rehearsed my reasoning and was quite content that I was doing the right thing. I went into my office, closed the door and picked up the telephone. I dialled the Commander's number, but it rang and rang until eventually the Chief Clerk picked up the phone. When I said I wanted to speak to the Commander, he replied that the Commander had set off first thing that morning to Cape Town to brief the Parliamentary Committee. He would therefore not be available until late that afternoon at the earliest. The clerk then asked politely if he could help in any way? I said, equally politely, 'Thank you, but not on this occasion'. I then rang the Army Headquarters to speak to Colonel David, but again the phone just rang and rang. I eventually got through to one of the South African clerks, who told me that the colonel was driving to Bloemfontein and would not be there until the afternoon. I was somewhat lost for words, having been so full of them earlier. Here I was, about to make a spectacular announcement, and bugger me, no one was there to listen!

Dejected, I drove back home to find Trisha looking very anxious. She had been trying to contact me, but my phone was always engaged. Little was she to know it was engaged fruitlessly. She said that when I had driven out that morning, no sooner had I left than our friend Ashleigh had arrived looking very flustered, standing on the threshold clutching a bag of bones. He hustled Trisha into the house, refusing coffee, and made her sit down. Many years before, Ashleigh had trained as a Sangoma,[2] and although we had only rarely been aware of his psychic abilities, on this occasion he immediately went into a trance. He then spoke very clearly to Trisha, saying, 'Huw is considering resigning today. Tell him that would be a mistake and he must not do it! You must stop him now before it's too late! Everything will work out fine.' And with that he got up and left.

Our departure from South Africa went as smoothly as it could have done. The packers arrived within a few days to box up our possessions, which had grown tremendously, swollen by numerous carved animals, pots and assorted memorabilia from our travels. In the final few days I had been given many presents, ranging from rugby shirts to a Zulu *assegai* (spear) and, as a complete surprise just before we left, a Martini Henry rifle from the Zulu Wars. The packers worked hard, and piece-by-piece our worldly goods were placed into an ISO container, sealed and the lorry disappeared down the driveway. The dog and cats had been rehomed, and we sat there with our suitcases, feeling somewhat forlorn. The end had come swiftly, and I am not sure that any of us were quite sure how we would find England when we returned. But unlike the period leading to our departure from Lincolnshire, there was very little time to ponder. We were off to Pretoria for a night in a hotel before being picked up and flown home: two adults, two young girls, eight suitcases and a Martini Henry rifle – this time the Bergen had been confined to the sea freight!

Epilogue

The luxury of writing a book is that you remember all those incidents, both good and bad, that have helped shape you and how you look at life and the world in general. Clearly, hindsight does enter into it to a greater or lesser degree, but you strive to be conscious that to write with hindsight is not always to tell the true story. I have changed some names for sensible reasons, and I am sure I may have made some errors or forgotten some nuances. I am also certain that I have appeared critical of some, especially on the British side; I think with reason. But without doubt, I think that I was incredibly lucky to have the opportunity to experience South Africa at that particular moment in its history. It was a time when one had to live by one's wits, with no rulebook to follow. It was undoubtedly the most exhilarating posting of my career. My wonderful family were often left to fend for themselves and we were accused of going native on several occasions, but as the Commander acknowledged sagely, if we had not gone native then we would not have stayed. It was a price worth paying.

It would be remiss of me not to touch on my family, who had shared this adventure with me. Whilst I was immersed in the integration process, they were living in Potchefstroom, which in the early days was far from welcoming. Indeed, after about two months of being cut dead by most of the local burghers, Trisha was ready to pack up and return to the UK. But suddenly, almost overnight, attitudes changed and we were made welcome. To this day we have friends still living in Potchefstroom. It was a major challenge for Trisha, being the only British wife in Potchefstroom, especially in a town with a history of anti-British sentiment, and also noting that the other BMATT families were enjoying the bright lights of Pretoria. The girls were of an age when everything was exciting and new. They went to the local English-speaking Model C school, which was the only fully mixed school in Potchefstroom. By 'mixed' I mean not only by gender, but by race.

They absorbed everything like little sponges, to such an extent that even to this day they still have a slight South African 'twang'. We had only one way to go if we were to stay, so perhaps we went a bit 'native' – I would perhaps call it 'hybrid'. But all was well, and as a family we had a fabulous time, making the most of everything that the wonderful country of South Africa had to offer us. The stories that could be told are plentiful, but for another time.

What has since happened to South Africa and the people we were privileged to meet? Starting at the top, the extraordinary President Mandela has passed away. He was the rock upon which the new South Africa was built. He epitomized the ANC's stated intent of trying to create a non-racial South Africa. Whether his successors have taken his torch forward is not for me to comment, but nobody has commanded so much respect in such a disarming and genuine way. He was not a superman, and maybe he was not the statesman so many in the world wanted him to be, but he was a statesman in South Africa, and that is where he needed to be a statesman. He rallied all to his dream of the Rainbow Nation. I saw this first-hand when I was fortunate enough to attend the Rugby World Cup final at Ellis Park in Johannesburg. The stadium was packed full, and the vast majority were South African supporters. The teams emerged onto the field to a huge cheer from the very lively and good-humoured crowd, and there was a real carnival atmosphere. The two teams lined up. Then, section-by-section, the crowd in the stadium saw President Mandela come down the tunnel and onto the pitch. He was dressed in the Springbok green and gold match jersey, with South Africa captain Francois Pienaar's number '6' emblazoned on the back. To say the crowd went wild is an understatement. Here was the freedom-fighter-turned-president wearing what many of his supporters would call one of the most flagrant symbols of the old Apartheid regime. He walked up to Francois Pienaar and shook his hand, and then proceeded to meet both teams. President Mandela then walked slowly, flanked by the presidents of the South African and New Zealand Rugby Unions, to take his place on the field for the national anthems. From all over the ground, the chant began – 'Nelson, Nelson, Nelson'. I looked around and could see everyone chanting, regardless of nationality or colour – most impressive of all, some of those who I would classify as die-hard Afrikaners were joining in. I realised that this was not just a rugby match; it was a ground-breaking event – a historic turning point.

I heard from a trusted agent of occasions when President Mandela chaired a meeting during one of the many integration crises, and having heard the various statements, he sat back and the lawyer came out of him. He summarized the arguments in his quiet voice, one that begged attention, but delivered his decision in the manner of a parable, an illustrative story infused with quiet and subtle humour that was the mark of the man.

General Siphiwe Nyanda, the fomer MK Chief of Staff, served on the Transitional Executive Council which oversaw the transition through the elections from the old National Party government to the new ANC government. He was integrated early and quickly rose through general officer ranks and senior appointments, including Chief of the Defence Force Staff, General Officer Commanding Gauteng Command, Deputy Chief of the SANDF and eventually Chief of the SANDF from 1998–2005. It was rumoured that when he stood down as Chief of the SANDF, it was more a question of his being 'pushed' by President Mbeki. General Nyanda was a close ally of Jacob Zuma, who was elected President of South Africa in 2009. Upon the assumption of President Zuma, Nyanda returned to public life as the Communications Minister. However, after a series of scandals which suggested that companies he owned had benefited from state tenders, he was promptly sacked by President Zuma, before being appointed as the president's personal representative in Parliament.

Very recently, General Nyanda returned to the public stage by being one of the signatories to a memorandum sent to the ANC Secretary General, Gwede Mantashe. The memorandum was from the 'Senior Commanders and Commissars of the former military wing of the ANC'. It is an interesting question as to why they felt compelled to write as former commanders and commissars of the MK, as opposed to referring to their post-Apartheid ranks and positions,

General Meiring was appointed as Chief of the SADF in 1993 and oversaw its transition to the SANDF. He served in that position until 1998, when he was forced to resign. His resignation was in quite peculiar circumstances: he provided a report to President Mandela on an organization called the Front African People's Liberation Army, suggesting that there was a plot by senior government figures to assassinate the president and key members of the judiciary, occupy Parliament and conduct other revolutionary activities. An investigation soon proved that the organization was fictitious, and the accusations and list of conspirators to be pure fantasy. There were many theories about why such a ridiculous report should be given directly to President Mandela by his Chief of Defence, but perhaps the most likely is that there was a wish to see the president act swiftly against those named in the report, including General

Nyanda. Fortunately, it was seen to be what it really was, and the only victim was General Meiring, although it did shine a spotlight on some of the ultra-conservative members of the SANDF and the intelligence community, who appeared to be undermining the road to political unification and reconciliation.

Many would make the observation that when an officer reaches a certain rank in the military, then he becomes more of a political animal than a military one. I think it is fair to say that this happens because there is an overt need to work within the state apparatus and to look at strategic issues within the political environment, otherwise there would be no chance to deliver policy. In South Africa, there was an inability to formally and finally break away from politics, whether it was the old guard hanging on or the new guard being unable to shake off their political past. Even now, almost thirty years on from integration, the thought of the SANDF being a-political is still a dream.

Abe Motsoaleka changed his name to Abe Notshweleka. He then went on from strength to strength, and in July 2014 retired from the South African Army in the rank of major general. Theunis Coetzee, Andre Eckard and Leon Phillipson all took early retirement. Patrick Zwane continued to serve as a lieutenant colonel before retiring. The officer, 'David', who had to decline command of P Battery because he was HIV positive, is still alive and kicking, having enjoyed an impressive career to date.

Although my Aunt Pat has passed away, my cousins still live in South Africa and have no intention of leaving!

The Commander of the School of Intelligence in Potchefstroom soldiered on for a while as the Personal Staff Officer to General Nyanda, but also took early retirement. After a period of consultancy, he enjoyed a very successful series of appointments with the United Nations in New York. I was lucky to have the opportunity to meet up with him on several occasions when I travelled to New York during the course of my last appointment in the Army.

As for me, I continued to serve. There was a short posting to Sandhurst, which I thoroughly enjoyed, followed by 'that' promotion. An equally short tour in the Army Personnel Centre in Glasgow saw me being appointed as Commanding Officer of my old regiment, the 22nd Regiment Royal Artillery (The Welsh Gunners). It was a rollercoaster of a ride, but I was posted on further promotion to a series of thoroughly exciting appointments, which embraced Istanbul, Ghana (as Commander of my own BMATT, ironically an appointment Colonel Paul Davis had held shortly after South Africa),

Rome and eventually the MOD. In between all this, there were operational tours to Cyprus, Bosnia and Afghanistan.

Over the years, I have run into many of the BMATT personnel around the world, including Al Sommerlad, who had the wager that he could have a conversation in Afrikaans and Zulu after a month in the country. We met in Sarajevo further on down the line, where he confirmed that he had won his wager! It reminded me of the quote I had heard on that same night in Pretoria: 'A hundred years ago it took a handful of us Boers to bring the British Empire to its knees, now you people have got the chance to do the same to the South African Army.'

I don't think we did, but what we did do was to help create a security force that was no longer perceived as a threat by the majority of its own people. We had played our bit in the Mandela Revolution and the creation of the Rainbow Nation.

Integration Schematic

INTEGRATION PROCESS SCHEMATIC (taken from the initial BMTT SA Flier)

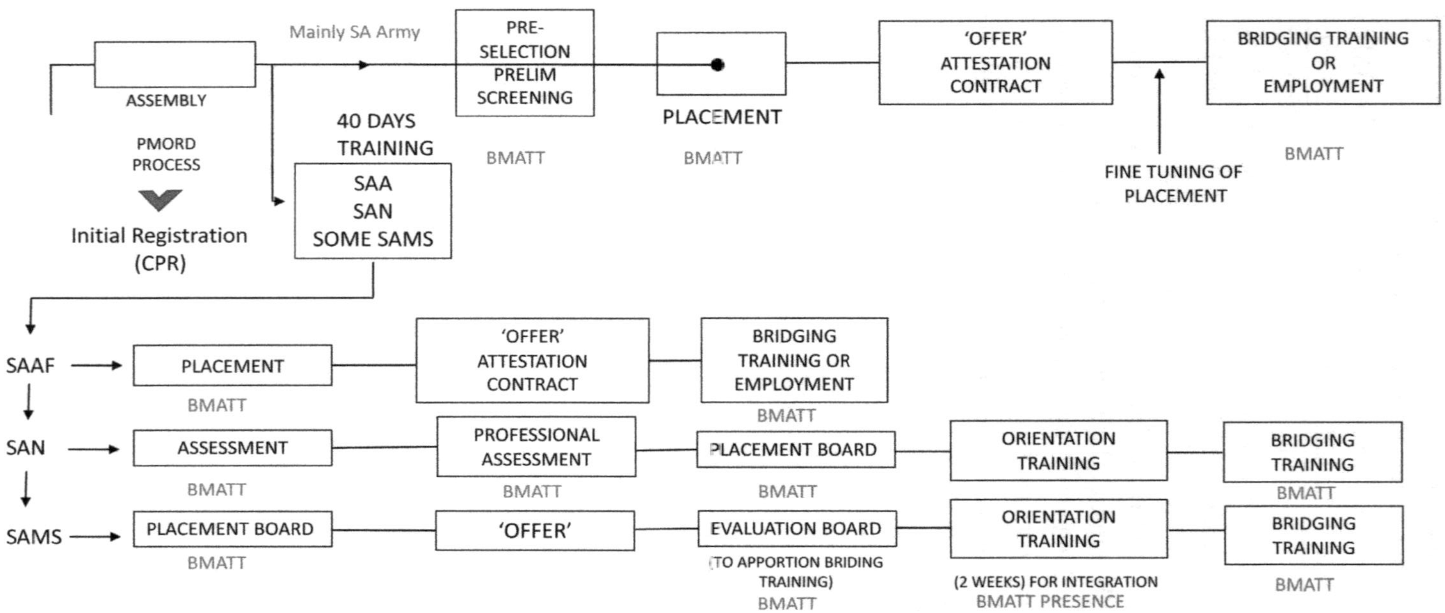

Bibliography

Barnard, Niël, *Secret Revolution* (Tafelberg, 2015).

Campbell, Susan Schuster, *Called to Heal* (Zebra Press, 1998).

Carlin, John, *Playing the Enemy: Nelson Mandela and the Game that made a Nation* (Atlantic Books, 2009).

Carthra, Gavin, *Post-War Security Transitions, Participatory Peacebuilding after Asymmetric Conflict, Part 3* (Routledge, 2012).

Cilliers, J., *An overview of the armed forces of the TBVC countries, African Security Review 13* (Institute for Security Studies, 1993).

Cloete, P.G., *The Anglo-Boer War: a chronology* (Lapa Publishers, 2000).

Crawford, Nicole, 'Helping South African veterans find jobs, heal anger', *Monitor on Psychology* Vol. 34, No. 9 (American Psychological Association, 2003).

Cumes, David, *Africa in my Bones* (Spearhead Press, 2004).

Gevisser, Mark, *Thabo Mbeki: The Dream Deferred* (Jonathan Ball, 2007).

Hamber, Brandon, *Truth: the Road to Reconciliation? Cantilevers: Building Bridges for Peace* (Centre for Study of Violence and Reconciliation, 2003).

Herskovitz, Jon & Laventure, Lisa, *Broken schools breed South Africa's 'lost generation'* (Reuters, US edition, Lifestyle, 2012).

Joubert, W.A., *The Law of South Africa* (Butterworth-Heinemann, 1976).

Kalley, Jacqueline Audrey, *et. al.*, *South African Political History: A Chronology of Key Political Events from Independence to Mid-1997* (Greenwood Press, 1999).

Le Roux, Len, *The post-*apartheid *South African military: Transforming with the nation* (Institute for Security Studies, 2005).

Mandela, Nelson, *Conversations with Myself* (Macmillan, 2010).

Mandela, Nelson, *Long Walk to Freedom* (Macdonald Purnell, 1994).

Mashike, J.L., *Age of Despair: the Unintegrated Forces of South Africa* (Oxford University Press, 2008).

Mashike, J.L., 'Blacks Can Win Everything, but the Army: The Transformation of the South African Military between 1994 and 2004', *Journal of Southern African Studies* Vol. 33, No. 3 (September 2007).

Meiring, G.L., 'Taking the South Africa Army into the future', *African Defence Review* Vol. 3, no. 14 (January 1994).

Mills, Greg, 'BMATT and Military Integration in Southern Africa', *South African Defence Review*, Issue No. 2 (1992).

Motumi, Tsepe & Hudson, Andrew, 'Rightsizing: The Challenges of Demobilisation and social reintegration in South Africa', in Jakkie Cilliers (ed.), *Demobilisation and Reintegration of Former Combatants in Africa* (Halfway House: Institute for Defence Policy, 1996).

Ngculu, J., *Umkhonoto we Sizwe manifesto. The role of Umkhonoto we Sizwe in the creation of a democratic civil-military relations tradition* (Ourselves to know, ISS, 2003).

O'Brien, Kevin, *Dismissed* in *Demobilisation and Reintegration of Former Combatants in Africa*, ed. Jakkie Cilliers (Halfway House: Institute for Defence Policy, 1996).

Pakenham, Thomas, *The Boer War* (Random House, 1979).

Twala, Mwezi & Bernard, Ed, *Mbokodo. Inside MK: Mwezi Twala – A Soldier's Story* (Jonathan Ball, 1994).

Vora, J.A. & Vora, E., *The Effectiveness of South Africa's Truth and Reconciliation Commission: Perceptions of Xhosa, Afrikaner and English South Africans* (Journal of Black Studies, 2004).

Wessels, Andre, *The South African Defence Force, 1994–2009: A Historical Perspective* (University of the Free State, 2010).

Williams, R.M., 'Integration or absorption? The creation of the SA National Defence Force, 1993 to 1999', *African Security Review* Vol. 11, No. 2 (2002).

Williams, R.M., 'The other armies: A brief historical overview of Unkhonto we Sizwe (MK), 1961–1994', *Military History Journal* Vol. 11, No. 5 (June 2005).

Wilson, Richard, *The Politics of Truth and Reconciliation in South Africa: Legitimizing the Post-*Apartheid *State* (Cambridge University Press, 2001).

Zwane, Pule, 'Challenges Facing the SANDF: From Integration to Affirmative Action', *African Security Review* Vol. 4, No. 1 (1995).

Media and Social Media

Cowell, Alan, In South Africa, a 'Lost Generation', *New York Times* (17 September 1990).

O'Malley, Padraig, *Afrikaner Weerstandsbeweging (AWB)*, The Nelson Mandela Centre of Memory site, (https://omalley.nelsonmandela.org/omalley/index.php/site/q/03lv02424/04lv02730/05lv03188/06lv03191.htm).

O'Malley, Padraig, *Address by State President P.W. Botha, August 15, 1985*, (https://omalley.nelsonmandela.org/omalley/index.php/site/q/03lv01538/04lv01600/05lv01638/06lv01639.htm).

Radio 702, 'Nonkululeko Britton, Nyanda and Former MK Cadres 'Compelled' to deal with Gupta State Capture Claims', (http://702.co.za/articles/12409/general-nyanda-guptagate 23 March 2016).

SABC Truth Commission Special Report, (http://sabctrc.saha.org.za/background.htm).

South African History Online, Robert Sobukwe Inaugural Speech, April 1959, (http://sahistory.org.za).

Andre Koopman, John Matisonn and Thami Ngidi, 'Bitter Army-ANC Clash Revealed', *Sunday Independent*, IOP News South Africa (25 September 1999).

un.org, 'On Freedom. Nelson Mandela's statement from the dock at the opening of the defence case in the Rivonia Trial, Pretoria Supreme Court, 20 April 1964', (https://www.un.org/en/events/mandeladay/court_statement_1964.shtml).

South African Government Records

BMATT (SA) Report on SANDF Integration as at 1 Oct 97 for the Parliamentary Integration Oversight Committee, (https://pmg.org.za/committee-meeting/6692/).

Joint Standing Committee on Defence Meeting Minutes of 23 Feb 1988, (https://pmg.org.za/committee-meeting/6692/).

Truth and Reconciliation Commission, Volume 1 Chapter 1, (https://www.justice.gov.za/trc/report/).

Truth and Reconciliation Commission, Amnesty Committee, Application in terms of Section 18 of the Promotion of National Unity and Reconciliation Act, No 34 of 1995, Linda Geoffrey Xaba (AM382/96), (https://www.justice.gov.za/trc/decisions/2000/ac20002.htm)

Truth and Reconciliation Commission, Amnesty Committee, Application in terms of Section 18 of the Promotion of National Unity and Reconciliation Act, No 34 of 1995, Adriaan van Straaten (AM58/96), Willem van Straaten (AM59/96), Gideon van Straaten (AM61/96) and Dawid van Straaten (AM62/96), (https://www.justice.gov.za/trc/decisions/trc-adt-1996.pdf).

Truth and Reconciliation Commission Volume 1 Chapter 4 Para 127, (https://www.justice.gov.za/trc/report/).

Truth and Reconciliation Commission, Human Rights Violations Committee, Case Number 01539, Klerksdorp, 23 Sep 1996, Mrs Susan J van der Merwe, (https://www.justice.gov.za/trc/hrvtrans/klerks/merwe.htm).

Notes

Chapter 1: We Live in Interesting Times

1. A sangar is a protected sentry post, normally located around the perimeter of a base. Its main function is to provide early warning of enemy/terrorist activity/attack in order to protect forces both within the base and those deployed within sight of the sangar.
2. A supersangar is an elevated sangar and may be indistinguishable from what is commonly termed a tower.
3. A multiple was a manoeuvre unit consisting of three teams of four men under the command of a junior officer or a senior non-commissioned officer.
4. 'Volunteer' is a term used by a number of Irish republican paramilitary organizations to describe their members.
5. The Barrett M82 is a 0.5-inch (12.7mm) recoil-operated, semi-automatic anti-material rifle.
6. The Mark 15 mortar was known as the barrack buster and fired a 1m-long metal propane gas cylinder containing about 75kg of home-made explosives. It had a range up to about 250m.
7. An artillery troop is between thirty and forty soldiers commanded by a young officer, the equivalent to an infantry platoon.
8. Many service children are sent to boarding school to provide them with continuity of education. The regular postings within the UK and abroad could not provide any continuity unless the husband served unaccompanied. The Ministry of Defence grant was substantial, and therefore once children had started at boarding school then it was a commitment that normally had to be seen all the way through to the completion of A-Levels – therefore the 'trap'.
9. The Army Command and Staff College, Camberley, trained officers in the administrative, staff and policy aspects of their profession. It was a competitive entry, and at this time officers attended prior to assuming command of a sub-unit. Officers spent one year at Camberley, and some

had spent up to a year prior to this at the Royal Military College of Science at Shrivenham. This course has been superseded by attendance on the Joint Command and Staff Course at the Defence Academy in Shrivenham. The teaching staff at UK military staff colleges are called the 'Directing Staff'.

10. The Royal Military Academy, Sandhurst, is the institution where initial officer training for the British Army is delivered.
11. For this generation of British Army officers there were very few medals available, except for the General Service Medal (Northern Ireland), the Falkland Islands medal or a Cyprus UN medal. Most people had one medal (a swisher), but many had no medals (Nobby No Medals).
12. Post Graduate Certificate of Education, a course that qualifies graduates to become school teachers.

Chapter 2: New World, New Role

1. The Transkei Defence Force was established in 1975, the Bophuthatswana Defence Force in 1979, the Ciskei Defence Force in 1981 and the Venda Defence Force in 1982.

Chapter 3: The Devil in the Detail

1. A Bergen is the British Army nickname for an Alpine-style backpack, which comes from the names of the original designer, Ole F. Bergan, and the Norwegian city of Bergen.

Chapter 4: First Days

1. In 2008 the area Voortrekkerhoogte was renamed Thaba Tshwane.
2. All armies have an order of precedence which gives regiments priority on parade. The most senior regiment will always parade on the right of the parade, hence the phrase 'right of line'.
3. A parka is a type of coat, often with a hood, to protect the wearer from the cold and wind.
4. The TBVC process being conducted separately.
5. The TBVC forces had been modelled on the SADF and had, to all extents and purposes, been territorial forces for the SADF. Their training and employment standards were similar, and the administration process required for verification and placement was much easier than those

of the non-statutory forces. In addition, the TBVC were considered by many of the non-statutory forces to be SADF, and therefore they could be classified previously as legitimate targets.

6. The Royal Regiment of Fusiliers wears a hackle, which in a clipped feather plume attached to a beret. It is white with a red tip. The original hackle belonged to the Royal Northumberland Fusiliers, who amalgamated with other fusilier regiments to form the Royal Regiment of Fusiliers. In 1829, King George IV ordered the white plume to be worn by all infantry regiments, and in order not to take away from the 5th (Northumberland) Regiment of Foot's distinction, their plume was differentiated by being made 'half red and half white, the red uppermost, instead of the plain white feather worn by the rest of the army per the 1829 order, as a peculiar mark of honour' (Royal Regiment of Fusiliers: Regimental history).
7. The Commissars, or political leaders, were essential within the structure of the MK. They had been based on the classic Communist insurgent cellular structure that was the role model at the inception of the MK. The Commissars were the 'generals', they were the leaders and were those who needed to bring on the body of the formations. Politically, they were essential to the future of the integration process. They were the spokesmen up and down the MK chain of command and had a huge vested interest in the integration process working smoothly and successfully. But to be fair, they had their hands full keeping their charges committed to the process.

Chapter 5: Into the Lion's Den

1. In 1994, the South African Artillery did not accept female applicants.
2. *Toyi-toyi* is a Southern African dance originating from Zimbabwe; it is claimed to have been started by the Zimbabwe People's Revolutionary Army (ZIPRA). It is used throughout South Africa as a form of protest. It is in essence the stomping of feet with chants, and when used by a crowd is very effective.

Chapter 6: Welcome to the Machine

1. The nomenclature was becoming quite complicated, as now once ex-SADF or ex-non-statutory personnel were taken into the SANDF then they were very much 'ex'. The ex-non-statutory force officer may

have been looking after the interests of the yet-to-be-integrated non-statutory force personnel, but he was no longer one of them. It was a difficult tightrope for many to negotiate.

2. Although candidates had been successful in placement, many stayed in the camp awaiting the exact details of when and where the Bridging Training was to take place.

Chapter 7: Dis-ease and Dad's Army

1. Special Pensions Section 189, Constitution of the Republic of South Africa, Act 200 of 1993.
2. The term 'Madiba' is the traditional Xhosa clan name for Nelson Mandela. It was used as a sign of respect throughout South Africa. He was also referred to as 'Tata' (Father) or 'Tata-Madiba'.

Chapter 10: The Truth, the Whole Truth and Nothing but the Truth

1. Truth and Reconciliation Commission, Amnesty Committee, Application in terms of Section 18 of the Promotion of National Unity and Reconciliation Act, No 34 of 1995, Adriaan van Straaten (AM58/96), Willem van Straaten (AM59/96), Gideon van Straaten (AM61/96) and Dawid van Straaten (AM62/96).
2. *Volkstaat*, 'people's state', is a term used to describe the envisioned independent Afrikaaner homeland.
3. Truth and Reconciliation Commission Volume 1 Chapter 4 Para 127.
4. Truth and Reconciliation Commission, Human Rights Violations Committee, Case Number 01539, Klerksdorp, 23 Sep 1996, Mrs Susan J van der Merwe.

Chapter 11: Scales of Justice

1. 'Black threat'.

Chapter 12: Affirmative Distraction

1. It was renamed the South African Army Battle School in January 2000.
2. In close air support, artillery, mortar, and naval gunfire support fire, 'danger close' is the term included in the method of engagement

segment of a call for fire which indicates that friendly forces are within close proximity of the target. The close proximity distance is determined by the weapon and munition fired.

3. The Ratel is the standard South African Infantry Fighting Vehicle and is considered to be an influential design, especially with its landline protection feature. It has many variants, including one for the artillery observer. *Ratel* is the Afrikaans name for the honey badger, which has the reputation for being a ferocious fighter.
4. A shebeen is an unlicensed establishment selling alcohol, typically regarded as slightly disreputable.

Chapter 13: I'm Sorry I'll Read that Again

1. Act No. 4 of 2000: Promotion of Equality and Prevention of Unfair Discrimination Act.

Chapter 14: Facing Reality

1. The South African Parliament sits in Cape Town, which is a historical legacy from the formation of the Union when there was disagreement between the four provinces as to which city would be the national capital. After years of negotiation, it was decided that Cape Town would be the legislative capital, Bloemfontein the judicial capital and Pretoria the administrative capital. BMATT HQ was based in Pretoria serving the Defence Headquarters, in effect the Ministry of Defence, and also had to report to the Parliamentary Oversight Committee in Cape Town.

Chapter 16: Farewell and Adieu

1. The technical head of the Royal Regiment of Artillery, and as far as promotion, command and postings are concerned, the kingmaker.
2. The witchdoctor is an integral part of the Zulu religion. There are two types: an Inyanga treats physical conditions and the Sangoma is concerned with the psych

Index